The Modern Language Association of America

MONOGRAPH SERIES

XIII

THE POETICAL DIALOGUES OF SOLOMON AND SATURN

Approved for publication in the Monograph Series of the Modern Language Association of America.

Carleton Brown
Christian Gauss
Raymond D. Havens
G. T. Northup
Lawrence M. Price

Committee of Award

THE POETICAL DIALOGUES OF SOLOMON AND SATURN

EDITED BY

ROBERT J. MENNER

PROFESSOR OF ENGLISH IN
YALE UNIVERSITY

NEW YORK
THE MODERN LANGUAGE ASSOCIATION
OF AMERICA
LONDON, OXFORD UNIVERSITY PRESS
MDCCCCXLI

KRAUS REPRINT CO.
Millwood, New York
1973

Solomon and Saturn.
The poetical dialogues of Solomon and Saturn.

Original ed. issued as no. 13 of Modern Language Association of America, monograph series.
Bibliography: p.
1. Solomon, King of Israel—Poetry. I. Menner, Robert James, ed. II. Title. III. Series: Modern Language Association of America. Monograph series, 13.
PR1770.A3M4 1973 829'.1 73-12784
ISBN 0-527-84500-0

Reprinted with the permission of Modern Language Association of America

KRAUS REPRINT CO.
A U.S. Division of Kraus-Thomson Organization Limited

Printed in Germany

TO THE MEMORY OF

ALBERT STANBURROUGH COOK

PREFACE

Ten years ago Dr. A. H. Smith and Professor Frederick Norman of the University of London asked me to edit *Solomon and Saturn*, on which I had published a paper in 1929, for their prospective series of Old English texts. A glossary had been made, notes written, and much material collected for the introduction by 1934, when I was obliged to abandon serious work on the edition for several years. In 1937, when I resumed my studies, it became obvious that a satisfactory edition of the dialogues could not be made within the limits agreed upon for the English series, since the poems are hardly intelligible without extensive comment. The sections of the book already written were therefore expanded and completely revised, and the original form abandoned. I am much indebted, nevertheless, to Dr. Smith and Professor Norman for their courtesy in considering various difficulties encountered in the early stages of the edition, and in particular for their efforts in trying to have certain obscure pages of Manuscript A photographed by ultraviolet light. These proved unsuccessful at the time because of the strict regulations governing Archbishop Parker's bequest to Corpus Christi College, Cambridge, but it is possible that some fragments of the text may ultimately be recovered by new methods of photography. To the late Sir Edwyn Hoskyns, Librarian of Corpus Christi College, Cambridge, and other officials of the college, I am indebted for their courteous consideration of the proposal to photograph portions of Manuscript A and for permission to have photostats made of the two Corpus Christi manuscripts.

The text of Manuscript B, Corpus Christi College, Cambridge, 41, is based on photostats. The text of Manuscript A, Corpus Christi College 422, is based partly on photostats and partly on a transcript of the certain pages made by my colleague, Professor John C. Pope, in the summer of 1933. At a time when I was unable to visit England, he spent many hours examining the obscure passages of Manuscript A to the great improvement of the text. In particular, the important new readings of lines 194f., 445f., and 474f. are entirely due to his skill and pertinacity. Because of the poor condition of Manuscript A and the imperfections of the photostats, the text of lines 193–199, 203–212, 229–230, 236–244, 334–344, 467–496, is wholly based on Pope's transcript, to which I have also resorted for the readings of several shorter passages and for confirmation of the readings of the photostats. Besides transcribing Manuscript A, Pope has given me invaluable help, as will be obvious from the notes, in metrical matters, notably in the division of the hypermetric lines.

To Professor Elliot van Kirk Dobbie of Columbia University, who is preparing an edition of *Solomon and Saturn* for the *Anglo-Saxon Poetic Records*, I am indebted for a list of readings of Manuscript A differing from those of earlier editors and for a precious reference to Mackay's article on the palm-tree. Professor Archer Taylor of The University of California was kind enough to send me his copy of the rare "bound page-proof" of Kemble's edition (see Bibliography, section III), and to inform me of the recent publication of a new edition of the Dutch chap-book of Solomon and Marcolf: Willem de Vreese and Jan de Vries (eds.), *Dat Dyalogus of Twisprake tusschen den wisen conicnk Salomon ende Marcolphus*, "Nederlandsche Volksboeken," VII, Leiden: E. J. Brill, 1941. To Professor F. P. Magoun, Jr., who read my manuscript for the Modern Language Association, and to the Monograph Committee of the Association I am indebted for various helpful hints and corrections. I am grieved that Carleton Brown, who established the Monograph Series in which this book appears and who showed great interest in my manuscript, is no longer living to accept my thanks for his helpful criticism, the last of many kindnesses. For information on special subjects I wish to thank Professors Erika von Erhardt-Siebold, Dorothy Bethurum, C. B. Morey, and Kemp Malone; and among my colleagues at Yale, Albrecht Goetze, Julius Obermann, C. B. Welles, and Karl Young.

Mrs. William C. De Vane and Professor Frederick A. Pottle read the Introduction and made helpful suggestions in matters of style and form. I am indebted to Miss Anna Hanson for her care and skill in typing the final draft of my book, to Mr. Harold D. Kelling for typing my original manuscript and for much assistance in the laborious task of revising the original form of the edition, to Mr. Paul M. Pickrel for drawing the runic characters from the photostats and for help in proof-reading the Introduction and Notes, and to Miss Florence E. Brown, Miss Margaret Mumford and Miss Dorothy H. Menner for help in verifying the references in the glossary. Finally, I wish to thank the staff of the Yale University Library for much efficient help and many kindnesses.

Those who have studied the poems of *Solomon and Saturn* will be aware of my obligations to earlier scholars. I should like to mention particularly my debt to Kemble, whose extraordinary learning makes his edition still valuable despite his arbitrary treatment of the text, to

Assmann and Holthausen in textual matters, and to Vincenti, whose important introduction was never followed by the promised text and commentary. It will be obvious from my own commentary that many difficult allusions are only partially or tentatively explained, and it is my hope that other medievalists will now be able to throw light on them. I have thought it better to suggest possible explanations than to shun the dark passages altogether.

Nǣnig manna wāt
hæleða under hefenum, hū mīn hige drēoseð
bysig æfter bōcum. Hwīlum mē bryne stīgeð,
hige heortan nēah hædre wealleð.

ROBERT J. MENNER

ELK LAKE, PA., August, 1941.

CONTENTS

	PAGE
PREFACE	vii
INTRODUCTION	1
I. The Manuscripts	1
II. The Two Poems	5
1. Differences between the Two Poems	5
2. The Prose Dialogue and Lines 497–505	8
III. Date	12
IV. Language	18
V. The Legend of Solomon in the Poems	21
1. The Origin and Spread of the Legend	21
2. Solomon, Marcolf, and Saturn	26
VI. The Background of Poem I	35
1. The Nature and Content of Poem I	35
2. The Use of the Pater Noster and the Palm Tree	37
3. Christian Use of Oriental and Germanic Sources	45
VII. The Background of Poem II	49
1. The Nature and Content of Poem II	49
2. The Dialogue and the Riddle	53
3. The Oriental Elements	59
4. The Germanic Elements	62
5. The Christian Elements	66
BIBLIOGRAPHY	71
TABLE OF ABBREVIATIONS	77
TEXT	79
NOTES	105
GLOSSARY	145
APPENDIX	168
INDEX	172

INTRODUCTION

I. THE MANUSCRIPTS

The poetic dialogues of *Solomon and Saturn* in Old English are found in two manuscripts, both in the library of Corpus Christi College, Cambridge. The more important, CCCC 422, known as MS A, contains not only Poem I, perhaps incomplete, and all that remains of Poem II, but also a dialogue between Solomon and Saturn in prose, which is found between the first poem and the second on pages 6 (middle) to 12 (bottom). CCCC 41, known as MS B, contains lines 1–93 of Poem I written on the margins of three pages of the Alfredian version of Bede's *Ecclesiastical History* (pp. 196–198).

MS A is a small vellum manuscript 7⅗″ × 5⅕″, originally in two distinct volumes, of which the first, of thirteen folios, contains the dialogues of *Solomon and Saturn*.[1] The writing is in a small, round, flat-topped hand, which Kemble curiously conjectured to be that of a woman. The date is given by James as ? X, and is probably of the late tenth century. James gives the collation as 1^8 (wants 7), 2^6. The original leaf 7, which was cut out of the first quire, as the remaining stub shows, was between the present pages 12 and 13. Page 12 ends with an incomplete sentence of the prose dialogue, 'ðōn is ðæt seofoðe'; and page 13 begins with a concluding fragment of nine lines of poetry (497–505) followed by the beginning of the second poem, the first manuscript line of which is in large capitals: HWÆT . IC . FLITAN . GEFRÆGN . It would naturally be supposed that the nine lines before the beginning of the second poem, though separated by the prose and the lost leaf from the first, represent the end of Poem I; but there is reason to believe that they actually

[1] The manuscript and its contents are fully described by M. R. James, *A Descriptive Catalogue of the Manuscripts in the Library of Corpus Christi College, Cambridge*, 2 vols. (Cambridge, 1912), II, 315–16; cf. Wanley's description in George Hickes, *Thesaurus*, III, *Antiquæ Literaturæ Liber Alter* (Oxford, 1705), p. 149a. My description depends on information supplied by Professor John C. Pope, which, in one or two respects, supplements and corrects that of Dr. James. The second and larger part of the volume, fols. 14–294, containing a calendar and missal, was known as 'the rede book of darlye' (in the Peak of Derbyshire), (James, II, 315). The liturgical texts, with prayers in Latin and directions for the ritual in Old English, are discussed by B. Fehr in the Liebermann *Festgabe, Texte und Forschungen zur englischen Kulturgeschichte* (Halle, 1923), pp. 20–67, where the *Ordo ad visitandum et unguendum infirmum* is printed.

represent the end of the second.[2] Although there is no evidence in the manuscript for the omission, gaps in the sense of the text of Poem II, between the present pages 18 and 19 (lines 299–300: *rēafað . . . swīðor*) and between 22 and 23 (lines 389–390), make it plain that two leaves, three and six, of the second quire have been lost. Since these leaves would have been conjugate, it is not surprising that there is no trace of them in the manuscript. The second quire might, therefore, on the basis of the textual evidence, be described as 2^8 (wants 3 and 6).[3]

Besides these losses the text of MS A has suffered other damages. Page 1, which contained lines 1–29, and part of 30, is largely illegible because it was originally pasted down to the cover. This page contained, as the portions read by Pope show, a first line in large capitals: S[ATV]RN[VS CWÆÐ H]WÆT,[4] followed by 21 ordinary lines. This page and several subsequent pages [5] have been treated with galls to bring out the damaged or faded handwriting, but most of the treated passages have not been rendered illegible. Finally, page 14 (between lines 192 and 193) has been erased and overwritten with a Latin excommunication in two hands of the twelfth century.[6]

MS B, a vellum manuscript 13⅟10″ × 8½″, is one of those given by Leofric to Exeter, as his inscriptions in Latin and Old English attest.[7] On the margins of a number of leaves are various fragments in Latin and English, many of them being blessings and charms. The most important of these fragments is the beginning of Poem I as far as the letter T, the first word of line 94 (pp. 196–198). The ugly insular handwriting shows the effects of points and sharp corners learned from the post-Conquest style of Caroline minuscules, and may

[2] See below, pp. 8–12.

[3] According to A. R. von Vincenti the missing leaves were not conjugate (*Die altenglischen Dialoge von Salomo und Saturn* [Leipzig, 1904], p. 46), but he apparently forgot that the first gathering lacks one leaf and comprises only pp. 1–14. The second gathering with the present MS pagination runs as follows: 1 (pp. 15–16), 2 (pp. 17–18), [3 lacking], 4 (pp. 19–20), 5 (pp. 21–22), [6 lacking], 7 (pp. 23–24), 8 (pp. 25–26).

[4] Vincenti, p. 45, read only S. . .RN. . . The first page was evidently illegible in Wanley's time, since he does not give the first lines, p. 149a, as is his custom.

[5] Notably, p. 13 middle, p. 14 bottom, pp. 15, 16, p. 18 middle, p. 23, pp. 25–26. Small holes, caused by rust, appear in the first five leaves, and make portions of some words illegible.

[6] This was edited by F. Liebermann, *Die Gesetze der Angelsachsen*, I (Halle, 1903), 435–436.

[7] James I, 81; Wanley, p. 114a; and M. Förster in the facsimile edition of *The Exeter Book of Old English Poetry* (London, 1933), pp. 11–12.

be dated at the end of the eleventh or beginning of the twelfth century. The fragment is important because of the illegibility of page 1 of MS A.

Though of later date, MS B, which contains only part of Poem I and none of Poem II, is plainly not derived from MS A, since B contains a line (67) omitted in A, and preserves at least one correct reading: *scyldum* 56, where A has *scyldigum*. In general A is much the better manuscript, for B has not only many late or careless spellings, such as *unit* 21 (A: *unnit*), *halie* 40 (A: *halige*), *bisi* 61 (A: *bysig*); but also numerous errors such as *wille* 13 for *sille*, *iraela* 14 for *israela*, and the curious *yorn* 88 (A: *ierne*). Some of the errors spoil the metre, such as the omission of the second *oððe* 11, *heofonrices* 52 for A's *heofona rices*, the omission of *neah* 62, and the incorrect word order *lufian wile* 86 for A's *wile lufian*. MS B sometimes substitutes a word that is obviously incorrect, as in *gehideð* 73 (A: *ahieðeð*), *wlenco* 82 (A: *welm*), or one that is less sensible than A's, as in *dreogeð* 60 (A: *dreoseð*), *deadra* 78 (A: *dumbra*).[8]

There is hardly sufficient evidence to determine whether both A and B go back to a common manuscript which is not the original. Both seem to have a mistake, A *dream*, B *dry*, for what must have been originally *dreor* in 44 (see note). The evidence of the spelling, now to be noted, appears to confirm the view that neither manuscript was copied directly from the original.

Characteristic differences in the spelling are the use of initial *þ* in B and *ð* in A: *þonne* 34 (A: *ðonne*), *þeos* 30 (A: *ðeos*); and the spelling *sawle* 66, 68 for A's *saule*. More significant differences are the two *sð* spellings in B for A's *st*: *wesðe* 22, and *eaðusð* 36, paralleled by *gesemesð* B 18, where A is illegible; and such spellings as *gyrde* 90 for A's *gierde*, and *symle* 85 for A's *siemle*,[9] especially the latter, since A has *ie* not only for genuine Early West Saxon *ie*, but frequently as a backspelling for *i*, while this *ie* never occurs in B.[10] Both the *sð* spelling preserved in B and the *ie* for *i* in A are characteristic of the late ninth-century Early West Saxon Hatton manuscript of the *Pastoral Care*. The presence of the two spellings shows, therefore, that both manuscripts go back to Early West Saxon texts, and quite possibly, in the case of Poem I, to an Early West Saxon text in which both *sð* and *ie* spellings occurred, *sð* spellings being preserved in B,

[8] Marks of length are not added in this section, since the readings of the MSS are being cited.

[9] On *i* and *ie* spellings, see the discussion under Date, p. 16; and on the *sð* spellings, p. 16 and note on line 22.

[10] For examples, see Language, p. 18, and for the importance of this spelling in the dating of the poems, Date, pp. 16f.

and *ie* spellings in A. The error, already mentioned, of *dream* in A and *dry* in B for an original *dreor* (44) shows that at one stage in the textual history A and B (or their ancestors) must have been copied from a manuscript in which *dreor* was at least poorly written, in which case the manuscript could have been the original, or was altered to some other word, in which case the common source of the error could only have been a copy. It must be remembered, furthermore, that since both B and A show occasional Anglian forms in addition to forms predominantly West Saxon, an Anglian original is probable.[11] B has some Anglian forms where A has West Saxon: *hwarfað* 35B (A: *hwearfað*), *gefetian* 69B (A: *gefeccan*); and A also has some Anglian forms where B has West Saxon: *seofan* 45A, 66A (B: *sefan*), and *wincendra* 77A (B: *winciendra*), although no absolutely certain Anglian forms occur in the same place in both manuscripts. Thus both seem to preserve occasional forms of the Anglian original, in spite of the fact that both are descended from copies or a copy written by an Early West Saxon scribe certainly not much later than the year 900.

The history of Poem II, which, as we shall see in the next section, is of different authorship from Poem I, and possibly older, has been hitherto left out of account, since Poem II does not occur in MS B, and there is therefore no way of telling whether the scribe of B, who stopped writing in the middle of Poem I, was copying a manuscript which contained only Poem I or both I and II. The language of A in Poem II differs hardly at all from that of Poem I, showing, for example, both Early and Late West Saxon forms with some Anglian forms, and distinctly Anglian vocabulary.[12] Poem II, therefore, must have been originally Anglian and gone through the hands of an Early West Saxon scribe, as did Poem I. Two possible ways in which Poem II may have been combined scribally with Poem I are represented by broken lines in the stemma below. The diagram is presented for the reader's assistance after this discussion, not as reflecting demonstrated relations, for which the evidence is hardly sufficient, but as the simplest possible explanation of the known facts. The true history of the manuscripts may easily have been more complicated. O I represents the original of Poem I, and O II the original of Poem II.

[11] Cf. the discussion under Language, pp. 18–21.

[12] Cf. pp. 18–21, below. It is to be noted that most of the peculiarly Anglian words are found in Poem II (cf. pp. 20f., below), but this is hardly significant since Poem I is so much shorter than Poem II, and Anglian phonological and morphological features appear in both the A and B manuscripts of Poem I.

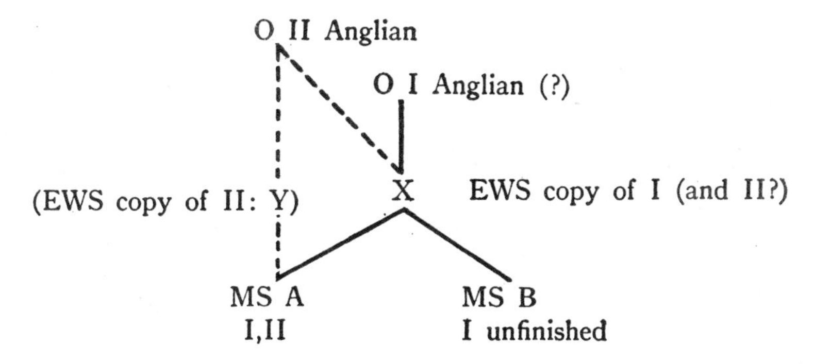

II. THE TWO POEMS

1. Differences between the Two Poems

Although Kemble entitled his edition *The Dialogue of Salomon and Saturnus*, he suspected that the poetical parts of the dialogue represented two distinct poems,[1] and since ten Brink's discussion, it has been generally recognized that there are two poetical dialogues.[2] The first lines of the poems, indeed, both beginning with the traditional *hwæt*, are enough to mark the two poems as distinct entities. This is further emphasized by the scribe of MS A, who writes the first manuscript lines of each in large capitals.[3]

The two poems are both dialogues between Solomon, representing the Judaeo-Christian tradition, and Saturn, representing pagan wisdom. In both Saturn is a Chaldean (I, 20; II, 198, and 318ff., and

[1] 'The poetical Salomon and Saturn, if indeed there be not two distinct poems of the name' . . . , p. 132.

[2] Ten Brink thought that the first was later than the second, *Geschichte der englischen Literatur* (Berlin, 1877), pp. 112–113; cf. the section on Date, p. 16, below. Vincenti, pp. 52–53, said that Poems I and II were by two different authors.

[3] The different methods by which the scribe of A blocks off the parts of the dialogue in I and II probably indicate different transmission for the two poems. In Poem I and the prose, the scribe does not begin the speeches of the debaters on separate lines unless the immediately preceding speech has ended on a line: thus *Salomon cwæð* 39, *Saturnus cwæð* 53 occur medially; whereas in Poem II each speech begins on a separate line with rows of crossed lines partly filling the space left at the end of the preceding speech. Furthermore, the large capitals covering the space of two lines that frequently appear in the proper names in II are absent in I, except for the first line, and in the prose. This might mean that the scribe had changed his practice, but it is more likely that he is simply reflecting the different practice of earlier separate manuscripts.

503), whose realm is beyond the river *Cōfor* (I, 20; II, 196). In I Saturn has searched the books of Libya, Greece, and India for the truth (1ff.); in II he has travelled through these Oriental lands and many more to find the keys of learned books (170–192). In both, Christian wisdom is triumphant over pagan. But there the resemblance ends. The poems differ greatly in substance and form. In Poem I (1–169) Saturn, whose lines number less than one-fifth of the whole, asks instruction of Solomon in the power of the 'palm-twigged' Pater Noster. Solomon thereupon explains how this instrument may overcome the Devil, describing in fanciful and sometimes grotesque detail the manner in which each letter of the prayer attacks and routs the Evil One, whose wily disguises and wicked deeds are listed in the last twenty lines of the poem as we have it. In Poem II (170–496 plus 497–505),[4] on the other hand, there is a real dialogue. Unlike Poem I, which begins directly with Saturn's request for instruction, Poem II begins with an introduction in which the author describes the two princes whose high debate he has heard. Saturn is here not merely the recipient of instruction, but a propounder of difficult riddles, all of which Solomon answers to his satisfaction. Saturn's own comment and occasional questions, comprising 105 lines to Solomon's 198, mark him as Solomon's equal, an antagonist learned in Oriental and Germanic lore, well worthy of his opponent. The fantastic superstition and childish literalism of Poem I give way in Poem II to cryptic questions on Oriental legend, to riddles on time and nature, and finally to lofty discourse on fate and foreknowledge, on good and evil and their rewards. The differences in theme and tone are in themselves enough to suggest that the two poems are not by one author. It is possible that the author of Poem I or his source merely used the familiar form of the Solomon and Saturn dialogue in order to give instruction in the value of the Pater Noster. If, as ten Brink supposed, and as certain stylistic features may indicate, Poem I is later than Poem II,[5] the author of Poem I may have taken from the second poem the characterization of Saturn as a Chaldean who had travelled far in search of wisdom. On the other hand, except for lines 20: 'Ofer Cōferflōd Caldēas sēcan' and 196: 'Ofer Cōforflōd cȳððe seccan,' verbal parallels are few, and the almost certain existence of an earlier Latin

[4] These nine lines, considered part of Poem I by previous editors, are discussed below, pp. 8–12.

[5] On the possible difference in date of the two poems, see below, p. 17. A fuller discussion of the differences between the two poems as dialogues will be found below, pp. 35–36.

dialogue, the original of Poem II, in which Saturn is characterized as a Chaldean prince, makes a borrowing from the Latin equally possible.[6]

The two poems are, furthermore, dissimilar in stylistic and metrical technique. Gnomic passages occur frequently in Poem II, but are lacking in Poem I, with one possible exception.[7] The more stately style of Poem II is likewise marked by the presence of twenty expanded lines in five different passages.[8] Poem I avoids the expanded line entirely. Poem I is somewhat more conventional in its use of poetic words. Those found elsewhere in the corpus of Old English poetry (marked with a dagger in the glossary) occur once to every five lines in Poem I, and once to every eight lines in Poem II; but words peculiar to either poet (marked with a double dagger in the glossary) occur only every ten lines in Poem I and every six lines in Poem II. Rhyming half-lines are found twice in Poem I: *ferigend, nerigend* (80), *weard, geard* (82); and assonance and rhyming inflectional endings are frequent: *morðre, sorge* (55), *stēoreð, healdeð* (51).[9] In Poem II one instance of rhyming half-lines occurs, *swingeð, hringeð* (258), and one rhyming phrase, *stēap and gēap* (405), and rhyming endings occur, in some cases accompanied by assonance, as in *blīcan, līxan* (227); but the inflectional rhymes, though more varied than in Poem I, where the *-eð, -að* ending predominates, occur only half as frequently.[10] Many of the rhymes in *-eð* in Poem I are the result of the author's predilection for parallelism and enumeration,[11] a practice avoided in Poem II, the only striking instance being in 427ff.[12] Double alliteration occurs much more frequently in Poem I (67% of the normal a-lines) than in Poem II (51%). These differences confirm the conclusion suggested by the differences in the subject-matter and tone of the poems: they are not by the same author.

[6] It is to be noted that neither the prose dialogue in MS A nor the unrelated prose Solomon-Saturn dialogue of Biblical riddles in Cotton Vitellius A XV (printed by Kemble, pp. 178–193, and Benjamin Thorpe, *Analecta Anglosaxonica* [London, 1834], pp. 95–100) characterizes Saturn as a Chaldean.

[7] See pp. 65–66, below.

[8] Lines 303–304, 318–322, (328b?), 329–330, 358–361, (427?), 443–449, (478).

[9] For further examples, see 7?, 40, 41, 49, 73, 74, 79 (note), 92, 94, 107, 124, 132, 138, 168. It should be noted that the rhyming is not so frequent as in *Judith*, for which cf. Kluge, *PBB*, IX (1884), 444.

[10] In lines 291?, 362, 422, 423, 424, 428, 429, 483, 486.

[11] In lines 39ff., 50ff., 55ff., 71ff., 92ff.

[12] Both poems have passages with many parallel nouns or nominal phrases: I, 77ff.; II, 183ff., the latter perhaps unavoidable because it is a list of place-names.

2. The Prose Dialogue and Lines 497–505

The insertion of the prose dialogue followed by a poetic passage, lines 497–505, between Poem I and Poem II in MS A causes a double complication. It is necessary to consider both the possibility of a connection between Poem I and the prose dialogue which immediately follows it, and the possibility that the nine lines of poetry which follow the prose belong to Poem II rather than to Poem I.

The following diagram will help to make clear the position of the poems and the prose in MS A:

Manuscript	Texts
Page 1 to Page 6, line 12, middle:	Poem I, 1–169
Page 6, line 12, middle, to Page 12 end:	Prose (incomplete)
Missing leaf between Pages 12 and 13:	Prose? Poetry?
Page 13, lines 1–7:	Lines 497–505 (Grein-Wülker's 170–178), end of Poem II (or I?)
Page 13, lines 8–23:	Beginning of Poem II, 170–192

The prose dialogue of Solomon and Saturn [1] begins with Saturn's question about how many shapes the Devil and the Pater Noster will take when they are contending together. When Solomon answers thirty, Saturn's further curiosity elicits an enumeration of these shapes: the Devil will appear successively in the likeness of a child, a dragon, darkness, a wild beast, a terrible dream, an evil woman, etc., while the Pater Noster will appear in the likeness of the Holy Spirit, the arrow *Brachia Dei*, light, Leviathan, a heavenly vision, a heavenly breast-plate, etc. Solomon then answers, in similarly fantastic vein, further questions on the angels who will track down the Devil and punish him, and on the head, heart, and garment of the Pater Noster. For example, '[the Pater Noster's] heart is twelve thousand times brighter than the seven heavens that are set over us, though they should all be kindled with the fire of Doomsday, and though all this earth should burn up from beneath them and it should have a fiery tongue and a golden throat and bright mouth within, and though the whole world from Adam's creation should be renewed, and each man should have the twelve wisdoms of Abraham and Isaac and Jacob, and each might live three hundred years, yet they could not discover the interpretation of his tongue, nor the greatness of his might.' This specimen of the style of the prose, savoring strongly of Hebrew methods of description,[2] is characteristic.

[1] Printed in Appendix, pp. 168–171; cf. further, pp. 55–56, below.

[2] Cf. the description in the *Tractate Berachoth*, A. Wünsche, *Der babylonische Talmud in seinen haggadischen Bestandtheilen* (Leipzig, 1886–89) I, 53. This kind of enumeration found its way into the West; cf. Wulfstan's description of hell, *Homily* XLIII (ed. Arthur Napier, pp. 214–215).

The prose dialogue follows immediately after line 169 of Poem I. Line 12 of page 6 in MS A reads as follows: 'me ðōn his feond cyme. Saturnus cwæð ac hu.' That is, there is no more separation between *cyme*, the last word in line 169 of Poem I, and *Saturnus cwæð*, the beginning of the prose dialogue, than there is between the speeches within Poem I or within the prose dialogue. This might make one suspect that the poem was a partial versification of the first portion of a longer prose piece, which was left in its original prose form after the description of the activities of the warrior-letters had been finished. It is true that the fantasy of Poem I to some extent resembles the descriptions of the prose dialogue; but the petty personifications of the poem are comparatively restrained beside the absurd exaggerations and colorful allegorical analysis of the prose. The Pater Noster of the prose is itself a gigantic creature, while only the letters of the Pater Noster are personified in Poem I. Furthermore, the transition from the poem to the prose is not a smooth one.[3] The description of the conquest of the Devil by the Pater Noster seems complete in Poem I, but the prose begins with an account of a renewed combat between the two in various shapes.[4] It seems quite possible that the shape-shifting of the Devil, described in the concluding lines of Poem I, led to the addition of comparable material from a prose dialogue of different origin.[5] The prose dialogue itself is not completed in the manuscript, stopping abruptly in the midst of Solomon's description of the seventh of twelve purple palls that are hung about the Pater Noster. Vincenti guessed[6] that the following leaf, which has been torn from the manuscript, was not sufficient to contain the conclusion of the prose piece, in which were to be described five more palls, 120 golden rings, and probably other parts of the gigantic Pater Noster's array,

[3] Cf. R. P. Wülker, *Grundriss zur Geschichte der angelsächsischen Litteratur* (Leipzig, 1885), p. 366, note 3, who remarks that the prose is not joined to the poetry in such a way as to indicate that the prose was composed as an amplification of the poem.

[4] Cf. Vincenti, p. 60.

[5] The exact relation of the prose dialogue on the Pater Noster to Poem I is obscure. I am inclined to think that there is no direct connection between the two: the prose is not a continuation of the poetry, nor the poetry an amplification of a first (lost) part of the prose. It is, of course, curious that there should be two separate Solomon and Saturn dialogues on the Pater Noster. It is possible that both go back in general form, though not in material, to some much earlier Solomonic dialogue on the Pater Noster; cf. the notes on 17a, 53a, for Latin loan-words common to Poem I and the prose. But it is conceivable that the prose, which is chiefly description, was turned into the form of a dialogue between Solomon and Saturn simply because Poem I or its original already had been.

[6] P. 64.

such as his shield and armor. The missing page, he thought, contained rather the conclusion of Poem II, of which only nine lines appear at the top of page 13. It is naturally impossible to be sure whether prose or poetry appeared in the missing leaf. It seems reasonable, however, to assume that the incomplete sentence of the prose at the bottom of page 12 ('ðōn is ðæt seofoðe') was continued, and not impossible that the description of the twelve palls was completed. On the other hand, Vincenti's assumption that the leaf contained poetry, or at least some poetry at the end, cannot be disproved, especially since the poetry on page 13 begins with the end of a sentence in the middle of a half-line (497a).

We now turn to the more difficult and more important problem of these nine apparently detached poetic lines which appear immediately following the prose, the original leaf between pages 12 and 13 having been torn out, and which immediately precede the opening of Poem II.[7] In these lines (497–505), after the sinner is (apparently) warned to desist before he discovers how the sinful souls will be punished in hell at Doomsday, the poet tells how the wise son of David has overcome (*forcumen and forcȳðed*) the prince of the Chaldeans, who had journeyed from afar. Yet Saturn was happy, as he never had been before; that is, though defeated in debate, Saturn rejoiced because he had learned Christian wisdom.

The earlier editors and commentators had very naturally assumed that, in spite of the intercalation of the prose fragment, these lines, which are obviously the conclusion to something, were intended as the conclusion to Poem I. Wülker, however, rightly noted that if they had not been preserved, one might assume that the first poem had concluded with line 169.[8] Lines 166–169, containing Solomon's injunction that any man when he draws his sword should pray that the Pater Noster and the palm-tree protect him, have, in fact, an air of finality. It remained for Vincenti to suggest that the lines really belong to the second poem, fittingly concluding it with the striking formula *forcumen and forcȳðed*, which had likewise been used at the beginning of Poem II in line 198.[9] Vincenti's suggestion, accepted by Brandl, seems inevitable for several reasons.

1. The second poem begins with the author's introduction of his characters (170ff.), and might fittingly conclude with comment upon

[7] Cf. the diagram, above, p. 5.

[8] *Grundriss*, p. 366, note 2.

[9] P. 64. Vincenti proposed to show in his 'Lautlehre,' which was never published, that the verses belonged linguistically to Poem II. Except for *was* 504 (cf. 173, 203), which might be merely scribal, I can find no phonological features which would inevitably connect the lines with Poem II rather than with Poem I.

them by the poet. The first poem has no such introduction, but begins directly with Solomon's words.

2. The use of the phrase *forcumen and forcȳðed* is especially striking in view of the rarity of the Anglian word *forcuman* [10] and the fact that the combination of the two words occurs nowhere else in Old English.

3. The lines can easily be accepted as continuing the last reflections of Poem II on fate and foreknowledge (416ff.), the punishment of Satan (441ff.), the Guardian Angel and his counterpart (477ff.). The last lines of page 26 begin the lament of the Guardian Angel about the sinner whose heart was steeled against righteousness. Vincenti rightly suggested that the transition to the subject of the Last Judgment would be a natural one.[11]

4. Even the phraseology of the lines seems reminiscent of Solomon's last speech in Poem II; cf. 496: 'sticað him tōmiddes' and 498–499: 'ðæt ðā sienfullan sāula sticien / mid hettendum helle tōmiddes.'

Over against all this the only connections of lines 497–505 with Poem I are the repetition of the phrase *sunu Dāuides* 502 (cf. 13), which, however, is hardly remarkable and is found also in II, 323, and the remark that Saturn, who has journeyed from afar, will return home rejoicing, which might conceivably be considered parallel to his willingness at the beginning of Poem I to return home if Solomon reconciles him with truth (18–20).[12]

Only one alternative to the acceptance of 497–505 as the conclusion of Poem II seems to be possible. It would be the assumption that the author of Poem I, being familiar with Poem II, modelled a concluding passage on the phraseology of the earlier poem (borrowing *forcumen and forcȳðed*). This assumption seems unnecessary in view of the presence of another adequate conclusion to I (163b–169) and the absence of any conclusion to II unless we accept lines 497–505. It would be rash, I believe, to throw aside so fitting a framework for the second poem.

Unfortunately, the manuscript casts no light on how such a curious confusion and misplacement could have arisen. But it seems possible that in an earlier manuscript, or perhaps even at the stage when the two poems existed in separate manuscripts, the final leaf of Poem II became detached from the end of the poem, and by some accident was later added to the prose following Poem I or attached to the beginning

[10] Cf. below, p. 20 and p. 21, note 21.

[11] P. 65. Vincenti may also be right in suggesting that the missing leaf contained the transitional passage.

[12] Part of the introduction of Poem II, it must be remembered, is missing, because of the erasure of page 14; cf. above, p. 2.

instead of the end of Poem II. The scribe of MS A, copying the works in this order, may thus have written the conclusion of Poem II at the top of page 13 immediately before its opening. The disappearance of the leaf preceding page 13 in the extant MS A makes any hypothesis about the cause of the misplacement of the lines pure speculation.

III. DATE

The poems of *Solomon and Saturn* have been assigned to a period as early as the beginning of the eighth century, the date conjecturally given by Grein,[1] and to one as late as the end of the tenth century, the date for which Brandl argues in some detail.[2] Ten Brink considered the dialogues contemporary with the poems on *Satan*, now usually called *Christ and Satan*, which he assigned to the end of the ninth or beginning of the tenth century.[3] Schipper thought that the original composition of the poems undoubtedly belonged to the 'classical period' of Old English literature.[4] Sweet, on linguistic grounds, thought that MS A must be a copy of a West Saxon manuscript of Alfred's time.[5] Only the earlier critics have put the poems in Alfred's time or before. Vincenti, whose commentary is the most elaborate since Kemble's, is an exception, chiefly because he is rather vague about the date.[6] He remarked that the *terminus a quo* must be the period in which Christianity had not yet won the final victory over heathendom, and since he believed Poem II to be Northumbrian, he suggested that this might be either shortly after 627, when the Northumbrians were not wholly Christianized, or after the Danish invasions. The reference to the flood preceding Doomsday (314ff.) might, he thought, point to the year 1000 as a *terminus ad quem*. Carl Richter, most of whose criteria are of little value in determining the date of poems admittedly so late, considered the dialogues very late (tenth century) because he found four instances in which liquid endings count as dissyllables and none in which they do not: *ēðelrīces* 106b, *hleahtor* 340a, *mōdor* 435b, *dohtor* 438a; and five monosyllables resulting from

[1] *Kurzgefasste angelsächsische Grammatik* (Kassel, 1880), p. 9.

[2] Paul's *Grundriss der germanischen Philologie*, 2nd ed., II.1 (Strassburg, 1908), 1092.

[3] *Geschichte der englischen Litteratur*, I, 112–114. Wülker, p. 367, mistakenly assumed that ten Brink put the poems in the period 800–850 because he pointed out the more conservative technique of the dialogues and the looser versification of the Alfredian *Metres of Boethius*.

[4] *Germania*, XXII (1877), 51.

[5] *Anglia*, I (1878), 153; see below, p. 16.

[6] P. 83; cf. p. 72.

contraction (and no dissyllables): *frēan* 34b, *getēo* 166b, *gǣð*[7] 126b, 274a, and *sīe* 415a.[8]

There can now be no question that the poems belong to the ninth or tenth century rather than to an earlier period. Many characteristics show this clearly: the frequent use of rhyme and assonance in Poem I;[9] the occasional tendency to a rather loose style savoring of prose in Poem I (4, 84ff., 92ff.); the absence in both Poems of the weak adjective without the article; the lack of early poetic words in both poems, and the presence of late Latin words (*istoriam* 4, *cantic* 17, 27, 49)[10] in I; the not infrequent stressing of unimportant words in alliteration (*ēac* 93, *swīðe* 214, *hīe* 237, *mid ðȳ* 476), and the placing of the alliterating verb before the noun (114b, 307b). But, when we find that Richter assigns only two poems, the *Metres of Boethius* and the *Paris Psalter*, to the ninth century,[11] and Brandl considers even the *Psalter* a tenth-century work,[12] it is plain that sufficient material does not exist to determine the stylistic and linguistic differences between the poetry of the second half of the ninth century and that of the first half of the tenth. The situation is further complicated by the possibility that the loose style of the *Metres of Boethius* is a characteristic rather of royal verse than of the ninth century, and by the probability that the stricter adherence to the older rules and the preservation of an older vocabulary in such poems as *Judith*, of the tenth century according to Brandl, and the *Battle of Brunanburh* (937) are due to the greater familiarity of their authors with the heroic poetry. The disinclination of critics to assign poetry to the ninth century, and especially to the late ninth century, it must be remembered, is the result of two assumptions, the first, probably correct, that most of the poetry not connected with Alfred's circle is Anglian, and the second, more doubtful, that in the troubled times of Alfred's wars with the Danes there was probably little opportunity for the composition of poetry by Anglian writers because of the limited section of Anglian territory still precariously kept under English rule.

[7] On the other hand, *gǣð* in 278a: 'ac him on hand gǣð heardes and hnesces' certainly looks as if it were dissyllabic in a C line.

[8] *Chronologische Studien*, [Morsbach's] *Studien zur englischen Philologie*, XXXII (Halle, 1909), 98.

[9] On this and on the stylistic differences between the poems, see above, p. 7.

[10] Cf. the note on *Pāter Noster* (12), which does not seem to be used in English before the tenth century.

[11] *Chronologische Studien*, p. 101.

[12] *Grundriss*, II.1, 1094. Brandl assigns 'pre-Alfredian' poems like the third part of *Christ* and the Exeter *Judgment Day* to a period decidedly later than Cynewulf without specifying that they are of the ninth century. He evidently considers that they belong to the period before 866 (p. 1050).

Before presenting possible evidence for a ninth-century date, it will be well to consider Brandl's arguments for a later one.[13]

1. Since both poems seem to be directed against the heathen, the choice must be made between the heathen before the eighth century or the Danish heathen of the tenth century for whom Ælfric wrote *De Falsis Deis;* and must naturally be in favor of the latter period, since the eighth century is out of the question. Brandl has previously mentioned [14] the influence of the Benedictine reform in the latter part of the tenth century, which led to the requirement that all Christians learn the Pater Noster and Creed, and was responsible for a number of translations, though not the earliest.

2. Lines 314–317, which contain a definite reference to the flood which is one of the signs of Doomsday, refer to the imminence (*Sōna bið gesīene*) of Doomsday, which was expected in the year 1000, and therefore Poem II must be placed shortly before that date.

3. The pseudo-learning about Oriental lands is an indication of lateness.

4. Poem I shows a decided preference for rhyme and assonance (cf. above, p. 7).

5. Both poems stress the verb before the noun. For examples, see above, p. 13.

6. Poem II shows, besides other irregularities of metrical structure, several cases of double alliteration in the second hemistich. (But see below, p. 15.)

The value of these arguments must be briefly considered.

1. To the first it might be replied that neither poem is necessarily interpreted as a composition designed to prevent the revival of heathenism. Poem I reflects the popular and superstitious view of the effectiveness of Christian prayers, a view that must have been present at all times among people of little education, and is only striking because it does not happen to be reflected elsewhere in the more sober Christian poetry modelled on the heroic tradition. Poem II represents a contention, it is true, between the pagan and Christian traditions, but there is nowhere a suggestion of direct appeal to the heathen, or even to backsliders from the faith. Both poems might as easily have served as a reminder during Alfred's reign, I to the less learned, II to the more learned, of the value of Christian practice and tradition as opposed to the beliefs of the heathen invaders.

2. This seems, at first sight, the most impressive of the arguments,

[13] *Grundriss*, II.1, 1092.

[14] P. 1089, in his introductory paragraph on the late poetry. Cf. further, p. 39, below.

since the lines undoubtedly refer to the flood before Doomsday.[15] It is true that references to the nearness of Doomsday are frequent in Old English writings of the tenth century,[16] but there is no specific mention of the year 1000 in any of them. What is more important, however, is that the proximity of Doomsday is mentioned in much earlier periods by Ephraem Syrus and Gregory the Great.[17] Line 781b of the second part of *Christ* ('Is þām dōme nēah') shows clearly that there is no need to assign a poem to the tenth century because it mentions the imminence of Doomsday.

3. The Oriental learning in Poem II is hardly of the type that is found in the late *Wonders of the East* or *Alexander's Letter*, except perhaps in the Vasa Mortis passage, and even this kind of apocryphal material, definitely a part of the legend of Solomon, may have been preserved in Celtic lands and transmitted to the Anglo-Saxons.[18]

4, 5. Points 4, 5 (and 6) cannot be taken to demonstrate tenth-century origin rather than late ninth-century, in view of the fact that the only poem of any length assigned by Brandl to the late ninth century, the Alfredian *Metres of Boethius*, is in many respects, for example the frequent stress on mere particles, less conservative stylistically than *Solomon and Saturn*.[19]

6. Of the two cases of double alliteration cited by Brandl (290b and 474b), the first passage shows other indications of corruption and may be emended (see note), and the second (*hū his hyʒe*) was incorrectly divided by earlier editors (see note). The incorrect alliteration of the second stress in 16b (*sī gebrydded*) and 350b (*se wyrsa leng*) may be due to scribal transposition.

It would be properly generous to the poets to attribute these deviations from the classical style to corruption of the manuscripts, as is done in similar cases in the older poems.[20] The corruption of the text, obvious in some instances (e.g. 108, 123), probably accounts for such metrically defective lines as 167, 290ff., 325, 328, and 386, since we

[15] Cf. 314ff. and note.

[16] Cf. Dorothy Whitelock, *Sermo Lupi ad Anglos* (London, 1938), p. 24, note 8. The accounts of romantic historians in the nineteenth century greatly exaggerated the importance of the year 1000 as the date of Doomsday; for bibliography on the subject in general see F. Ermini, 'La fine del mondo nel'anno mille e il pensiero di Odone di Cluny,' *Studien zur lateinischen Dichtung des Mittelalters, Ehrengabe für Karl Strecker* (Dresden, 1931), pp. 29–36.

[17] Ephraem Syrus, *Hymni et Sermones*, ed. T. J. Lamy, IV, 402; Gregory, *Dialogues* IV, 41, *Pat. Lat.*, LXXVII, 397.

[18] Cf. below, p. 25.

[19] Cf. ten Brink, *Geschichte der englischen Litteratur*, I, 112–114; Brandl, pp 1065–66.

[20] M. Rieger, *ZfdPh.*, VII (1876), 5–7.

can hardly suppose poets normally so conscious of metrical technique to have suffered such extraordinary lapses in a few cases. Sievers considered the irregularity of 325 (see note) intentional. Nowhere in either poem do we have such a serious departure from the traditional technique as the alliteration of *sc* and *s* so frequent in the *Psalms;* nor do we find *st* ever alliterating with *s* as in the *Battle of Maldon*.

The evidence for a ninth-century date presented by Sweet has been disregarded by most critics and is mentioned by none, but some of it cannot be easily brushed aside. Sweet thought that the constant *ie* in such words as *hīe, hiene, nīeten, gesīene,* was alone enough to prove that the existing MS A must be a copy of a West Saxon manuscript of Alfred's time.[21] It is true that *ie* is by no means constant in other words, since we sometimes find both *i* and *y* for *ie*,[22] and it is further true that *ie* occurs frequently when it is obviously a back-spelling, not only in *sienful*, which Sweet notes, but in many other words such as *brieceð, hieltas, siemle.*[23] But the point is that the genuine *ie* in such numbers must at the very least indicate a copy of the early tenth century, and the numerous back-spellings can be paralleled only in the late ninth. It is generally assumed that *ie* spellings ceased about the middle of the tenth century, there being none, for example, in *Judith*.[24] But actually, Kügler's study shows that, apart from the pronominal forms, the dated documents indicate an earlier disappearance, varying according to the origin of the *ie* from 900 to 934.[25] Again, the only manuscript in which the back-spelling *ie* is at all common is the Hatton MS of the *Pastoral Care*, which dates from the end of the ninth century.[26] Now we should expect this sort of spelling to occur at a period when genuine *ǐe* had become *ǐ*, but there is no evidence that it persisted after Alfred's time. That the dialogues go back to a copy with peculiarities characteristic of the Hatton MS of the *Pastoral Care* is further shown by the preservation in MS B of the *sð* spellings for *st*, as in *ēaðusð*,[27] which is likewise found only sporad-

[21] *Anglia* I, 153.

[22] Cf. Language, below, p. 18.

[23] Cf. Language, below, p. 18.

[24] Brandl, *Grundriss*, II.1, 1091.

[25] H. Kügler, *ie und seine Parallelformen im Angelsächsischen*, Berlin, 1916. The last *ie*-spellings found by Kügler are 1) *ie* $<$ *ea*^{i}, 931, none after 924 in the Parker Chronicle (p. 68); *īe* $<$ *ēa*^{i}, 934 (p. 73); *ie* $<$ *io*^{i}, none after Alfred (p. 80); *īe* $<$ *īo*^{i}, 909 (p. 86); *ǐe* from initial palatalization, none after Alfred (p. 60).

[26] H. Sweet, *King Alfred's West-Saxon Version of Gregory's Pastoral Care, EETS*, L, p. xiii. On the analogical *ie*, see Bülbring, *Anglia Beiblatt*, IX (1889), 96f., *Elementarbuch*, § 306, Anm. 1; Luick, § 263, Anm. 2; and Kügler, p. 26.

[27] Cf. the discussion of this point with reference to the relation of the MSS, pp. 3–4, above, and note on line 22.

ically outside the late ninth-century Hatton MS. It is possible, of course, that some scriptorium whose manuscripts are not preserved continued these practices to a later time; but one cannot, from the extant evidence, avoid the conclusion that both spellings point, as Sweet thought, to the existence of an earlier manuscript of the late ninth century. Other interesting archaisms pointed out by Sweet, who was criticizing Kemble for normalizing his text, are the *e* of *hefonum* (458, cf. 60A) for LWS *eo* with back-mutation, *twēga* for *twēgra* (426) and *neahtes* (386), *meahta* (220) for LWS forms in *-iht*, although these by themselves would not necessitate the assumption of a ninth-century original.[28]

The evidence for an Early West Saxon copy of the late ninth century, or at least very early tenth century, seems, on the whole, more compelling than Brandl's philological and metrical arguments for a late tenth-century date discussed above. If, as seems probable, the original poems were Anglian,[29] the composition of the poems would necessarily be pushed further back than this Early West Saxon copy. It is usually assumed that Anglian composition is incompatible with a late ninth-century dating because of the Scandinavian invasions and the occupation of a large part of Anglian territory. Actual composition in Northumbria at this period of Scandinavian rule may be unlikely.[30] But it would be possible in Western Mercia, and the presence of Mercian authors like Werferth at Alfred's court teaches us the likelihood of composition in Wessex by writers from Mercia or Northumbria.

That Poem I was composed later than Poem II is not improbable, as has been mentioned above.[31] The use of late Latin borrowings such as *cantic*, *istoriam*, the more extensive use of rhyme and assonance, and the repetition and parallelism,[32] all point in this direction.

[28] Still other archaisms mentioned by Sweet are: *(ge)brengan*, *gehwelc*, both of which might be either EWS or Anglian; *gǣst* for *gāst*, which may not necessarily be early; the *e* in the suffixes of *eallenga* and *nǣnegu*, which are EWS, but may occur later (on the phonology, cf. Luick, § 325); and *ēc*, *ēge*, which really represent either Anglian smoothing or LWS monophthongization (cf. Language, p. 18).

[29] Cf. Language, pp. 19–21, below.

[30] It seems to me, however, that Schücking was right in pointing out (*PBB*, XLII [1916/17], 364–365) that the usual assumption of a total disappearance of literature in the North is not necessarily justified by the cultural conditions. The converted Guthred provided a new home for the monks who until 883 had wandered about with the bones of St. Cuthbert, and other centers of religious influence remained (R. H. Hodgkin, *History of the Anglo-Saxons*, 2nd ed. [Oxford, 1939], II, 650–651).

[31] P. 6.

[32] These features are all discussed in greater detail above, p. 7.

IV. LANGUAGE

The language of the two manuscripts is, for the most part, West Saxon, with occasional Anglian forms probably inherited from the original text. The chief differences between MS A, which contains all of Poem II and, except for illegible portions, all of Poem I, and MS B, which contains lines 1–93 of Poem I, have already been discussed in connection with the value and relation of the manuscripts.[1] The uncertain date of the poems occasionally increases the difficulty of distinguishing Anglian and Saxon forms, since several characteristics such as *ĭo* and the unbroken *a* before *l* plus consonant, which could only be Anglian if the poems were of the late tenth century, might conceivably be Early West Saxon, if the poems were of the late ninth century.[2] Many of the spellings noted might be either Anglian or Kentish on the one hand, or West Saxon or Kentish on the other; but since no certain instances of Kentish forms are to be found, I shall usually refer to non-West-Saxon spellings as Anglian and to non-Anglian as West Saxon.

Typical West Saxon forms are characteristic of both manuscripts of Poem I as well as of Poem II. West Germanic *ā* is regularly *ǣ*: *wǣron* 198A; *mǣrðo* 163A, *mǣrþa* 67B; *rǣd* 482A; an exception like the poetical word *mēce* is not significant, since it was borrowed unchanged in West Saxon transcriptions of Anglian poetry. Breaking occurs regularly: *treahteras* 5B; *ealle* 28B; *weard* 83A,B, 253A. Palatalization of *e* occurs in *ongieldað* 132A; and with further development to *i*: *gillan* 259A. The i-umlaut of *ĕa* sometimes appears as EWS *ĭe*: *nīeten* 22B, *gehīere* 317A; *niehtes* 240A; *miehtum* 320A, and likewise the i-umlaut of *eo*: *scierpeð* 138A. But frequently we find *i* or *y* for *ĭe*: *gehīran* 313A, *gehȳrde* 416A; *gyrde* 90B, *gierde* 90A. The scribe of A differs from B in having numerous back-spellings in both I and II with *ie* for original *i*, and even for *y*: for *i*, *brieceð* 95A beside *bebriceð* 287A, *hieltas* 215A, *gielpne* 199A, *siemle* 85A, *symle* 85B, beside *simle* 146A, and *symle* 166A, 235A; for *y̆*, *āhīeðeð* 73A, but *hīðan* 445A, *sienfullan* 498A. The relevance of this characteristic, which MS A shares with the Hatton MS of the *Pastoral Care*, for the dating of the poems has already been discussed.[3] OE *y̆* from *ŭ*ⁱ frequently appears as *ī*: *īða* 29B, but *ȳða* 81A,B; *hige* 60A,B, but *hyge* 474A. Conversely the appearance of *y* for *i* is also common: *fīra* 208A, but *fȳra* 202A, *-gewrytum* 8B, *bryceð* 404A. The Late West Saxon development of *y* after *w* appears not infrequently: *swylce* 4B, 43A; but *swilce* 43B,

[1] See above, pp. 3–4.

[2] Cf. Luick, § 261, § 146 and Anm. 2.

[3] See Date, p. 16.

118A; and *hwȳlum* 61B, but *hwīlum* 61A; *cwyde* 17B, but *cwide* 63A. *Syllice* 149A, 261A is typical Late West Saxon for earlier *sel-*, though *sille* (MS *wille* 13B) might be either Anglian or Late West Saxon.

The morphology is, in general, also West Saxon, with the exception of a few forms to be noted in the next paragraph, which may be Anglian, and the regular Anglian or poetical present indicative third singular in *-eð*.

Anglian forms, though not numerous, occur often enough to suggest that the text was at one time written in Anglian. Anglian (or possibly Early West Saxon) lack of breaking is to be found in *bald* 175A, 234A and *baldlīce* 298A, *aldor* 348A; and *hwarfað* 35B. *Sceppend* has Anglian, or at least not strict West Saxon *e* in 56B, but LWS *y* (< *ie* < *ea*ⁱ) 56A.[4] Anglian i-umlaut of *ēa* appears in *nēd* 303A.[5] *Welm* 82A shows Anglian *i*-umlaut of *æ* beside LWS *wylm* (< *ie* < *ea*ⁱ) 74A,B, and the same may be true of *meltan* 55A, as opposed to *miltan* 55B. Anglian *a*-umlaut of *e* appears in *seofan* 66A beside *sefa(n)* 66B and 430A. Forms such as *ēc* 333A, 456A beside *ēac* 4B, 296A, and *ēge* 487A, *ēgna* 464A might as well represent Late West Saxon monophthongization as Anglian smoothing.[6] The *īo* of *tuīon* 426A (cf. *twēon* 418A) might occur in any dialect at an early period, but if the poem were of the tenth century would probably be Anglian, and perhaps rather Northumbrian than Mercian.[7] *Hīo* 291A, 292A, beside the usual *hēo*, also has a Northumbrian look if the poem is late.[8] The isolated *heartan* 104A (cf. *heortan* 156A) and *āweorp* 454A might be respectively North Northumbrian and South Northumbrian, since *eo/ea* confusion is characteristic of Northumbrian;[9] but occasional confusion of this sort might occur in almost any manuscript. In such words as *gīfrust* 48A (*-ost* 48B), *-twigude* 39B, *werud* 160A, *u* is rather Anglian than West Saxon.[10]

In morphology, *mec* 18B, 19B beside *mē* is Anglian or poetical; and similarly *ūsic* 450A beside *ūs* 329A.[11] The use of the accusative form *mec* for the dative in 18B (*mec gesund fare*), if it is not a scribal error because of the earlier *mec*, accusative, in the same line, would be Northumbrian.[12] *Heht* 268A, 449A is Anglian or poetical beside *hēt*

[4] Luick, §§ 189, 197.
[5] Luick, § 194.
[6] Luick, §§ 278, 238.
[7] Luick, § 261.
[8] Sievers-Cook, § 334.
[9] Luick, § 228, Anm. 2, § 136.
[10] Luick, § 326.2.
[11] Sievers-Cook, § 332.
[12] Sievers-Cook, § 336, note 4.

267A. The Anglian participle in *-ende* for *-iende* appears in *wincendra* 77A beside the metrically more difficult *winciendra* 77B. It would be metrically desirable in *hangiende* 105A, and may appear in *weallende* 204A (see note), 212A. The unsyncopated verbal forms in the present indicative third singular, which occur almost without exception,[13] and are often required by the metre, as in *bēateð* 274A, *rǣdeð* 362A, *āðrēoteð* 420A, are more likely to be Anglian than Late West Saxon, and the absence of i-umlaut and of *i* < *e* as in *wegeð* 52B (but *wigeð* 52A, 124), is Anglian or 'less pure' West Saxon.[14] Manuscript *scīnað* for *scīneð* 214A, *healdeð* for *healdað* 252A, and *besceadeð* for *besceadað* 332A, and the curious change from the plural to singular in 153Aff. (see note) might possibly reflect an original in Northumbrian, where the confusion of *-eð* and *-að* was normal. The neuter gender of *bōc* 6B is striking, and might reflect a Northumbrian original, since *bōc* occurs as a neuter in that dialect.[15]

The vocabulary is perhaps a safer test of origin than phonology and accidence. Excluding Anglian words that apparently became traditionally poetic and are found normally in Southern poems, one still finds quite a number that seem to indicate Anglian provenience. *Gēna* 241A, *ðecele* 410A, and *forcuman* 198A, 503A are all listed by Jordan as specifically Anglian,[16] and to these *līxan*, *winnan* in the sense of 'laborari' 384A (cf. 275),[17] and *(eormen)strȳnde* 322 may be added.[18] The curious *gewesan* 'converse,' 'debate' 172A, seems to be used in a

[13] *Wyrcð* 492 seems to be required by the metre; see also the note on *līehð* 172A.

[14] Sievers-Cook, § 371.

[15] Uno Lindelöf, *Beiträge zur Kenntnis des Altnorthumbrischen* (Helsingfors, 1893), p. 233. The accusative feminine singular *winrōd* 227A (see note) might also represent a Northumbrian inflection, since this form occurs in the *Lindisfarne Gospels*, and the lack of *e* in this declension is extremely common in Northumbrian (H. C. A. Carpenter, *Die Deklination in der nordhumbrischen Evangelienübersetzung der Lindisfarner Handschrift*, *Bonner Studien* II [Bonn, 1910], p. 152).

[16] *Eigentümlichkeiten des anglischen Wortschatzes*, *Anglistische Forschungen*, XVII (Heidelberg, 1906), pp. 48, 58, 59–60.

[17] Günther Scherer, *Zur Geographie und Chronologie des ags. Wortschatzes* (Berlin diss., 1928), pp. 15, 17; cf. p. 42, where Scherer assigns the poems to the Anglian dialect on the basis of four words: *ēþian*, *hlēoþrian*, *þæcele*, *winnan*. It should be noted, however, that the first two occur, not in the poems, but in the prose dialogues, *ǣþung* in the Cotton Vitellius A XV dialogue, ed. Kemble, p. 180, line 10, *(ofer)hlēoðrað* in that of our MS A, Appendix, p. 170, line 34. One word *clūd*, listed by Scherer as Saxon (p. 21), probably occurs in 185 (see note), but he observes that *clūdig* occurs in Orm. The value of the test of vocabulary is somewhat diminished by the fact that some Anglian words occur in the Alfredian *Metres of Boethius* (Scherer, p. 42), but the number in *Solomon and Saturn* is certainly striking.

[18] M. Deutschbein, 'Dialektisches in der Übersetzung von Bedas Kirchengeschichte,' *PBB*, XXVI (1901), 172; cf. Klaeber, *Anglia* XXV (1922), 292.

sense paralleled only in Anglian.[19] Finally, MS *weallað* 143A (see note) is certainly a mistake for *wǣleð*, a word specifically Anglian.[20]

The test of vocabulary thus confirms the view that the occasional Anglian forms point to an Anglian origin; but there does not seem to be enough evidence to prove Vincenti's contention, probably based on such forms as *hīo* and *heartan*, noted above, that the poems were written in Northumbrian.[21] In spite of the lack of distinctive Mercian forms, it seems venturesome to attempt to assign definitely either of the poems, transcribed as they are into a predominantly West Saxon dialect, to a Northumbrian rather than to a Mercian dialect.[22]

V. THE LEGEND OF SOLOMON IN THE POEMS

1. The Origin and Spread of the Legend

Solomon, the wise and mighty ruler of the Old Testament, whose only weakness was the love of those foreign women who turned his heart to strange gods (I Kings XI, 1–9), became in Talmudic and Cabbalistic writings a great magician who held sway by means of his magic ring over the creatures of nature and the demons of the underworld.[1] Solomon came to be considered the author not only of Proverbs, Ecclesiastes, The Song of Songs, The Book of Wisdom, and Ecclesiasticus (Jesus Sirach), but of many books of magic, such as the famous *Clavicula Salomonis*.[2] The legend of Solomon was destined to become one of the most popular in Europe, and influenced many a

[19] Bosworth-Toller cites *giwosa* 'conversatio' only for the Durham Ritual, and *gewesness* 'dissensio' only from the *Ecclesiastical History*, IV, 4, ed. J. Schipper, p. 369, note 44.

[20] Jordan, p. 57.

[21] Vincenti based his confidently stated opinion (p. 49, and p. 85, where only Poem II is mentioned) on his unpublished phonology. It may be noted that *forcuman* appears to be chiefly Northumbrian, although it does occur in the *Corpus Glossary* (Jordan, p. 58, Bosworth-Toller and *Suppl.*).

[22] On the relation of the date and the dialect, see above, pp. 17–18.

[1] On the legend of Solomon in Hebrew and Arabic, see Louis Ginzberg, *Legends of the Jews* (Philadelphia, 1909–38), IV, 125–126; VI, 277–303; and Ginzberg's article *Solomon* in the *Jewish Encyclopedia;* G. Salzberger, *Die Salomosage in der semitischen Literatur*, I Teil (Berlin, 1907); on its later development, C. C. McCown, *The Testament of Solomon* (Leipzig, 1922); St. John D. Seymour, *Tales of King Solomon* (London, 1924); on special subjects, see the further bibliographical notes in this section; and for references to phases of the medieval legend not directly connected with the Old English poems, G. Ehrismann, *Geschichte der deutschen Literatur* II.1 (1922), 314–328.

[2] *Jewish Ency.*, art. *Solomon*, pp. 446–448; E. Schürer, *Geschichte des jüdischen Volkes im Zeitalter Christi*, 4th ed. (Leipzig, 1921), III, 413–414, 419–420; cf. III, 221.

medieval tale from that of Merlin to that of Robert of Sicily.[3] The later Middle Ages made of the worldly Solomon a hero of courtly romance, whose story proved that even the wisest of men must submit to the power of love.[4] But the religious tradition represented him as the ideal king, known for his wisdom and magnificence, who prefigured in the Old Testament the Christ of the New.[5] In the Old English dialogues this conception persists in the king whose wisdom, now Christianized, triumphs over that of his opponent; but traces of the magician remain in the curious power of the runic letters of the Pater Noster over the Devil (Poem I), and in the subduing of the demonic Vasa Mortis (238–272).[6]

In the vast literature concerning Solomon transmitted to Western Europe by the Orient, dialogues between Solomon and another person play an important part. The dialogues are ultimately derived from two phases of the legend of Solomon: first, tests of his wisdom by human beings, and secondly, conversations with demons over whom he acquired power. The germs of an exchange of wisdom are found in the Old Testament itself where the Queen of Sheba 'came to prove him with hard questions' (I Kings X, 1–3; II Chron. IX, 1–3). The Queen's riddles and Solomon's answers are duly recorded in Hebrew legend.[7] Similarly, the exchange of letters between Solomon and Hiram, King of Tyre, (II Chron. II) developed into a contest of wisdom between the two, a story cited by Josephus from Menander of Ephesus and from Dius.[8] According to these versions, Hiram, unable to solve Solomon's riddles himself, enlisted the aid of one Abdemon, or Abdemon's son, who received the name Abdimus in the story as recorded by the twelfth-century William of Tyre, to be mentioned shortly.[9]

Solomon's power over demons became an important theme in

[3] M. Gaster, 'The Legend of Merlin,' *Folk-Lore*, XVI (1905), 407–426, reprinted in *Studies and Texts* (London, 1925–1928), II, 963–984.

[4] Cf. Heinrich von Veldeke, in *Des Minnesangs Frühling*, ed. F. Vogt (Leipzig, 1911), p. 74:66, lines 16–18.

[5] For example, Augustine, *Enarratio in Psalmum* 126, *Pat. Lat.*, XXXVII, 1668; Isidore, *Allegoriæ*, *Pat. Lat.*, LXXXIII, 113. On Solomon and Christ, see below, pp. 47–48.

[6] Cf. below, pp. 28–29.

[7] Ginzberg, *Legends of the Jews*, IV, 145–149, VI, 290–291; S. Schechter, *Folk-Lore*, I (1890), 349–358; Seymour, *Tales of King Solomon*, pp. 137–148; W. Hertz, *Gesammelte Abhandlungen* (Stuttgart-Berlin, 1905), pp. 413–455. It should be noted that the Queen of Sheba, called Bilqis in Arabic legend, partakes of the nature of a demon, having the feet of a demon in some legends; cf. Gaster, 'The Legend of Merlin,' *Folk-Lore*, XVI (1905), 418.

[8] *Antiquities of the Jews*, VIII, 5.

[9] See below, pp. 28–29.

Hebrew and Arabic tradition. In Rabbinic legend Solomon commands his chief man Benaiah to capture Ashmedai (Asmodeus), king of the demons, by means of a magic ring.[10] Thereupon Ashmedai is obliged to reveal to Solomon important secrets of the supernatural world. This story is of special relevance, for it is not only part of the general tradition of Solomon's conversations with mighty seers, human and supernatural, out of which the medieval dialogue grew, but also the ultimate source of the Vasa Mortis passage in our poem (238–272), in which Solomon orders the son of Melot to bind the demon worshipped by the Philistines.[11] In Arabic legend Solomon talks with the king of the djinns Sachr, the Arabic counterpart of the Hebrew Ashmedai, who tells him of the spheres of fire, water, and air, and of the seven worlds and the seven seas, and of the old world-dragon.[12] The story of Solomon's power over demons appears in a slightly different form in the Hebrew legend according to which Solomon is carried by an eagle to the 'mountain of darkness,' where the fallen angels Azza and Azzael, lying chained in iron fetters, are forced to reveal the heavenly mysteries to the king.[13]

An early reflection of these stories of Solomon's mastery over demons is the Greek *Testament of Solomon*.[14] In this text of the third or fourth century, Solomon summons a host of demons of horrible shapes, including Ornias, Beelzeboul, and Asmodeus, who reveal their names and powers to him and are forced, as in the Hebrew legends, to help him build the Temple. Jewish elements are overlaid with Christian in the *Testament*, and the possibility of Solomon's becoming the counterpart of Christ as a subduer of demons, and thus a representative of Christianity, as in our poems, is foreshadowed by the introduction of references to Christ's power over demons.[15]

[10] Ginzberg, art. *Asmodeus*, *Jewish Ency.*; *Legends*, IV, 165–169, VI, 299. The passage in the *Tractate Gittin* which contains this legend is translated in Vogt, pp. 213–217 (*Anhang*).

[11] See the notes on lines 244ff., 265ff., and pp. 59–61, below.

[12] Vogt, p. liii, citing Hammer[-Purgstall], *Rosenöl*, I, 205, which I have not seen. Vincenti, p. 11, cites another Arabic legend from *Rosenöl*, in which Solomon converses with Simurg about fate and prophecy (cf. *Solomon and Saturn*, lines 293–377).

[13] Ginzberg, *Legends*, IV, 149–150; cf. I, 148.

[14] C. C. McCown, *The Testament of Solomon* (Leipzig, 1922), with valuable introduction; English translation by Conybeare, *Jewish Quarterly Review*, XI (1899), 1–45. The *Testament* also contains romantic elements, such as Solomon's fall through his wicked marriage with Sulamith, the Shunammite woman, through whom he worshipped Moloch (XXVI, 1–7).

[15] XI, 6; XII, 3; cf. McCown's *Testament of Solomon*, pp. 49–50, 68–78, and below, p. 47.

A lost *Contradictio Salomonis* has been supposed by many writers to be the actual source of the Old English dialogues.[16] A book of that title is condemned in the so-called Gelasian decree, now thought to be a product of the early sixth century.[17] But although the title *Contradictio Salomonis* might indicate a debate between Solomon and some other person, it is to be noted that the earlier group of MSS has *Interdictio Salomonis.* Besides, as Vincenti rightly pointed out,[18] this sixth-century *Contradictio* could hardly, in any case, be the immediate and sole source of a poem which contrasted Germanic and Christian wisdom. The mention of the *Contradictio* is at least welcome testimony from an obscure period to the continued popularity of the apocryphal literature concerning Solomon, and if really a debate, might well be the ancestor of the medieval dialogues.

The gap of five centuries in actual literary remains between the Greek *Testament of Solomon* and the Old English poems, which are certainly no earlier than the late ninth century, is thus a large one. In spite of the loss of the *Contradictio* and the lack of other texts, certain early allusions to Solomon and reflections of earlier stories in later popular Slavic literature enable us to fill this gap in Solomonic literature. The interest of pilgrims to the Holy Land in the legend of Solomon makes it probable that stories about him were first brought to Western Europe over the pilgrim routes.[19] As early as the fourth century the *Peregrinatio* tells how a deacon in the church of the Holy Sepulchre pointed out not only the relics of the Cross, but the ring and horn of Solomon;[20] and two centuries later the seal-ring with which Solomon conquered the demons is more precisely mentioned in the *Breviarius de Hierosolyma.*[21] It is probable that Byzantine Greek sources helped to spread the legend of Solomon in Western Europe, as they certainly did in Slavic lands. The great popularity

[16] Von der Hagen, in Hagen and Büsching, *Deutsche Gedichte des Mittelalters*, I (Berlin, 1808), iv; Grimm, *Kleinere Schriften* (Berlin, 1869), IV, 46: 'unbezweifelbar unser Buch'; Kemble, p. 12; M. Förster, *Archiv für das Studium der neueren Sprachen*, CVIII (1902), 27.

[17] The best edition is by Ernst von Dobschütz, *Das Decretum Gelasianum*, *Texte und Untersuchungen zur Geschichte der altchristlichen Literatur*, XXXVIII, 4 (Leipzig, 1912); the book is mentioned in line 333, p. 57, and discussed briefly on p. 319, where the editor considers it a magical book.

[18] Pp. 122–124.

[19] This was first pointed out by Konrad Burdach, *Archiv für das Studium der neueren Sprachen*, CVIII (1902), 131–132.

[20] *Itinera Hierosolymitana*, Chap. 37, ed. P. Geyer, *Corpus Scriptorum Ecclesiasticorum Latinorum*, XXXIX, 88.

[21] Geyer, p. 154. The tradition was still repeated in the twelfth century (Burdach, p. 132).

of stories about Solomon in Russia and the Balkans can be explained only by the supposition that Byzantine literature supplied Southeastern Europe and Russia with these tales.[22] A certain Kitovras, who is Solomon's brother in the Russian romantic tales, and who takes the place of Ashmedai in the Russian story of the binding of the demon, has been shown by Jagić to be a Slavic transformation of Greek κένταυρος, evidently one of the forms assumed by the demon in a Greek version.[23] The popularity of the legendary Solomon in Byzantine literature is attested not only by frequent allusion to his power as a magician,[24] but by various pseudepigraphical writings, all later, however, than the Old English poems, such as the famous *Clavicula Salomonis*, which appears with various titles in Greek.[25] The exact means by which the legend of Solomon was transmitted to England can only be guessed at. The possibility that a Latin version of the Solomonic dialogues came to England from Ireland must not be overlooked, for the Celtic church, because of its isolation and independent tradition, may have preserved apocryphal legends savoring of demonology which disappeared elsewhere when condemned by ecclesiastical authority.[26] Some of the phraseology in Poem I is, as we shall see, reminiscent of Irish religious literature,[27] and both poems contain apocryphal material that seems more characteristic of Irish than of English tradition.[28]

Whether the dialogue of Solomon and Saturn came to the Old English poets through the Celtic church or from the continent, there is little doubt that the immediate sources of both Old English poems were written in Latin. Apart from the fact that Poem I concerns the Latin form of the Lord's Prayer, such loan-words as *cantic* (17, 24, 49), *organ* (33, 53), and especially *istoriam* (4) and *prologa prima* (89)

[22] A. Wesselofsky, *Slavianskiia skazaniia o Solomonie i Kitovrasie* [*Slavic Tales of Solomon and Kitovras*]—in Russian—(St. Petersburg, 1872); V. Jagić, 'Die christlich-mythologische Schicht in der russischen Volksepik,' *Archiv für slavische Philologie*, I (1876), 82–133; Vogt, pp. xli–lii; M. Gaster, *Literatura populară română* (Bucharest, 1883), pp. 78–91, 324–329; M. Murko, *Geschichte der älteren südslawischen Litteraturen* (Leipzig, 1908), pp. 89, 91, 99, 100.

[23] Jagić, pp. 109–110; Vogt, p. xlvi.

[24] Cf. McCown, *Testament of Solomon*, pp. 94–95; for reference to the many medieval amulets depicting Solomon's power over demons, see McCown, p. 77, note 5.

[25] K. Krumbacher, *Geschichte der byzantinischen Literatur*, 2nd ed. (Munich, 1897), pp. 802ff.; J. A. Fabricius, *Codex Pseudepigraphus* (Hamburg, 1722), pp. 1046–47, and cf. p. 46, below.

[26] Cf. M. Förster, *Archiv für das Studium der neueren Sprachen*, CVII (1901), 27–28.

[27] See below, pp. 42–43.

[28] See the notes on lines 66ff. and line 90.

attest a Latin original. The Latin form of the name Saturn not only appears invariably in the headings of speeches in both poems, but is used in the text of the second (174), where the name Vasa Mortis (272) also occurs. Unfortunately no Latin texts resembling either dialogue in content have as yet been discovered, for the later Latin dialogues of Solomon and Marcolf, to be discussed in the next section, have little in common with the Old English poems. One may hazard the guess that even if Latin sources should be found they would contain only a part of the material of the Old English dialogues. This is especially probable in the case of Poem II, in which many of the characteristic themes of Germanic poetry are interwoven with Oriental legends. However much amplified, the Old English poems are dependent on lost Solomonic Christian dialogues in Latin, which in turn were presumably adapted from Greek originals that had their ultimate source in the Hebrew legends of King Solomon.

2. Solomon, Marcolf, and Saturn

a) *The Medieval Legends of Solomon and Marcolf*

It is only in the Old English poetic and prose dialogues that the opponent of Solomon is Saturn. In the medieval Latin dialogue, which differs entirely in tone from the Old English, a Marcolfus replies in merry and often indecent fashion to the serious proverbs of Solomon. The nature of the later medieval dialogues is well described in the comment of the early thirteenth-century Swabian poet Freidank: 'Salmon wîsheit lêrte, Marolt daz verkêrte.' [1] The Latin *Salomon et Marcolfus*,[2] which appears in manuscripts of the fourteenth and fifteenth centuries and in many early printed editions, consists of two parts, of different authorship, the first, the dialogue proper, being a series of proverbs in which Marcolf parodies Solomon's wise sayings, many of which are drawn from the Bible, and the second a collection of anecdotes about Marcolf and Solomon, in most of which Marcolf offers ingenious proof of his curious or riddling pronouncements. The Latin collection of proverbs, or at least a similar one under the same name, was in existence as early as the tenth century, the nucleus of the anecdotes as early as the twelfth, and the two may have been combined by the thirteenth.[3] A German *Spruchgedicht*, *Salomon und*

[1] H. Bezzenberger, *Frîdankes Bescheidenheit* (Halle, 1872), str. 81.

[2] Ed. W. Benary, in A. Hilka's *Sammlung mittellateinischer Texte* 8 (Heidelberg, 1914).

[3] On the date, see Benary, pp. viii–ix, and especially Paul Lehmann, *Die Parodie im Mittelalter* (Munich, 1922), pp. 236–237. Benary is inclined to think that the anecdotes are a later addition to the dialogue of proverbs (p. viii), partly because the

Markolf (variants Marolf, Morolf) of the thirteenth century, is a translation of the Latin.[4] Marcolf likewise appears in the Morolf of the German fourteenth-century romance *Salman und Morolf*,[5] where, as the brother of Solomon, he twice rescues Solomon's wife Salme from kings who have seduced her. This romantic tale is closely related to the Russian stories about Solomon's wife, in which Solomon's brother is not Morolf, but Kitovras.[6] Another variant of the romance appears in an appendix to the German *Spruchgedicht*.[7] But the dialogue and romance are not directly related, although they both ultimately reflect the Oriental stories of Solomon's power over demons,[8] and both contain the figure of Marcolf-Morolf. The opponent of Solomon in French dialogues of the thirteenth, or possibly late twelfth century, is Marcoul or Marcon. Of these dialogues there are two chief types, one in which Solomon presents the code of chivalry, and Marcoul the views of the common man or *vilein;* and a second in which Marcoul's answers are all drawn from the life of harlots.[9]

The romance of Solomon's wife and the dialogues of Solomon and Marcolf continued to be popular for centuries. It would be impossible

---

proverbs are mentioned earlier by Notker (see below, p. 28), and partly because some manuscripts of the Latin contain the proverbs without the anecdotes. But it might be argued that the riddling nature of the humorous anecdotes shows that this section is inherited ultimately from the early Solomonic riddle-contests, despite many changes and accretions; cf. William of Tyre's remarks, below, pp. 28f., which bridge the gap between the contests mentioned by Josephus (see above, p. 22) and the anecdotes of the dialogue.

[4] W. Hartmann, *Salomon und Markolf* (Halle, 1934), pp. xxxvi–vii; this edition supersedes von der Hagen's in Hagen und Büsching, *Deutsche Gedichte des Mittelalters* I (Berlin, 1808).

[5] Ed. Friedrich Vogt (Halle, 1880).

[6] See above, p. 25.

[7] Lines 1631–1902 of Hartmann's edition. On its importance, see Vogt, pp. lxiff., who shows, by comparison with the Russian stories, that it contains more original elements than the romance or *Spielmannsepos*.

[8] Vogt, pp. xlv–vii, shows that the Oriental stories of Solomon and the demons are reflected in various elements in the Russian version of the romance: 1) winged centaurs, 2) the horn by which Solomon summons birds and beasts, and his ring, 3) the identity of Kitovras and Ashmedai.

[9] The first type was printed by G. A. Crapelet, *Proverbes et Dictons Populaires* (Paris, 1831), pp. 187–200; this is attributed in manuscript to Count Mauclerc of Brittany (d. 1250), cf. *Histoire Littéraire de la France*, XXIII (1856), 686–688. The second type, called sometimes *La Disputacion de Marcoux et de Salmon*, was printed by M. Méon, *Nouveau Recueil de Fabliaux et Contes*, I (1823), 416–436, and was translated into English and printed by Pynson, ca. 1530, as *The Sayings or Proverbes of King Solomon* (*Short Title Catalogue* 22899). On the French versions, see Cosquin, *Romania*, XL (1911), 374–377.

here to enumerate the various later versions in German, Danish, Norwegian, Swedish, Portuguese, Italian, and Greek.[10] Even in England Marcolf was well known in the late Middle Ages, being cited in connection with Solomon by both Audelay and Lydgate.[11] The name of Marcolf was still familiar in the sixteenth century to such different men as Luther and Rabelais;[12] and in the *Anatomy of Melancholy* (III, 2.5.3) Burton, like them, couples him with Solomon.

b) *Early References to Marcolf*

Marcolf, who thus supplants the Saturn of the Old English versions in all the later medieval dialogues, is so intimately bound up with the origin of the Old English poems and the figure of Saturn that it will now be necessary to examine the earliest references to him and the source of his name in order to understand the reason for his appearance as Saturn's *alter ego*. That his name was connected with the Solomon legend before the time of the Old English poems is obvious from the occurrence of the Old English equivalent *Marculf* in line 180 of Poem II, where among the many Oriental countries visited by Saturn in search of wisdom is *Marculfes eard*.

Marcolf is first mentioned as debating with Solomon in a passage of Notker Labeo (d. 1022), who, in commenting on the *fabulationes* of Psalm 118, mentions uncanonical writings of the Jews and heretics, and cites among such fables in secular letters Marcolf's 'striving against the proverbs of Solomon; in all of which are only fair words without truth.'[1] Writing ca. 1181–84, a century and a half later, William of Tyre, after citing from Josephus[2] the passage about Hiram's enlisting the aid of Abdemon's son [Abdimus] to solve Solomon's riddles, continues: 'Et hic fortasse est, quem fabulose popularium narrationes

[10] Kemble's Introduction, though antiquated in details, is still invaluable as a guide to these versions; for a rapid survey see Vincenti, pp. 14–23, which may be supplemented by Vogt and Benary. For the German see C. H. Herford, *Studies in the Relations of England and Germany in the Sixteenth Century*, pp. 253–272; for the French, Cosquin, *op. cit.*, and for the Italian, Gina Pagani, 'Il Bertoldo di Giulio Cesare Croce ed i suoi fonti,' *Studi Medievali*, III (1908–11), 533–602.

[11] Audelay, *Poems*, ed. E. K. Whiting, *EETS*, CLXXXIV, 12, Poem 2, lines 66–67, cf. 988–989; Lydgate, *Order of Fools*, in *Minor Poems*, ed. H. L. MacCracken, *EETS*, CXCII, 449; cf. p. 564.

[12] Cf. Kemble, pp. 70, 82; Luther refers to Marcolphus in his *Table Talk* or *Colloquia* (Leipzig, 1621), f. 409; Rabelais in Bk. I, Chap. 33.

[1] 'Habent ouh soliche sęculares literę. Vuaz ist ioh anderes daz man marcholfum saget sih éllenon uuider prouerbiis salomonis? An diên allen sint uuort scôniû âne uuârheit.' Paul Piper, *Die Schriften Notkers und seiner Schule* (Freiburg, 1882ff.), II, 522.

[2] Cf. above, p. 22.

Marcholfum vocant, de quo dicitur quod Salomonis solvebat aenigmata, et ei respondebat, aequipollenter iterum solvenda proponens.' [3] That William of Tyre was not alone in connecting Marcolfus with Josephus's story of Solomon, Hiram, and Abdemon, is shown by a marginal note in the Paris codex of the *Apology* of Guido of Bazoches (d. 1203), in a passage where he cites the story of the cat and the candle from the Latin anecdotes following the dialogue. Solomon's opponent is called simply 'quodam cum eo sofistice confligente' in the text, but the marginal note reads: 'De Salomone rege et Abdemone Tyrio, qui Marculphus vulgariter appellatur.' [4] Other late twelfth-century references to Solomon and Marcolf are to be found in the Provençal poet Raimbaut d'Orange (fl. 1150–1173), who praises his mistress for knowing more than Solomon or Marcol,[5] and in Serlo of Wilton, who, writing in Latin, gives satirical praise to the lines of a certain Robert who had expounded the life of Marcolf and Solomon's disputes with him.[6]

It is hard to tell from these allusions when the serious type of Solomonic dialogue represented by the Old English *Solomon and Saturn* became the humorous type represented by the Latin, German, and French dialogues of Solomon and Marcolf. It has been argued that Notker would not have spoken of Solomon and Marcolf disputing (*éllinon*) or of *scôniû uuort* if he had been commenting on the extant ribald Latin dialogue of later times; [7] and certainly his words and

[3] *Historia Rerum in partibus transmarinis gestarum*, Lib. XIII, Cap. 1, *Recueil des Historiens des Croisades, Historiens Occidentaux*, I.1 (Paris, 1844), 556–557. The name Abdimus, given by William of Tyre to Abdemon's son, is not in the Greek of Josephus, and apparently comes from the early Latin version, which substitutes Abdimum for the Greek 'Αβδήμονα in the account Josephus cites from Dius; see the textual variants in B. Niese, *Flavii Josephi Opera* (Berlin, 1895), II, 209. It should be noted that William of Tyre's phrase 'erat Abdimus, Abdaemonis filius, in vinculis' (*ibid.*) does not reflect the Solomonic legend of the demon 'in chains,' since *in vinculis* is an error for *iuvenculus*, which stands in the Latin version (*Josephi Judei historici Opera* [Paris, 1513], VIII, 7, fol. 71v) corresponding to the Greek νεώτερος. M. Gaster in *Folk-Lore*, XVI (1905), 418, suggested that the name Abdemon in Josephus may have contributed toward introducing a demon into the legend, but the process is more likely to have been the opposite.

[4] W. Wattenbach, 'Die Apologie von Guido von Bazoches,' *Sitzungsberichte der kgl. preuss. Akad. der Wissenschaften* (Berlin, 1893), I, 405; cf. P. Lehmann, *Die Parodie im Mittelalter*, pp. 236–237.

[5] A. Kolsen, *Dichtungen der Trobadors* (Halle, 1916ff.), p. 225, in a canzone beginning 'Apres mon vers,' ll. 13–18.

[6] B.Hauréau, *Notices et extraits de quelques MSS. latins de la Bibliothèque Nationale*, I (1890), 307, cf. p. 123; E. Faral, *Romania*, XL (1911), 93–96.

[7] Kemble, p. 13; Schaumberg, p. 33; Pagani, *Studi Medievali*, III, 537–538. Lehmann, *Die Parodie*, pp. 22–24, 235–237, seems to take it for granted that Notker refers to a parody, and even suggests that the famous *Contradictio* (cf. above, p. 24) was a parody.

those of Raimbaut d'Orange and William of Tyre seem to refer to serious matter. Guido of Bazoches refers to a comic story, but this is not part of the dialogue proper. The first definite reference to the comic dialogue is that of Freidank in the early thirteenth century, whose remarks that Marcolf perverted (*verkêrte*) Solomon's wisdom have already been cited.[8] After his time the tradition of the comic Marcolf was so well established that a serious dialogue between him and Solomon may be considered impossible.

c) *Origin of the Name Marcolf: Marcolus, Markolis-Mercurius*

The ambiguity of the early references to the Latin dialogue, which, as we have just seen, may indicate a serious debate between Solomon and Marcolf, would be enough to make one hesitate to assign the later dialogues of Solomon and Marcolf to an ancient tradition differing from the serious debates between Solomon and Saturn. The presence in the Old English dialogue (180) of a Marculf, who is ruler of an eastern realm visited by Saturn, is a further indication of a connection between *Solomon and Saturn* and the Solomonic dialogues with Marcolfus, who is described as 'a parte orientis venientem.'[1] Finally, the identity of Saturn and Marcolf becomes more intelligible from a curious statement in the seventh-century compilation ascribed to Aethicus Cosmographicus, in which the Turks are said to worship Saturn by building a mighty pile of stones, and to call it 'Morcholon in their language, that is star of the gods, which they call Saturn by a derived name.' The Latin reads as follows in Kemble's text from Cotton Caligula A 3, fol. 4: 'Appellaverunt lingua sua Morcholon, id est stellam deorum, quod derivato nomine Saturnum appellant.'[2] But it is to be noted that the majority of manuscripts have a form with *a*: Marcholom, Marcholon, or Marcholum.[3] From this passage it is plain that Marchol and Saturn were identified as early as the seventh century.

What is the origin of the name Marcolfus or Marcholus? It is now considered by most investigators of the legend of Marcolf that Marc(h)olus was the original Latin form of the name, which was

[8] P. 26.

[1] Benary, *Salomon et Marcolfus*, p. 1, line 3.

[2] Kemble, p. 119. The text of H. Wuttke, *Die Kosmographie des Istrier Aithikos* (Leipzig, 1853), III, 32, p. 19, is almost unintelligible, reading 'phyrram fonte[m] glutinantes' etc. instead of Kemble's 'pyrrham fortem et glutinatam,' correctly taken from MS Cotton Caligula A 3, fol. 4; and that of d'Avezac, *Mémoires présentés . . . à l'Académie des Inscriptions et Belles-Lettres*, I, Tome 2 (1852), 473, is no better. On Aethicus, see M. Manitius, *Geschichte der lat. Literatur des Mittelalters*, I, 229ff.

[3] Wuttke, p. 97.

transformed into Marcolfus (Markolf, Marculf), because of the frequency of the Germanic name Marculf, which appeared in Latin as Marculfus (Marcolfus).[4] In the genealogy of the Latin dialogue the Marcol who is said to be the father of Marcolfus may be a remnant of the more original form.[5] Marcolus, in turn, is generally admitted, since Schaumberg's investigation, to be identical with the Hebrew idol Markolis,[6] who is considered by Hebrew scholars to be nothing but a borrowing of the Latin Mercurius.[7] The identity of Markolis and Mercury is plain from the many references of Jewish writers and commentators to the worship of the Markolis-statue consisting of three stones, and to the custom of casting a stone at it, practices which are simply a reflection of the well-known Greco-Roman worship of Hermes-Mercury.[8] In the Proverbs of Solomon XXVI, 8, Jerome's version, which reads 'sicut qui mittit lapidem in acervum Mercurii,' can only be derived from the Midrashic interpretation of the difficult Hebrew as Markolis.[9] The identity of Markolis-Mercury with the Marcholus (Morcholos) of Aethicus is clear from his reference to the monument of stones, in spite of the fact that the author does not recognize the origin of Marcholus and identifies him with Saturn.

d) *The Alternation of Saturn and Marcolf and the Question of Priority*

The Marcolf who is Solomon's opponent in the later medieval dialogues is thus the god Marcolus-Markolis-Mercury, and corresponds

[4] Cf. Schaumberg, pp. 48, 60; ten Brink, I, 112 (translation I, 88). For the Germanic name, which occurs with special frequency in Frankish territory in Carolingian times, see Schaumberg, p. 48, and E. Förstemann, *Altdeutsches Namenbuch, Personennamen*, 2nd ed. (Bonn, 1900), p. 1098. For the interpretation of the name, see note on line 180b.

[5] Benary, p. 4, lines 8–10: 'Marcuil genuit Marcuart; Marcuart genuit Marcol; Marcol genuit Marcolfum.' The French form Marcol(s) might be derived from either Marcolus or Marcolfus.

[6] Schaumberg, pp. 52–59; ten Brink, I, 112 (translation I, 88); Vogt, p. lxv; Ehrismann, *Geschichte der deutschen Literatur des Mittelalters*, II.1, 326.

[7] J. Levy, *Neuhebräisches und Chaldäisches Wörterbuch* (Leipzig, 1886–89), III, 261. Kemble's rejection (pp. 8–9, note) of the identity of Mercury and Markolis was based on insufficient evidence.

[8] Levy, III, 261; Preller-Robert, *Griechische Mythologie*, 4th ed. (Berlin, 1884), p. 401; Hofmann, 'Ueber Jourdain de Blaivies, Apollonius von Tyrus, Salomon und Marcolf,' *Sitzungsberichte der phil.-hist. Cl. der k. bayrischen Akademie der Wissenschaften zu München*, I (1871), 424–430; Schaumberg, pp. 52–59.

[9] Hofmann, p. 426, thought that Jerome's use of Mercury here must have been suggested to him by one of his Hebrew teachers as equivalent to the Midrashic Markolis in this passage (for this reading see Levy, p. 261, end of article). Naturally the idol Mercury-Markolis could have become familiar to the Jews only after the Roman conquest of Palestine.

to the Saturn who debates with Solomon in Old English. How did Saturn and Marcolf happen to exchange places? The identification of Marcolus with Saturn in Aethicus may perhaps be considered sufficient explanation of the existence of Solomon-Saturn and Solomon-Marcolf dialogues side by side. Too precise an explanation need hardly be sought when it is remembered that the identification of one god with another was a favorite and facile practice in ancient and medieval times, and that the name of Saturn in particular was often transferred to the gods of strange peoples.[1] But it has been suggested by Hofmann and other scholars[2] that since Moloch was regularly identified with Kronos-Saturn as a devourer of children,[3] and since the name Moloch, the form of the Septuagint Μόλοχ, is in Hebrew found also as Milcom, Malcom, Malcol,[4] a confusion of the very similar names Malcol and Marcol led to the identification of Saturn with Marcol. Whether or not this plausible and ingenious explanation of the manner in which Saturn and Marcol(f)us became identified is accepted, Aethicus stands witness to the fact that at least two centuries before the composition of the Old English dialogues, Marcolus was considered equivalent to Saturn.

The question of the priority of Marcolf or Saturn as Solomon's opponent still remains. Was Marcolf in the later dialogues substituted for Saturn, or was Saturn in the Old English dialogues substituted for Marcolf? At first sight, the earlier date of the Old English poems seems to indicate that Saturn was the original and Marcolf the substitute, but the presence of the name Marculf as an Eastern ruler

[1] Cf. Cicero, *De natura deorum* III, 17; Isidore, *Etymologiae*, VIII, 11, who identifies Saturn with Bel and Ninus. So great was the passion for syncretism that John Selden was tempted to exclaim: 'Sol, Jupiter, Saturnus in Baale et Moloch . . . inextricabile hallucinatione confundebantur,' *De Diis Syriis* (ed. Leipzig, 1668), p. 51.

[2] Hofmann, pp. 431–432; Schaumberg, p. 60; ten Brink, I, 89; Vincenti, pp. 98–101, all of whom accept an influence of Moloch-Malcol. Schaumberg's attempt to corroborate the confusion of Marcol with Malcol-Moloch by the citation of a Latin thirteenth-century dialogue between Milcol and Salomo cited in *Histoire Littéraire de la France*, XV, p. xvi, is hardly convincing, since the name is actually Micoll, not Milcoll (see *Hist. Litt.*, *ibid.*, and the poem as printed by Signa. Pagani, *Studi Med.*, III, 539–540, from the Vatican MS Reg. 344, f. 40), and the connection with Melcol, variant of Moloch, is possible only if one assumes that Micoll must be an error for Milcol, not for Marcol.

[3] Cf. Lactantius, *Div. Inst.* I. 21, Minucius Felix, *Octavius*, XXX, 5 (on the Carthaginian sacrifice), and in general, W. H. Roscher, *Ausführliches Lexikon der griechischen und römischen Mythologie* (Leipzig, 1890–97), art. *Kronos*, col. 1501–07.

[4] Hofmann, p. 431. The name Moloch is now considered a miswriting of Melek (*Jewish Ency.*, s.v. *Moloch*); on the many variations found in Greek and hence in Latin see J. Hastings, *Dictionary of the Bible*, and Schaff-Herzog, *Encyclopaedia of Religious Knowledge*, s.v. *Moloch*.

in the Old English, and the allusion of Notker to Marcolf certainly not more than a century and a half later than the Old English poems, and probably less, show that the earlier date of the versions which happen to be extant is not of primary importance. A Solomonic dialogue with Marcolf may well have antedated by several centuries the oldest references to it, and hence be more ancient than the Old English versions.[5] Arguments for an early connection of Saturn with Solomon might be found, first, in the legend of Saturn's being bound by Jupiter, which might have been connected with the demon bound by Solomon in the Solomonic legend,[6] secondly, in the reputation of Saturn-Kronos as the oldest and wisest of the gods, and thirdly, in the representation of Saturn as a prince of the Chaldeans, which probably arose through an early identification of Saturn with Nimrod or Ninus.[7] Almost all students of the legend since Schaumberg's time, however, have followed him, without adducing much evidence, in supposing that the original figure was Marcolf, for whom Saturn is substituted in the Old English poems.[8] Reasons for assuming the priority of Marcolf, though they are seldom definitely stated, are, first, the widespread use of the name Marcolf in the countries of Western Europe and the limitation of Saturn to England; secondly, the development of notable differences in the character of the Morolf of the romance and the Marcolf-Morolf of the dialogues, a development which presupposes a considerable antiquity for the figure of Marcolf; [9] thirdly, the close connection between the Biblical proverbs of Solomon and the Solomonic proverbs of the Latin (and German) dialogues, a similarity which is taken to indicate the priority of the Solomon-Marcolf type of dialogue to that of the Solomon-Saturn.[10] Thus the evidence for the priority of either Saturn or Marcolus-Markolf seems very incon-

[5] It should be noted that Kemble's remark that Marcolfus replaced Saturn (p. 130, cf. p. 118), refers primarily to the versions as we have them, and that his whole discussion of Saturn is obscured by his adoption (pp. 120–130) of Grimm's view, now rejected, that Saturn-Sætern was a Germanic god; cf. Vincenti, pp. 107–122, and E. A. Philippson, *Germanisches Heidentum bei den Angelsachsen, Kölner Anglistische Arbeiten*, IV (Leipzig, 1929), pp. 176–177.

[6] Cf. pp. 59f.

[7] See note on line 20. Marcolf likewise comes *a parte orientis* to visit Solomon; see above, p. 30.

[8] Schaumberg, p. 61; Vogt, p. lv; ten Brink, I, 113 (translation I, 89).

[9] Vogt's argument, p. lvi; Vogt, p. lviii, assumed that the hero of the Byzantine story was called Markolis, or at least by some transformation of that name.

[10] Schaumberg's argument, p. 61; but this seems hardly cogent, since the proverbs and figure of Marcolf are certainly far removed from the Bible, unless it is taken for granted that the parodistic answers of Marcolf replace an earlier serious debate with Marcolf, which may be indicated by the earlier references (cf. above, pp. 29ff.).

clusive. It must be remembered that the name of Solomon's opponent is variable even in the Oriental legends, being Hiram or the Queen of Sheba in Hebrew, and among demons, Asmodeus in Hebrew and Sachr in Arabic, and that the names of many demons, such as Ornias, Asmodeus and Beelzeboul, appear in the *Testament of Solomon*, and a still different name, Kitovras, in the Russian stories.[11] The name of Solomon's mortal or demonic opponent in debate is thus constantly shifting, and the interchange of Saturn and Marcolf is therefore hardly surprising. It would, of course, be possible to argue that there arose two quite separate traditions of Solomon-Marcolf and Solomon-Saturn debates, without any other connection than their ultimate origin in the legend of Solomonic contest with Hiram or conversation with Asmodeus. Still, it would be an unlikely coincidence that two independent traditions of Solomon-Marcolf and Solomon-Saturn should have existed side by side for centuries, and that the figures of Saturn and Marcolus should have come to be considered identical, as in Aethicus, for reasons apparently altogether unconnected with the Solomon legend.[12] It is therefore probable that the Solomon-Saturn dialogue and the Solomon-Marcolf dialogue both go back to the same original, but whether Marcolus was substituted for Saturn or Saturn for Marcolus can now hardly be determined.

e) *Primitive Traits of the Solomon Legend in the Figures of Saturn and Marcolf-Morolf*

The form of both the Solomon-Saturn and the Solomon-Marcolf dialogues shows the direct descent of both from the contests of wit between Solomon and Hiram or the Queen of Sheba. In subject-matter there is little in common between the Old English dialogues, on the one hand, and either the dialogue of Solomon and Marcolf or the romance of Solomon and Morolf, on the other. Yet both Marcolf-Morolf and Saturn as characters exhibit certain traits which unmistakably point to the Solomonic legends of the East, and especially to the legend in which Solomon's opponent is a demon or a person possessed of demonic powers. In Marcolfus faint traces of this ancestry remain in his horrible appearance,[1] and perhaps in his cunning malevolence.[2] In the German romance, Morolf as Solomon's brother has

[11] Cf. above, pp. 22f. and p. 25, and Vogt, p. lv.

[12] It seems improbable that Marcolus and Saturn were identified in Aethicus simply because the two played similar rôles in two different legends of Solomon.

[1] Benary, pp. 1–2.

[2] Schaumberg, pp. 37–40, thought that the humorously satirical character of Marcolfus was influenced by the tradition of Æsop; cf. Ehrismann, *Geschichte der deutschen Literatur*, II.1, 326, and Vogt, p. lvi, note, who is skeptical.

lost much of his earlier character, though Kitovras, his counterpart in the more primitive Russian version of the romance, preserves a great deal more of the demonic power of his original, having rule over men by day and beasts by night.[3] Morolf's descent is manifest only in his many disguises, his magic trickery and his power over dwarfs. Just as Marcolfus has come *a parte orientis* (line 3),[3a] so Saturn, as we have noted, is a prince of Chaldea (20, 503), and has traversed all the kingdoms of the East in search of wisdom (3–4, 170–192). A remnant of the demonic power of Solomon's opponent appears in the characterization of Saturn as the descendant of the fearful race of giants who built the Tower of Babel and strove against God (lines 318–322).[4] In keeping with the general difference in tone between the dialogues, Saturn has preserved the more regal and philosophic aspects of the character of Asmodeus, prince of demons, while Marcolf has preserved only his trickery and cunning subtlety. But if the characters of Saturn and Marcolf thus exhibit only faint traces of the original legend from which they sprang, the Old English dialogues retain in the triumph of Solomon over Saturn a more definite feature of the Hebrew story. The use of the runic letters of the Pater Noster in Poem I is simply a transformation of the inherited power of Solomon's magical ring and magical prayers. Finally, the Vasa Mortis episode in which Solomon binds the demon of that name is a direct inheritance of the Oriental story. These influences will be discussed in the next sections.

VI. THE BACKGROUND OF POEM I

1. The Nature and Content of Poem I

The subject-matter and tone of the two poems are so different that it will be best to treat them separately.[1] Poem I, although couched in the form of a dialogue, is not a contest of wisdom like Poem II, but a conversation in which Saturn seeks to be persuaded of the virtue of the palm-twigged Pater Noster and receives the requested information from Solomon. Saturn makes only three speeches. In the first (1–20) he declares his willingness to receive—and pay for—the truth that he has been unable to find in the books of other peoples; in the second (36–38) he asks who may open the door of Heaven for him and learns from Solomon that it is the Pater Noster (39–52); in the third (53–62) he asks how this wonderful song is to be used.

[3] Vogt, p. xliii. [3a] Benary, *Salomon et Marcolfus*, p. 1.

[4] Cf. the notes on this passage and 203ff.; and cf. Vogt, p. liv.

[1] On differences in style see the discussion of authorship, above, pp. 5–7.

Solomon, in a long reply, which constitutes nearly three-fourths of Poem I (63–169), never once addresses Saturn, and the pleasant fiction of the dialogue in which Solomon instructs Saturn seems to become imperceptibly the instruction of his ignorant contemporaries by the author. For this reason, the history of the dialogue form will be reserved for discussion in connection with Poem II, a true dialogue.[2]

Solomon's long speech describes in detail the value of the Pater Noster. It is first said to be not only wisdom of the heart and honey of the soul (66), leach of the lame, door of the deaf, tongue of the dumb, and shield of the sinful (77–80), but also—and more strangely—hereditary lord of the waves, the ocean of the poor fish and serpents, and grove of the wild beasts (81–82). There follows an elaborate description of the power of each rune or letter of the Pater Noster, and especially of the manner in which each letter, personified as an angelic warrior, can punish or overcome the Devil and his emissaries. P is a warrior who has a long rod, a golden goad, with which he continually scourges the Devil (90–92a); A follows on his track and likewise strikes the Devil down (92b–93); T injures him by stabbing at his tongue, twisting his throat and smashing his cheeks (94–95); and the rest of the letters behave similarly (96–145). The poet certainly included all the letters of the prayer, but some, as we shall see, have disappeared from our text. Solomon then ends his speech by declaring that the prayer can put to flight all devils no matter how ingeniously they change their shapes or make their attacks, whether they seize the sailor, bite cattle in the likeness of serpents, pull the horse down in the water, or fetter the hand of the doomed warrior in battle (146–160). Therefore, he says, no man should draw his sword without uttering the prayer of the Pater Noster (161–169).[3]

In the list of the letters of the Pater Noster the poet probably followed the familiar form of the liturgy, which has 'panem nostrum quotidianum,' instead of the Vulgate 'panem nostrum supersubstantialem' (Matt. VI, 11); but the order of the letters would be the same in either case.[4] The poet's text may be represented as follows: Pater nos(ter), qui (es)· (in) c(ae)l(is): (sancti)f(icetur) (no)m(en) (tuum). (A)d(veniat) (re)g(num) (tuum). (Fiat voluntas tua, sicut in caelo,

[2] Section VII, 2, below, pp. 53–57.

[3] On the conclusion of Poem I, see above, p. 10. The prose (see Appendix) which follows immediately in the manuscript is superficially in the form of a dialogue throughout, but consists merely of questions by Saturn which are answered by Solomon; cf. below, pp. 55–56.

[4] Ælfric has *cotidianum* (*Cath. Hom.*, I, 264), as have the poetical paraphrases II, 13 and III, 68 (Grein-Wülker, II, 229, 235).

et in terra.) (Panem nostrum) (quotidianum) (da) (no)b(is) h(odie).[5] The letters in parenthesis are those which have already occurred earlier in the prayer and are hence not repeated by the poet; after *hodie* only letters already used are found. If the poet adhered strictly to the order of the prayer we should therefore expect: P A T E R N O S Q U I C L F M D G B H. But only sixteen of the nineteen letters actually appear in MS A, and the order is not followed exactly. Of the letters to be expected, *o* of *nos*(*ter*), *i* of *qui*, and *b* of *nobis* are not found in the manuscript, which has the following order: P A T E R N S Q U L C F M G D H. The poet's own copy probably had: P A T E R N [O] S Q U [I] L C F M G D [B] H. Of the letters missing it is obvious that O and I are omitted by scribal error, since O is required by both sense and metre in line 108, and I by the metre in line 123 (see the notes on these lines). The missing B is perhaps to be inferred from 136–137, or 141 (see notes), but probably disappeared through a similar but more serious scribal lapse. The only deviations in the poem from the sequence of letters in the Latin are the changes of C L to L C, and of D G to G D. The first transposition was apparently made for the sake of the metre in order to have L, pronounced *el*, occur in the first half of the line for vocalic alliteration: 'Đonne hine [Ī and] L, and se yrra C' (123). The reason for the transposition of D and G is obscure. The poet tended to group letters, such as the 'twins of the church' N, O (108), Q and U (118), I, L and C (123), and F and M (127). In MS A all the letters except N, H (and the omitted O, I, and B) are preceded by the corresponding runes.

2. The Use of the Pater Noster and the Palm Tree

The prayer which Christ himself taught his followers to use (Matt. VI, 9–13) was, from the earliest times, naturally considered the most important and sacred of all Christian prayers. The fathers of the Church looked upon its seven petitions as the summary of all things that man can ask of God,[1] and its place in the liturgy of the Church made it familiar to every Christian. Instruction in the Pater Noster was recommended at a very early period. The *Doctrine of the Apostles* (*Didache*), of the first or second century, enjoined Christians to recite

[5] The *u* of *qui*, which appears in the MS as *v*, naturally stands for both *u* and *v* and is not repeated. The *ae* of *caelum* is considered a repetition of *a*, *e*, and not a separate letter.

[1] Tertullian, *De Oratione*, ed. A. Reifferscheid and G. Wissowa, *Corpus Scriptorum Ecclesiasticorum Latinorum*, XX.1 (Vienna, 1890), 180–200; Cyprian, *De Dominica Oratione*, ed. G. Hartel, [Vienna] *Corpus*, III.1, 265–294; cf. F. Cabrol, *Liturgical Prayer* (London, 1925), p. 88; V. Thalhofer and L. Eisenhofer, *Handbuch der katholischen Liturgik*, 2nd ed. (Freiburg, 1912), I, 303–305.

the Pater Noster three times a day.[2] The fathers exhorted the faithful to use it daily.[3] In England in 734 Bede urged that Bishop Egbert instruct the uneducated laymen as well as priests to learn the Lord's Prayer in their own language ('sua lingua discere, ac sedulo decantare').[4] The Council of Clovesho in 747, like many a medieval synod, required priests to learn and teach the Pater Noster in the native tongue of the people.[5] Beginning with 794 several of Charlemagne's capitularies require that all Christian people learn the Lord's Prayer and Creed.[6] A capitulary of Theodulf of Orleans, Alcuin's contemporary at Charlemagne's court, adds the remarkable warning that unless Pater Noster and Creed are committed to memory a man 'catholicus esse non poterit,' [7] a phrase that finds its way into several Old English works of the tenth century.

The Lord's Prayer was frequently translated into Old English verse and prose.[8] Two poetical versions, the brief translation of eleven lines in the Exeter Book and a longer paraphrase in Junius 121, may belong to Alfred's time, and a still more elaborate paraphrase is somewhat later.[9] The two paraphrases contain the clauses of the Pater Noster in Latin followed by amplifications in Old English verse. Of the many prose renderings those by Ælfric and Wulfstan may be noted.[10] But these translations, although they attest the importance attached to

[2] Cap. VIII, 3, ed. A. Harnack, *Texte und Untersuchungen zur Geschichte der altchristlichen Literatur*, II, 27.

[3] Cyprian, *De Dominica Oratione* 12, [Vienna] *Corpus*, III. 1, 275; Augustine, *Sermones*, LVIII, *Pat. Lat.*, XXXVIII, 399.

[4] *Opera Historica*, ed. C. H. Plummer, I, 409.

[5] Haddan and Stubbs, *Councils and Ecclesiastical Documents*, III, 361, 366.

[6] Boretius and Krause, *Capitularia Regum Francorum*, *Monumenta Germaniae Historica*, p. 77 (28.33), cf. p. 103, (35.30); and A. Hauck, *Kirchengeschichte Deutschlands* (Leipzig, 1890), II, 240, and note 1.

[7] Cap. XXII, Migne, *Pat. Lat.*, CV, 198. On the great popularity of the Capitula of Theodulf in England at the end of the tenth and beginning of the eleventh centuries, cf. further, p. 39, and K. Jost, *Anglia*, LVI (1932), 293. A tenth-century translation of the Capitula was printed by B. Thorpe under the title *Ecclesiastical Institutes*, *Ancient Laws and Institutes of England* (London, 1840), pp. 466ff., see esp. pp. 477–478, and the passage on the Pater Noster and other large sections were used in the enlarged rule of St. Chrodegang, ed. Napier, *EETS*, CL.

[8] On the Lord's Prayer in Old English see A. S. Cook, 'The Evolution of the Lord's Prayer in English,' *American Journal of Philology*, XII (1891), 59–66; 'New Texts of the Lord's Prayer and Hymns,' *MLN*, VII (1892), 21–23; Brandl, *Grundriss*, II.1, 1050, 1094, 1114; Heusinkveld and Bashe, *Bibliographical Guide*, pp. 126–127.

[9] The three are printed in Grein-Wülker, II, 227–238; the latest edition of the Exeter Lord's Prayer is in Krapp-Dobbie, *Anglo-Saxon Poetic Records*, III, 223–224.

[10] *Wulfstan*, ed. Napier, p. 125; Ælfric, *Cath. Hom.*, II, 596; cf. the latter's homily on the Pater Noster, *Cath. Hom.*, I, 258–274.

the Lord's Prayer in Christian teaching, are without any hint of such a superstitious use of it as appears in *Solomon and Saturn*.

The tenth-century Benedictine reform in England brought a renewed insistence on the instruction in Pater Noster and Creed,[11] which is reflected in the writings of Ælfric, Wulfstan, and in the laws. Ælfric in the *Catholic Homilies* said that each Christian man must know his Pater Noster and Creed,[12] and Wulfstan specifies that the Christian must learn them in English if he knows no Latin.[13] Theodulf's warning that a man who refuses to commit them to memory cannot be *catholicus* now reappears in the Canons of Edgar, Wulfstan, and the Laws of Cnut, all three saying that such a man 'ne bið wel cristen.'[14]

The laymen who were taught the significance of the Lord's Prayer could not always comprehend its deeper meaning and sometimes regarded it chiefly as a powerful means of warding off spiritual or physical evil. Even the interpretations of the learned tended to emphasize its value in man's warfare against the Devil and his temptations. In particular, the final petition 'Sed libera nos a malo' (Ἀλλὰ ῥῦσαι ἡμᾶς ἀπὸ τοῦ πονηροῦ) was often interpreted by early fathers such as Origen and Cyprian as referring to the Evil One, not simply to evil; and, indeed, many modern critics consider that the words of Jesus refer to Satan.[15] Cyril of Jerusalem in the fourth century, expounding the Lord's Prayer in its place in the liturgy after the Great Intercession for the Living and the Dead, interprets πονηρός as the Devil.[16] Later commentators of the Western Church, despite Augustine's more spiritual interpretation,[17] often cling to this view or emphasize the value

[11] On the possible connection of the Benedictine reform with the date of the poem, see above, p. 14.

[12] I, 274, ed. Thorpe.

[13] Ed. Napier, p. 39.

[14] B. Thorpe, *Ancient Laws*, Canons of Edgar 22, p. 397; F. Liebermann, *Die Gesetze der Angelsachsen*, I, 302; cf. K. Jost, *Anglia*, LVI (1932), 292–293; and p. 38, note 7.

[15] *De Oratione* 30, ed. P. Koetschau, *Die griechischen christlichen Schriftsteller*, Origenes, II, 393; cf. Origen, *Selecta in Psalmos*, Hom. II, § 4, *Pat. Gr.*, XII, 1332, Hom. V, § 7, *Pat. Gr.*, XII, 1366; Cyprian, *De Dominica Oratione*, 25, 27; cf. 'from the Evil One' of the Revised Version. According to F. H. Chase, Tertullian is slightly ambiguous, but comparison with other passages in Tertullian shows that *malo* is masculine rather than neuter ('The Lord's Prayer in the Early Church,' *Texts and Studies*, I.3 [Cambridge, 1891], pp. 133–136). Chase insists, after an exhaustive examination, that τοῦ πονηροῦ of Matthew VI, 13 must be properly interpreted as masculine and a reference to Satan.

[16] *Catechesis*, XXIII, *Mystagogica*, V, 18, *Pat. Gr.*, XXXIII, 1123; cf. Chase, pp. 144–145.

[17] *Pat. Lat.*, XXXVIII, 386; cf. *Pat. Lat.*, XXXIV, 1284.

of the Lord's Prayer as a whole in combating the wiles of Satan.[18] The sober Ælfric, though he translates *a malo* 'fram yfele,' immediately adds 'ālȳs ūs fram dēofle, and fram eallum his syrwungum.' [19]

Thus both the conclusion of the prayer itself and the phraseology of the commentators might impress simple and ignorant Christians, especially those accustomed to the use of pagan incantations and charms, with the supreme value of the Pater Noster in warfare against the Devil. The superstitious use of the Pater Noster as a kind of magical formula is well attested from the fifth century to the present day. The practice of reciting the Pater Noster in applying remedies for diseases was still common in the sixteenth century in England,[20] and was widespread in German country districts at the end of the nineteenth century.[21] The extension of the meaning of Paternoster in such an expression as the *white paternoster*,[22] mentioned by Chaucer's Miller (299), is testimony to the importance of the Pater Noster proper in popular medicine and exorcism.

The earliest examples of the use of the Lord's Prayer in magic formulas occur in the Greek papyri. A papyrus of the fifth or sixth century, used as an amulet against evil spirits and illness, incorporates part of the Pater Noster in a strange combination of Christian and Jewish elements, including Solomonic exhortation.[23] One of the sixth century, likewise folded as an amulet, makes use of the entire prayer.[24]

[18] Peter Chrysologus, *Pat. Lat.*, LII, 393; Cassian, *Sermo* LVI, *Pat. Lat.*, XLIX, 799; Alcuin, *Disputatio Puerorum:* 'Id est, a diabolo, a peccato, et ab omni malo tentamento,' *Pat. Lat.*, CI, 1144; Radbertus, *Pat. Lat.*, CXX, 297–298.

[19] *Cath. Hom.* I, 270; cf. the conclusion of the Junius 121 *Lord's Prayer* 31–32: 'and wið yfele gefrēo ūs ēac nū ðā / fēonda gehwylces' (Grein-Wülker, II, 230).

[20] G. L. Kittredge, *Witchcraft in Old and New England* (Cambridge, Mass., 1929), pp. 36–37.

[21] A. Wuttke, *Der deutsche Volksaberglaube der Gegenwart*, 3rd ed. (Berlin, 1900), §§ 419, 481, 483, 495f., and Index s.v. *Vaterunser*. The best general account of the Pater Noster in superstitious use is the article *Vaterunser* in E. Hoffmann-Krayer, *Handbuch des deutschen Aberglaubens*, 1927ff. E. F. Knuchel cites a custom of Swedish peasants who draw the Lord's Prayer in a circle about a person to protect him from evil powers (*Die Umwandlung in Kult, Magie, und Rechtsgebrauch, Schriften der Schweizerischen Gesellschaft für Volkskunde* XV [Basel, 1918], p. 63).

[22] Cf. the Parson's *Devil's paternoster* (439), and *NED*'s definition of *paternoster* 2a: 'any form of words repeated or muttered by way of a prayer, imprecation or charm.' It is curious that in Italian folklore the recital of a *green* Pater Noster (*paternoster verde*) is connected with the knot of Solomon (Jack La Bolina, 'Il Gruppo di Salomone e il "Paternoster" verde,' *Revista delle Tradizioni Popolari Italiane* I (1893), 75–77; cf. 389–392).

[23] K. Preisendanz, *Papyri Graecae Magicae* (Leipzig and Berlin, 1931), II, 206 (P 17); cf. Leclercq, art. *Oraison Dominicale* in Cabrol and Leclercq, *Dictionnaire d'Archéologie Chrétienne*.

[24] Preisendanz, II, 197 (P 9).

The famous fragmentary tablet of Megara, of the fourth century, is probably the oldest evidence of a semi-magical use of the Lord's Prayer.[25] The Latin Pater Noster is naturally found in similar incantations and exorcisms.[26] Martin of Bracara in the sixth century called the Creed and Pater Noster 'incantationem sanctam' which the rustics had abandoned for 'diabolicas incantationes.'[27] Interesting testimony to the power of the very letters of the Pater Noster is to be found in the ritual of the ordeal by means of consecrated bread and cheese (end of the eleventh century?) in which the priest is instructed to write Pater Noster on both the bread and cheese to be swallowed by the suspected thief ('scribe *Pater Noster* in utroque').[28]

In Old English writings the superstitious use of the Pater Noster is amply attested by the frequent mention of it in the charms. 'Of the Church prayers employed to replace Heathen spells,' writes Grendon, 'the majority are Paternosters, which are prescribed for recital in about one fourth of the charms.'[29] In the charm against infectious disease 'Wið flēogendum attre,' a litany and Pater Noster are to be sung over butter, together with corrupt Old Irish words.[30] In the charm for a strange swelling, the Pater Noster is to be sung six times over one's little finger together with a sentence beginning *Fuge diabolus*.[31] The first charm shows the reluctance with which heathen incantations were abandoned even when Christian prayers were added, while the second illustrates the practice permitted by the Church of using Christian prayers in herb-gathering and medicine, provided that heathen spells were excluded. In the tenth-century Old English ver-

[25] Preisendanz, II, 211 (O 4).

[26] R. Heim, *Incantamenta Magica Graeca Latina, Jahrbücher für classische Philologie, Supplementband* XIX (Leipzig, 1893), p. 525. The famous *sator*-rebus, a magic square, has been explained as a cross composed of the letters of Pater Noster plus A and O, representing Alpha and Omega (F. Grosser, *Archiv für Religionswissenschaft*, XXIV (1926), 164–169; cf. G. de Jerphanion, *Recherches de Science Religieuse*, XXV (1935), 188–225). But the fact that two *sator*-inscriptions have been found at Pompeii, and must therefore be dated before 79 A.D., casts doubt upon the explanation of the square as a Christian symbol based on the Latin form of the prayer (M. della Corte, and G. de Jerphanion, *Pontificia Accademia Romana di Archeologia*, Ser. III, *Rendiconti* XII (1936), 397–400; 401–404).

[27] C. P. Caspari, *Martin von Bracara's Schrift De Correctione Rusticorum* (Christiania, 1883), p. 35.

[28] F. Liebermann, *Die Gesetze der Angelsachsen* I, 425, Iudicium Die, Rituale XIVa.

[29] Felix Grendon, 'Anglo-Saxon Charms,' p. 151, in *Journal of American Folk-Lore*, XXII (1905), 105–237.

[30] Grendon, p. 196; cf. F. P. Magoun, *Archiv für das Studium der neueren Sprachen*, CLXXI (1937), 30; for other examples see Grendon, pp. 188, 212.

[31] Grendon, p. 186.

sion of the Penitential of Bishop Halitgar of Cambrai (d. 831), the Christian is instructed not to gather herbs with a charm, but with Pater Noster and Creed or some other prayer to God.[32] Ælfric wrote 'Ne sceal nān man mid galdre wyrte besingan, ac mid Godes wordum hī geblētsian, and swā ðicgan.'[33] Christian incantations were thus substituted for heathen, with the consent of the ecclesiastical authorities. There would have been nothing shocking to medieval churchmen in the principle of reciting the Pater Noster to ward off the attacks of demons, as expounded in *Solomon and Saturn* (I, 146–169), though some would probably have smiled at the fantastic elaboration of the theme in the personification of the letters.[34]

The personification of the letters and the detailed description of battles are an extraordinary feature of the poem to which it is hard to find an exact parallel. The battles are vaguely reminiscent of those in the *Psychomachia* of Prudentius. The personification of the letters is partly an inheritance of ancient Greek and Hebrew alphabetical mysticism and partly an adaptation of runic magic.[35] But still more curious is the tendency to hypostasize the Pater Noster itself and consider it capable of a person's action (cf. Saturn's *hwā*, 36). The closest parallels to this, apart from the prose dialogue, are to be found, I believe, in the medieval Irish prayers and litanies, where the *lorica* becomes a kind of all-inclusive protector, and a prayer may come to be spoken of in extravagant terms applicable only to a person.[36] The figures of speech applied to the Pater Noster in lines 66–83, 'wisdom of the heart,' 'honey of the soul,' 'leech of the lame,' 'savior of the people,' 'hall of the Creator,' are such as are ordinarily used only of Christ or the Virgin Mary.[37] The extravagance of expression is reminiscent of Irish religious literature, and, indeed, the whole tone of this

[32] J. Raith, *Die altenglische Version des Halitgar'schen Bussbuches (sog. Poenitentiale Pseudo-Egberti)*, *Bibl. der ags. Prosa* XIII (Hamburg, 1933), § 23, p. 30. At a later time St. Thomas Aquinas decided that the ancient practice of wearing protective amulets with sacred words about the neck was permissible, provided there were no unknown words and no invocation of demons, though it would be more laudable to abstain from the practice altogether (*Summa* II, ii, 96, art. 4).

[33] *Cath. Hom.* I, 476.

[34] On the magic power of the runes and the connection with Hebrew and Germanic magic, see below, pp. 45ff., pp. 48ff.

[35] See below, pp. 45–49.

[36] See note on lines 66ff., where the Irish 'besom of devotion' is cited. On the type of prayer called *lorica*, see Dom L. Gougaud, 'Etude sur les Loricae Celtiques,' *Bulletin d'ancienne littérature et d'archéologie chrétiennes*, I (1911), 265–281; II (1912), 33–41; 101–127; and Charles Singer, 'The Lorica of Gildas The Briton,' in *From Magic to Science* (New York, 1928), pp. 111–132.

[37] See note on lines 66ff.

section of the poem savors of Hisperic Latin. This may be another indication that the dialogues of Solomon and Saturn have come to Old English through Celtic sources.[38]

The description of the Pater Noster as *gepalmtwigede*, 'palm-branched' (39), is quite unparalleled outside of Poem I.[39] The combination of Pater Noster and *palmtrēow* in line 167, where the warrior is exhorted to sing the Pater Noster and pray the palm-tree as though they were one and the same thing, shows that the poet's association of the two is a very definite and intentional one. *Palmtwig* in Old English is the normal equivalent of *ramus palmae*, 'palm-branch,' as appears from Ælfric's description, paraphrasing Revelation, of the angels standing before God's throne 'healdende palmtwigu on heora handum.'[40] The literalness of the poet's description may indicate that he had actually seen tablets of the Pater Noster with ornamentation of palm-branches; for the palm, as we shall see, was an important symbolic motif in Christian art. The fact that the Pater Noster has silver leaves and is adorned with gems (63–64) may likewise imply a written Pater Noster elaborately ornamented.[41] It is possible, however, that the expression is merely figurative, referring to the palm as the symbol of victory over the Devil.

In the ancient East the palm was a symbol of life, fertility, and immortality.[42] Among the Jews its significance may have varied somewhat, but the lulab, the palm-shoot, appears to have represented life and salvation, especially salvation from the Adversary.[43] In early Christian times the Greek conception of the palm as an emblem of victory combined with the tradition of Jewish symbolism to make the palm the sign of Christ's victory over death and the Devil. Jerome and Ambrose interpreted the palm as a sign of victory,[44] and Augustine more specifically wrote that the palm-branches of Palm Sunday signify

[38] On the possibility of Celtic transmission of apocryphal material, see above, p. 25. *The Book of Cerne*, with its Old English gloss of the Latin *lorica* of Loding and other Irish prayers, testifies to the fact that Hiberno-Latin of this type was still familiar in England at the beginning of the ninth century; cf. Dom A. B. Kuypers, *Book of Cerne* (Cambridge, 1902), pp. 85–88 and *passim*.

[39] It seems unlikely that the palm-branched Pater Noster is connected with the *paternoster verde* of Italian folk-lore mentioned above, p. 40, note 22.

[40] *Cath. Hom.*, I, 538; cf. the *blōwende palmtwigu* of Palm Sunday in *Blickling Homilies*, VI, *EETS*, LVIII, 67.

[41] See below, p. 44. It is conceivable that a Pater Noster inscribed on a tablet was decorated with the actual palm-branches of Palm Sunday.

[42] Cameron Mackay, 'The Sign of the Palm Tree,' *Church Quarterly Review*, CXXVI [No. 252] (1938), 187–212, esp. pp. 203–209.

[43] Mackay, *ibid.*, pp. 194–195.

[44] *Pat. Lat.*, XXV, 1537; XVII, 669.

victory because Christ was about to overcome death and triumph over the Devil, the prince of death,[45] an interpretation repeated by Bede and Alcuin,[46] and paraphrased by Isidore of Seville.[47] The development of the impressive service and procession of Palm Sunday made every Christian aware of the importance of the palm as a symbol of his faith. In the first text of the Latin service for Palm Sunday in the western church, the sacramentary of Bobbio (ca. 700), there is not only a reference to the palm as a symbol of Christ's triumph over the Devil, but a prayer that all who carry the blessed branches home with pious devotion may be safe from the attacks of the enemy.[48]

In early Christian art the palm, which in the Old Testament had been one of the symbolic ornaments of Solomon's temple (I Kings VI, 32), and is especially significant in Ezekiel's vision (Ezek. XLI, 18–26), appears on gravestones as a sign of victory over death or of immortality.[49] Palm-branches surround the sacred monogram of Christ's name,[50] and often appear on either side of the figure of Christ or his Apostles.[51] It is therefore quite possible that the motif so frequent in Christian art was sometimes used to adorn the Pater Noster.[52] Even

[45] *Tract. in Johannem*, LI, 2, *Pat. Lat.*, XXXV, 1764.

[46] Bede, *Expositio in Johannem*, cap. 12, *Pat. Lat.*, XCII, 787; Alcuin, *Comment. in Johannem*, cap. 29, *Pat. Lat.*, C, 909. Alcuin wrote some hexameters in honor of the palm as a sign of Christ's victory, *Pat. Lat.*, CI, 650, and Aldhelm wrote an enigma on the Palm (No. 91, *Opera*, p. 139, ed. R. Ehwald, *Monumenta Germaniae Historica*, Berlin, 1919).

[47] *Etymologiae*, XVII, 7; cf. his *De Ecclesiasticis Officiis* I, 28, *Pat. Lat.*, LXXXIII, 763.

[48] E. A. Lowe, *The Bobbio Missal, Henry Bradshaw Society*, LVIII (London, 1920), p. 170, where the uncorrected text is difficult; cf. A. Franz, *Die kirchlichen Benediktionen im Mittelalter* (Freiburg, 1909), I, 480, where the text, corrected on the basis of others, reads: 'Haec quoque creatura arboris olivarum una cum palmis . . . benedicatur benedictione perenni, ut quicunque pia devotione pro expellendis languoribus sive etiam pro expugnandas omnes insidias inimici in cunctis habitationibus suis eas adportaverint aut biberint, ab omni sint impugnatione inimici securi.' Cf. the addition to the benediction of palms in MS O (before 850) of *The Gregorian Sacramentary* (ed. H. A. Wilson [London, 1915], p. 46, note): 'ut omnes qui eos laturi sunt ita benedictionis tue dono repleantur, quatinus et in hoc seculo hostis antiqui temptamenta superare, et in futuro cum palma victorie et fructu bonorum operum valeant apparere.'

[49] Art. *palme, palmier*, and illustrations, in Cabrol and Leclercq, *Dictionnaire d'Archéologie Chrétienne*.

[50] *Ibid.*

[51] E. L. Cutts, *History of Christian Art* (London, 1893), p. 208.

[52] The only possible example known to me is an illustration in the Utrecht Psalter. Appearing above the words of the Pater Noster at Matthew VI, 9–13, is a picture of Christ praying with his disciples, and there are branches at either side which might possibly be intended to represent palms; see E. T. DeWald, *The Illustrations*

in the absence of testimony from Christian art, it is plain that the significance of the palm as the symbol of victory over the Devil was so well known in the Middle Ages that the Pater Noster, described in Poem I as a specific means of combatting the Devil's attacks, was fittingly adorned with palm-branches. Pater Noster and palm-tree together protect the Christian warrior in his battles against both spiritual and human adversaries (39ff., 163ff.).

3. Christian Use of Oriental and Germanic Elements

The Christian development of the Oriental symbol of the palm-tree was probably attached to the source of Poem I from a tradition that was quite independent of the Solomonic dialogues. In general, it is plain that Poem I, in contrast to Poem II, has retained little of the earlier material of the Solomon legend, and merely uses the dialogue as a convenient framework. Even the framework becomes unimportant in the latter half of the poem.[1] Saturn's search for learning is described by himself (1–9) and he speaks of returning to the land of the Chaldeans beyond the river *Cōfor* (18–20), but this might have been borrowed from the Latin original of Poem II or even from Poem II itself. Saturn's promise of thirty pounds of gold and his twelve sons (14–15), if Solomon convinces him of the truth of Christianity, is probably a faint reminiscence of the original riddle-debates between Hiram and Solomon, in which each agreed to pay a large fine of money if he were unable to solve the other's riddles.[2] The most important inheritance from the Solomon legend is so disguised as to be hardly recognizable. The use of the letters of the Lord's Prayer, and more especially of the runic letters, is the Germano-Christian transformation of the Oriental legends in which Solomon by means of his magic ring conquers the demons of the underworld.[3]

Belief in the mystic and magic power of letters was widespread in the ancient world, and the Greeks and Hebrews anticipated the Germanic peoples in their use of the alphabet in charms and incantations.[4]

---

of the Utrecht Psalter (Princeton University Press), Plate CXLII. This illustration was pointed out to me by Professor C. H. Morey, who consulted the Princeton Index of Christian Art.

[1] Cf. above, pp. 35f., on the differences between the two poems, and below, pp. 49f., on Poem II.

[2] Dius, according to Josephus, *Antiquities of the Jews*, VIII, 5, recorded that both Solomon and Hiram at different times forfeited large sums of money; on these legends cf. p. 22, above.

[3] See above, p. 23.

[4] F. Dornseiff, *Das Alphabet in Mystik und Magie*, Στοιχεῖα, *Studien zur Geschichte der antiken Welt*, VII, 2nd ed. (Berlin, 1925); L. Blau, *Das altjüdische Zauberwesen*

The Jews not only used the psalms for magical purposes, but wove mystical names of God out of the letters of the psalms.[5] Psalm XCI, perhaps originally composed as an incantation, was called the 'Song against Demons' and used as a protection against them in amulets.[6] The use of letters in magic formulas played a large part in Gnosticism and the Cabbalistic writings. Solomon is a prominent figure in Jewish and Hellenistic magic, because in the popular mind his reputation as a magician came to be considered even more important than his reputation for wisdom. His name occurs constantly in exorcistic formulas, often in connection with alphabetic magic.[7] Solomon was said in Arabic legends to be the inventor of the Arabic and Syriac scripts.[8] His seal, engraved on the ring with which he subdued demons, was sometimes depicted as containing unintelligible words and the combinations of vowels common in Judaeo-Hellenistic magic.[9] Josephus tells us that Solomon bequeathed to his successors the use of exorcisms by which demons are driven away, and adds that he himself, in the presence of Vespasian, saw a Jew cast a demon out of a man by means of a ring and incantations in which the name of Solomon was repeated.[10] Origen refers in all seriousness to the conjurations written by Solomon which are used to drive out demons,[11] and according to a Byzantine historian, as late as the reign of Manuel Comnenus (d. 1180) a certain Aaron owned a *βίβλον Σολομώντειον* by means of which legions of demons could be summoned.[11a] Solomon's own power over demons, described in great detail in the *Testament of Solomon*,[12] was thus transmitted to others by means of magical books supposedly written by himself. The famous Hebrew *Key of Solomon*, translated into Latin under the title *Clavicula Salomonis* and only one of many magical

(Strassburg, 1898); E. Schürer, *Geschichte des jüdischen Volkes im Zeitalter Christi* (Leipzig, 1909), III, 407–420; F. R. Schröder, *Germanentum und Hellenismus* (Heidelberg, 1924), pp. 5–14.

[5] K. Kayser, 'Gebrauch der Psalmen zu Zauberei,' *Zeitschrift der deutschen morgenländischen Gesellschaft*, XLII (1888), 456–462; M. Gaster, 'Samaritan Phylacteries and Amulets,' *Proceedings of the Society of Biblical Archaeology*, XXXVIII (1916), 78–79.

[6] *Jewish Ency.*, art. *Bibliomancy.*

[7] Schürer, *Geschichte des jüdischen Volkes*, III, 419; K. Preisendanz, *Papyri Graecae Magicae* (Leipzig and Berlin), II, 190ff., esp. P3, P10, P17.

[8] *Jewish Ency.*, art. *Solomon*, p. 446.

[9] McCown, *Testament of Solomon*, p. 77, notes, pp. 86–87, pp. 100–101; cf. *Jewish Ency.*, art. *Solomon's Seal*, and note on line 136.

[10] *Antiquities of the Jews*, VIII, 2, 5; cf. McCown, *Testament*, p. 92.

[11] *In Matt.* XXVI, 63, ed. E. Klostermann, *Die griechischen christlichen Schriftsteller*, Origenes XI, 230.

[11a] Nicetas Choniates, *Pat. Gr.* CXXXIX, 489.

[12] See above, p. 23.

books attributed to Solomon,[13] uses the letters of the Hebrew alphabet, both by themselves and in particular combinations, together with the names of many strange powers, in verses and incantations.[14]

In Poem I Solomon is still, in a sense, a magician, and the exorcist of demons by means of the potent letters of the Pater Noster. The ease with which the ancient Hebrew king could assume this Christian rôle is explained partly by the respect that both early and medieval Christians accorded him as a subduer of demons. Solomon and Jesus were both famous as exorcists, and even their names were powerful weapons against demons.[15] But if the Jews considered Solomon a rival to Jesus and some Christians disputed the powers of Solomon,[16] most Christians preferred to adopt Solomon as a forerunner and collaborator of Jesus in the warfare against demons. Solomon's name appears together with that of Christ in amulets and magic formulas from the fourth century.[17] Solomon's seal remained so famous that it appears in the medieval Christian formulas for exorcism, where the Devil is said to have suffered the torments of God *sub sigilla Salomonis.*[18] If the medieval respect for Solomon as a master of demons is nothing but an inheritance from Jewish legend, the interpretation of Solomon as a symbolic forerunner and representative of Christ is, of course, a definitely Christian development.[19] Several connections were made here by the fathers of the Church. Christ was identified with Solomon as being 'great David's greater son.' Psalm LXXI (LXXII), which described the future glories of Solomon, was interpreted as referring symbolically to the coming of Christ.[20] Christ

[13] See above, p. 21, note 2, for books attributed to Solomon, and cf. L. Thorndike, *History of Magic and Experimental Science* (New York, 1923), II, chap. XLIX, especially for later medieval books attributed to Solomon.

[14] S. L. M. Mathers, *The Key of Solomon* translated (London, 1909), pp. 32, 39, 42, and *passim;* cf. H. Gollancz, *Sepher Maphteah Shelomo* (Oxford, 1914)—a facsimile edition of the Hebrew.

[15] Cf. Mark IX, 38; Luke IX, 49; Acts XIX, 13; and Matt. VII, 22; Luke X, 20; and W. Heitmüller, *Im Namen Jesus* (Göttingen, 1903), pp. 223–257.

[16] McCown, pp. 76–77.

[17] K. Preisendanz, *Papyri Graecae Magicae,* II, 190–191 (P 3); II, 198–199 (P 10); II, 206 (P 17); cf. Cabrol and Leclercq, *Dictionnaire d'Archéologie Chrétienne,* art. *amulettes.*

[18] A. Franz, *Die kirchlichen Benediktionen im Mittelalter,* II, 592, and note 9, Gallican Missal and Exorcism of St. Martin. A. Dieterich, *Abraxas* (Leipzig, 1891), p. 142, notes that people still believe in the power of the plant called Solomon's Seal to cure epilepsy.

[19] Cf. above, p. 22.

[20] Jerome, *Commentarioli in Psalmos,* ed. G. Morin, *Anecdota Maredsolana,* III.1 (1895), 58; cf. pseudo-Jerome, *Pat. Lat.,* XXVI, 1027; Augustine, *Pat. Lat.,* XXXVI, 901; Cassiodorus, LXX, 505; cf. p. 22, note 5, above, and R. Harris and A. Mingana, *The Odes and Psalms of Solomon* (Manchester, 1920), II, 70.

was identified with the Wisdom of the Sapiential Books.[21] He was the builder of the temple of the Church as Solomon was the builder of the temple of Jerusalem.[22] To men familiar with these traditions there was nothing strange in the appearance of Solomon as a defender of Christianity and nothing incredible in his rôle as exorcist of demons by means of the Pater Noster.

It is significant that the warrior letters in MS A are given their runic form, for the magic power of the rune was a deep-seated belief of the Germanic peoples, and the word *rūn* itself still meant 'mystery,' 'secret' as well as 'letter.' [23] The runes were reputed to be of divine origin, discovered by Odin himself who, according to the *Hávamál* (138ff.), released himself from the World-Tree by their power, becoming master of words and deeds. The potency of runes is seen especially in inscriptions on grave-stones and weapons, for the Fuþark itself or certain of its letters sufficed to ward off demons and to strengthen weapons.[24] A short sword of about 800 found in the Thames has the runic alphabet inscribed upon it,[25] testifying to the fact that Sigrdrifa's instructions to Sigurd to inscribe victory-runes on his sword was a common practice.[26] But runes could be used for evil purposes, as well as good, and an enemy could blunt the edges of a hero's weapons by magic incantations and inscriptions.[27] Like Grendel, who had cast a spell upon weapons (*Beowulf* 804), the Devil in Poem I can write on the warrior's sword 'many death-bringing marks and baleful letters'

[21] Rabanus Maurus, *Pat. Lat.*, CIX, 671; Walafridus Strabo, *Pat. Lat.*, CXIII, 1167.

[22] Ambrose, *Pat. Lat.*, XV, 1585; Augustine, *Pat. Lat.*, XXXVII, 1168.

[23] On the magic power of the runes see Kemble, 'On Anglo-Saxon Runes,' *Archaeologia*, XXVIII (1840), 328–338; Helmut Arntz, *Handbuch der Runenkunde* (Halle, 1935), Chap. IX, 'Runen und Magie,' pp. 230–272, and the publications of Sigurd Agrell on the magical origin of runes, especially 'Das Ursprung der Runenschrift und die Magie,' *Arkiv for Nordisk Filologi*, XLIII (1927), 97–109; *Die spätantike Alphabetmystik und die Runenreihe* (Lund, 1922); and for a convenient summary, H. Shetelig and H. Falk (translator E. V. Gordon), *Scandinavian Archaeology* (Oxford, 1937), Chap. XIII and index. For the meanings of *rūn* in Old English, see Richard Jente, *Die mythologischen Ausdrücke im Altenglischen, Anglistische Forschungen*, LVI (Heidelberg, 1921), pp. 327–333.

[24] Cf. Arntz, pp. 252–258; A. Dieterich, 'ABC-Denkmäler,' *Rheinisches Museum für Philologie*, LVI (1901), 85–87, gives a list of objects on which the runic alphabet was inscribed.

[25] [British Museum] *Guide to the Anglo-Saxon and Foreign Teutonic Antiquities* (London, 1923), p. 96; cf. also the knives of Gjersvik and Fløksand discussed by Arntz, and the spearheads illustrated in Hoops, *Reallexikon*, art. *Runenschrift*, table 1.

[26] *Sigrdrifumál* 6.

[27] See the note on line 161ff.

(161–162), evil spells which only the recital of the Pater Noster can defeat. In the passage just cited from the *Sigrdrifumál*, Sigurd is urged to call twice on Týr; for Týr, the god of war, had given his name to the T-rune. The fact that some of the runes (Týr, Óss, the English Ing) were named after gods, together with the practice in the Old English and Scandinavian runic poems [28] of describing the characteristics of runes somewhat as though they were persons, may have facilitated the kind of personification of runic letters found in *Solomon and Saturn*. At any rate, the power of the rune was as familiar a tradition to the English as the power of the letter had been to the Hebrews.

Thus, though the runic letters of Poem I are simply those of the Christian prayer, their very appearance as the personified conquerors of demons represents the last vestige of an ancient pagan Germanic tradition, according to which the runes themselves possessed magic power.[29] The native superstition of the pagan English has been pressed into the service of Christianity, just as has the persistent Oriental tradition of King Solomon's power over demons.

VII. THE BACKGROUND OF POEM II

1. The Nature and Content of Poem II

The second dialogue is much superior to the first in literary power. It is, in the first place, a true dialogue in which Solomon and Saturn ask each other questions. The poet provides a proper framework by announcing the debaters at the beginning and declaring at the end that Solomon has triumphed. It is true that Solomon is distinctly the master (*Saloman wæs brēmra*, 173b), and the debate is destined to be unequal. Solomon asks only two or three questions of Saturn,[1] and except for the gnomic passages in which both take part, the rest of the dialogue consists of questions by Saturn and answers by Solomon. The dialogue is thus hardly a balanced *contentio*.[2] But the poem never loses its dialogic character to become merely instructional, as does Poem I. Saturn's rôle of pagan prince is maintained throughout. His questions are those natural to a pagan acquainted only with Oriental and Germanic beliefs, and he knows of Christ only by hear-

[28] Bruce Dickins, *Runic and Heroic Poems* (Cambridge, 1915).

[29] Kittredge calls the use of the runic Pater Noster in our poem 'a manifest transference from the runic sorcerer of heathen days' (*Witchcraft in Old and New England*, p. 31).

[1] In lines 201b–202, 330b, and possibly before line 300, in the omitted leaf. Solomon's questions in 329f., 335f., are merely rhetorical.

[2] On the *Rätselwettkampf*, see below, p. 57.

say.[3] In the first part of the poem his questions are sometimes those of a man already aware of the answers, as in the riddle of Old Age (273ff.), and even when he declares himself curious, as in the question about the strange creature who turns out to be the Philistine God (238ff.), he seems to be testing Solomon's knowledge rather than seeking enlightenment. As the dialogue proceeds, Saturn is apparently convinced of Solomon's wisdom and asks for explanations of matters that he does not truly comprehend and that Christianity may explain.

Poem II differs from Poem I, in the second place, in subject-matter. It is of more serious import, ranging from curious Oriental legends to such favorite themes of Old English poetry as the exile's misery and the passing of life, and from the Christian interpretation of good and evil to universal problems of fate and foreknowledge. Solomon consistently but unobtrusively, for the most part, points out to Saturn how the Christian view of life answers the troubling questions concerning the unequal blessings of the earthly life (331–338), the mingling of joy and sorrow (339–343), the wicked man's length of days (350–354), and the heavy hand of Wyrd (416–433).[4]

Finally, the second dialogue is not only superior to the first in general conception, but frequently rises above it in passages that reveal its author as something more than a mere versifier. The poet was capable both of writing in dark, riddling vein and of composing a vivid description of falling snow or a poignant picture of the homeless exile. His gnomic observations and his prophetic warnings sound a solemn and mysterious note that lifts his poem above conventional moralizing.

Since the sequence of ideas in Poem II is often obscure, an outline is here given for the reader's convenience.

170–272. The poet introduces the characters of his dialogue by saying that he has heard of two sages contending in ancient days about their wisdom: Solomon was the more famous, though Saturn had unlocked the keys of many books and visited many lands (170–192). The end of the introduction is missing because the second page of MS A has been erased and written over.[5] The interrupted text resumes in the middle of a speech by Solomon (193–202), in which he says that he will keep silent, presumably if he is unable to answer Saturn's questions, being well aware that Saturn will then return beyond the river *Cōfor* to boast of his victory. Solomon recalls that

[3] Cf. Vincenti, p. 83; and below, pp. 67–68.

[4] The Christian elements are discussed more fully below, pp. 66–69.

[5] Cf. above, p. 2, and note on line 299 for the total number of missing lines.

the Chaldeans [Saturn's ancestors][6] were so proud that a warning befell them near the field of Shinar, a reference to the Tower of Babel. This suggests to Solomon a question about the land where no human being may tread. Saturn's answer (203–215), one of the most difficult passages in the poem,[7] suggests that a certain *Weallende Wulf*, after slaying twenty-five dragons, was himself slain, and from this fearful site of the dragon-conflict poisons have spread throughout the world. After a brief comment by Solomon (216–220), Saturn propounds a riddle about the dumb one who dwells in a vale (221–228). This is a Christian book of some sort,[8] but Solomon contents himself with an indirect answer, as he often does in the poem, merely remarking that books are famous and will work wonders (229–233), a thought in which the two wise men completely agree (234–237). Saturn now mentions a creature about whom he has been curious for fifty years (238–243), and Solomon, with no further hint of its nature, divines that Saturn is thinking of the strange demon Vasa Mortis, guarded by the Philistines and bound at Solomon's own command (244–272), a plain reminiscence of the original Hebrew legend of Solomon's binding of the demon.[9] Hitherto, the themes of discourse, such as the Tower of Babel and the Wolf, both connected with Nimrod, and Vasa Mortis, connected with the Philistines, have been definitely of Oriental origin, following naturally upon the opening description of the Oriental lands visited by Saturn. The reader is again to be reminded of Saturn's Oriental origin by references to his Chaldean ancestors (318–322) and to his debates with the Philistine wise men (421–426). But for the most part the debate now shifts to themes natural to Germanic poetry, the passing of life, the power of the elements, the might of Wyrd, all of which are given a Christian interpretation by Solomon.

273–322. Saturn propounds a riddle about Old Age (273–282), which is easily answered by Solomon (283–292). Saturn's next question as to why the snow falls (293–299) remains unanswered in our text because of a missing leaf between pages 18 and 19.[10] When the text resumes, Solomon is talking about something that is mightier than cunning war (300–302), possibly Death, and Saturn's solemn answer, 'Night is the darkest of weathers, Necessity the bitterest of fates, Sorrow the heaviest burden, Sleep most like to Death' (303–304), suggests to Solomon a thought on the fading of the leaf and the transi-

[6] Cf. 318–322, where the builders of the Tower are identified with Saturn's ancestors.

[7] See the note on 203ff., and below, p. 61.

[8] See the note on lines 221ff.

[9] See below, pp. 59–61, and the note on lines 265ff.

[10] See above, p. 2.

toriness of life, which proves the folly of the wicked who offend God by storing up earthly treasures (305–313). Saturn is reminded of the Flood preceding Doomsday (314–317) and Solomon prophesies the fate of the proud on that day, expressing the hope that Saturn is not following in the wicked ways of his ancestors, who roused God's wrath by striving vainly against his might in building the Tower of Babel (318–322).

323–354. The dialogue now becomes livelier in a series of short speeches of two to four lines. Solomon answering Saturn's question explains that 'accomplished fates' are the four ropes of the doomed man (323–326).[11] A foolish question of Saturn's on who will judge Christ at Doomsday is properly rebuked by Solomon, who in turn asks a question of difficult interpretation, perhaps on what is and is not (327–330),[12] to which Saturn gives an indirect answer (shadow) in a counter-question on why the sun does not shine brightly on the whole creation but shadows mountains and moors (331–334). Solomon replies by hinting that the similar problem, why earth's riches are not equally divided among men, is resolved by God's ultimate rewards (335–338). Saturn, who is disturbed because the companions weeping and laughter are always together, is told that man offends God by continual mourning (339–343). Saturn then asks why we cannot all proceed straight to God's kingdom, and is told that some things, such as fire and frost, cannot dwell together (344–349). Saturn's question as to why the worse man lives longer receives the indirect answer that no man can postpone the dread journey, at the end of which, it is implied, the injustices of earthly life will be remedied (350–354).

355–383. A series of longer speeches is now introduced by Saturn's question on a similar problem of good and evil fate—how it happens that twins may have entirely different lives (355–361). Solomon, in reply, remarks that the mother has no control over the fate of her children, and must grieve helplessly over the wretched lot of a wayward son; each child must pursue his own destiny (362–377). The Christian modification of this Germanic conception appears only after Saturn's next question asking why a young man does not choose a good lord and follow wisdom; for Solomon's reply indicates that the 'ēadig eorl' can choose a mild lord, who is probably meant to be Christ (378–383).[13]

[11] See the note on line 325a.

[12] See the note on line 330b.

[13] See the note on line 381.

384–505. Saturn's next question apparently introduces a series on the powers of nature. The first question on the restless motion of water (384–389) remains unanswered because of a second missing leaf between pages 22 and 23.[14] The text, as we have it, continues with Solomon's speech in answer to what must have been another question on fire, a speech that explains the nature of fire and light, with Christian applications (390–415). The ancient problem of the relative power of fate and foreknowledge, which Saturn says he has heard the Philistine philosophers debate, is presented to Solomon (416–426), who declares that Wyrd is changed with difficulty, but the wise-hearted man may temper it by seeking human and divine aid (427–433). Saturn then inquires why Wyrd, the origin of all wickedness and the daughter of death, should dwell with us (434–440), and Solomon, in a long passage, explains that Satan's revolt against God is the source of all our woes (441–466). Saturn asks if anyone can bring about his death-day before the appointed end of his life has come (467–471). Solomon's long reply concerns man's guardian angel, and his counterpart the evil spirit who watches man to incite him to evil (472–496). Since the manuscript of the poem ends here, it is not possible to say what intervenes between this passage and the concluding fragment on page 13(A) preceding the beginning. If those who believe this fragment is the proper conclusion of Poem II [15] are right, the final part of Solomon's speech (or of a naturally succeeding speech on Doomsday) appears in the statement that sinful souls will be thrust into hell with the fiends (497–501). A brief conclusion of four lines then contains the poet's own remark that the wise son of David had conquered the prince of the Chaldeans, who rejoiced in spite of his defeat (502–505).

2. The Dialogue and the Riddle

To understand the significance of Poem II one must remember that it combines the traditions of patristic and Germanic literature. The medieval dialogue is a literary form inherited from the Romans and the Greeks. The Platonic dialogue of philosophical speculation, with its vivid contrasts in character and intellect, often became among the more practical Romans a didactic treatise in which one person merely instructed another.[1] The early Christians were quick to adopt the familiar form of the dialogue in their controversies with heathen philosophers and heretics. Just as St. Paul had followed the example

[14] See above, p. 2.

[15] See above, p. 11.

[1] On the classical dialogue see R. Hirzel, *Der Dialog, ein literarhistorischer Versuch* (Leipzig, 1895).

of Socrates in seeking open debate in the market-place of Athens, so Justin Martyr took over the literary form of the dialogue in theological debate with the Jew Trypho.[2] A still earlier Greek dialogue between a Christian and a Jew by Aristo of Pella has been lost.[3] In Latin, the *Octavius* of Minucius Felix, written in the early part of the third century, follows closely the tradition of antiquity, and imitates in particular the fine art of Cicero's *De Natura Deorum*.[4] In this dialogue, Octavius, a Christian, argues with Caecilius, a friend who is still a heathen, about the God of the Christians and their supposed superstitions. The arguments of Octavius are based on a Christian-Stoic philosophy which attempts to reconcile reason and faith. At the end, Caecilius, like Saturn in our poem, acknowledges himself vanquished, but claims a victory for himself in that he has triumphed over error, just as Saturn rejoices in spite of his defeat (502–505). Origen's dialogues against heretics are lost, but by the fourth century the apologetic dialogue of Latin writers is often directed against heretics, as in Jerome's dialogue of a Luciferian and an orthodox Christian, or the larger work against the Pelagians.[5] Augustine's preference was for more general and abstract subjects, but these might vary from easy and delightful philosophical conversations with friends, like *De Ordine*, to more abstruse arguments quite different from real conversations, like *De Libero Arbitrio*.[6] The problem of fate and free-will, which Augustine tried to solve by the doctrines of original sin and grace, was debated in a later dialogue that had as profound an effect on the popular philosophy of the Middle Ages as did Augustine on its theology—the *De Consolatione Philosophiae* of Boethius. Though the poet of *Solomon and Saturn* II discusses the old question of the flourish-

[2] Πρὸς Τρυφῶνος Ιουδαίου Διάλογος, ed. J. K. T. Otto, *S. Iustini . . . Opera* (Jena, 1847–50), IV. On the early Christian Greek and Latin dialogues, see, besides Hirzel, Hermann Jordan, *Geschichte der altchristlichen Literatur* (Leipzig, 1910), Chap. VI.

[3] A. Harnack, *Geschichte der altchristlichen Literatur*, I.1, 92–95; Jordan, *op. cit.*, p. 245. Later dialogues of the sort are the fifth-century *Altercatio inter Simonem Judaeum et Theophilum Christianum*, ed. F. Bratke, *Corpus Scriptorum Ecclesiasticorum Latinorum*, XLV, 1904, and the pseudo-Augustinian *De Altercatione Ecclesiae et Synagogae Dialogus*, of the late fifth century (*Pat. Lat.*, XLII, 1131), which was to have a far-reaching influence on the allegory of ecclesiastical art (from the ninth century) and on the medieval drama; cf. H. Pflaum, *Die Religiöse Disputation in der europäischen Dichtung des Mittelalters* I, *Der allegorische Streit zwischen Synagoge und Kirche* (Geneva, 1935).

[4] The *Octavius*, at one time supposed to be the earliest Christian-Latin work of importance (cf. Jordan, pp. 254–255), has been often edited—by J. P. Waltzing (Louvain, 1909); G. Rauschen (Bonn, 1913).

[5] *Pat. Lat.*, XXIII, 155–182; 495–590.

[6] *Pat. Lat.*, XXXII, 977–1020; 1221–1310.

ing of the wicked and the power of fate in poetic rather than philosophic fashion, he would hardly have written just as he did if Augustine and Boethius had not speculated on these problems before him.[7]

Christian writers continued to use the dialogue for all kinds of purposes in the succeeding centuries. Gregory the Great's *Dialogues*, which deserve the name only because the deacon Peter occasionally asks Gregory a question, consist chiefly of tales of miracles intended for edification and warning. On the other hand, John the Scot's remarkable *De Divisione Naturae*, of the ninth century, is a true philosophical dialogue, in which the pupil asks penetrating questions of his master, and argues ingeniously. Scarcely to be called dialogues proper are the numerous 'question and answer' books[8] which go back to the Greek *aporiae* of the Homeric critics and the exegetical *quaestiones* of the fathers. The dialogues of Alcuin are mostly of this instructional type, for example the *Grammatica* between master and disciple,[9] the *De Rhetorica* between Charlemagne and Alcuin,[10] and the *Disputatio* between Alcuin and Charlemagne's young son Pippin.[11] The most popular of the medieval dialogues of inquiry and response was the *Altercatio Hadriani et Epicteti*.[12] Such *didascalia* are as far removed from the classical dialogue as they are from the poetic dialogues of Solomon and Saturn, but they deserve mention here because the two prose dialogues of the same name are clearly of this mechanically didactic type. In the prose dialogue of Solomon and Saturn in Cotton Vitellius A XV,[13] Saturn asks Solomon fifty-nine questions, most of

[7] On the relation of the poet's discussion of Wyrd to Boethius and Christian thought, see the note on lines 419a, 434ff., and below, pp. 62–63.

[8] On this type of literature, see Max Förster, 'Two Notes on Old English Dialogue Literature,' *An English Miscellany presented to Dr. Furnivall* (Oxford, 1901), pp. 86–106; cf. Förster on the oldest (sixth-century) medieval Latin 'question and answer' book, *Romanische Forschungen*, XXVII (1910), 342–348; and especially the valuable introduction to A. W. Daly and W. Suchier, *Altercatio Hadriani Augusti et Epicteti Philosophi, Illinois Studies in Language and Literature*, XXIV (Urbana, 1939).

[9] *Pat. Lat.*, CI, 850–902.

[10] *Pat. Lat.*, CI, 919–950.

[11] *Pat. Lat.*, CI, 975–980, and Wilmann's edition in *ZfdA*, XIV (1869), 530–555. Daly, *Altercatio Hadriani*, p. 84, thinks the *Disputatio*, the authorship of which has been questioned, may well be by Alcuin.

[12] Cf. note 8, above.

[13] Printed by Kemble, *Dialogues of Solomon and Saturnus*, pp. 178–193, and earlier by B. Thorpe, *Analecta Anglo-Saxonica* (London, 1834), pp. 95–100; in later editions, pp. 110–115. This dialogue closely resembles the Old English *Adrian and Ritheus* which was also printed by Kemble, pp. 198–207, and the Middle English *Questions between the Master of Oxford and his Clerk* (printed by C. Horstmann, *Englische*

which are on Biblical subjects, such as how old Adam was when he was created, what man first built a city, what bird is most blessed, and so on. The prose dialogue about the Pater Noster between Poem I and Poem II in MS A has already been discussed.[14] This, too, consists of mechanical questions and answers, although the answers are much more elaborate than most of those in the prose dialogue of Cotton Vitellius XV, and the whole gives the impression of being a fantastically elaborate description of the Pater Noster merely turned into dialogue form. In these cases the great popularity of the Solomonic dialogues attached the names of Solomon and Saturn to dialogues of a catechistic type.

The poetic dialogues, to which we now return, can only be understood in the light of the Christian use of the dialogue proper. They follow, as we have seen, an old tradition of Christian literature in adapting the dialogue to didactic purposes. Poem I is more deliberately and obviously written for the sake of instruction, since its chief purpose seems to be to urge upon the ignorant the value of the Lord's Prayer. Poem II contains something of the dignity of the philosophical dialogue and debates matters of larger interest. Neither poem seems addressed to the heathen or to heretics. The period at which a contention between Christian and Jew or Christian and pagan was of immediate concern for the promotion of the Christian faith had passed. The presence of heathen Danes in the land may, of course, have given some contemporary point to the contest of Solomon and Saturn,[15] but the debate of two such patriarchs could hardly have had the same direct appeal to the contemporaries of Alfred as did the dialogues of the fathers who chose contemporary characters for their Christian apologies and often reflected the actual debates of the times. In the early Christian period, when Christians debated seriously with Jews in life as well as in literature, Solomon would hardly have been chosen as the representative of Christianity.[16] But at a later period,

Studien, VIII, 284–287) of which Kemble printed a shorter version, pp. 216–220. All these apparently go back to the same Latin original (cf. Förster, 'Two Notes,' *Furnivall Miscellany*, p. 87, note 8).

[14] See above, pp. 8–10.

[15] Cf. above, p. 14.

[16] Alcuin in a letter to Charlemagne reports that he had heard in his youth a debate between a Jew and Master Peter of Pavia (*Pat. Lat.*, C, 313), but such public debates could hardly have had the same importance in the eighth century as in the second and third. In the twelfth century the interest in this kind of 'debate' revived and we find not only allegorical debates between Church and Synagogue (cf. above, p. 54, note 3) but also debates between Jew and Christian (cf. H. Walther, *Das Streitgedicht in der lateinischen Literatur des Mittelalters* [Munich, 1920], pp. 100–102; and the dispute of a Heathen, a Jew, and a Christian printed by him, pp. 227–229, and another between a Jew and a Christian, pp. 230–232).

between the sixth and the ninth centuries, let us say, a *contentio* between Solomon and Saturn or some other wise king could have been modified to become a poem illustrating the historic triumph of Christianity over paganism. Such a dialogue was the Latin original of Poem II. The acceptance of Solomon as defender of Christianity against the pagan philosopher Saturn implies that the battle was fought and won long ago. Unlike the usual representative of Christianity in an apologetic dialogue, Solomon in Poem II seldom argues Christian doctrine directly. The poet is by no means, as we shall see, intent on presenting a purely Christian point of view throughout, and differs from other Christian writers of dialogues in embodying much material not directly relevant to the main theme. This is partly, of course, because the dialogue is a poem, and not like the reasoned prose of apologetic writers.[17] It is descended not only from the classical dialogue, but also from those Germanic poems so well represented in the *Edda*, the verbal contests of gods and heroes.

The peculiar character of the Solomon and Saturn poems lies in the fact that they are not only didactic dialogues but contests of wit and wisdom. In this respect Poem II is closely related to riddle-literature. The medieval dialogue, in the words of Frederick Tupper, is 'at once enigmatic in phrasing and didactic in its purpose.'[18] It is likely to be not so much a philosophical colloquy in the manner of the Greek dialogue, as a contest in which the contestant matches his knowledge with another's, often for some heavy stake. This kind of *Rätselwettkampf* was well known to antiquity, the most famous example being the legendary contest between Homer and Hesiod.[19] The ancient riddle was not merely a pleasant pastime, but a literary form used for serious purposes. The oldest riddles are often of mythical origin and preserve primitive views of life and nature.[20] The riddle-contest sometimes involved life and death, as in the story of Calchas and Mopsus told by Strabo,[21] or the *Hervararsaga*, in which King Heiðrek forfeits his life because he is unable to answer the last question

[17] Poetic dialogues in Latin are rare until the *débats* of the twelfth century.

[18] *The Riddles of the Exeter Book* (Boston, 1910), p. xx.

[19] See A. Rzach, *Hesiodi quae feruntur omnia* (Leipzig, 1884), pp. 235–250. Homer's death of mortification because of his inability to answer the riddle of the fisherman is recounted in this *Agon* or *Certamen*, *idem*, p. 250. A similar contest between two bards is found in the Irish (tenth-century?) *Colloquy of the Two Sages* between Néde and Fechertne (*Revue Celtique*, XXVI [1905], 4–53). For the types of riddle-contest see F. J. Child, *The English and Scottish Popular Ballads* (Boston and New York, 1882ff.), I, 1; and Tupper, *The Riddles of the Exeter Book*, p. xix.

[20] Cf. K. Ohlert, *Rätsel und Rätselspiele der alten Griechen*, 2nd ed. (Berlin, 1912), p. 1.

[21] *Geography*, XIV, 1, 27.

addressed to him by the disguised Odin.[22] Saturn forfeits not his life, but, at least by implication, a religion that he is not unwilling to lose. We cannot tell whether a real wager appeared in Poem II because the section of the introduction that would have contained it is missing, but there is a definite wager in Poem I where Saturn promises to give thirty pounds of pure gold and his twelve sons, if Solomon persuades him of the truth of Christianity, a possible reminiscence of the wagers in Solomon's contests with Hiram.[23]

The 'hard questions' propounded by Saturn to Solomon are, for the most part, not riddles, properly speaking. Only the questions on the Book (221–235), on Old Age (273–292), and possibly on the Shadow (330–334), are technical riddles that might be solved by the wit of the contestant.[24] The contest is one of knowledge and wisdom rather than one of intellectual cunning. The questions on the Vasa Mortis, fate, the nature of fire, and the flourishing of the wicked can be answered by Solomon because of his superior knowledge of esoteric lore or his wise interpretation of the problems of life in the light of Christian faith. In this respect the second dialogue resembles not so much the riddle-contest of Solomon and Bilqis, Queen of Sheba, nor that between Heiðrek and Odin, in both of which genuine riddles appear, as the *Vafþrúðnismál* of the *Elder Edda*, in which Odin and the giant Gagnrath propound questions to each other on cosmological matters, mythological stories of the origins of life and the future destruction of the gods.[25]

Even when the questions asked by Saturn are not riddles in the strictest sense, the enigmatic tone of the riddle-contest remains in the speeches of both disputants. The clarity of direct intellectual argument characteristic of both the Platonic and patristic dialogue is deliberately avoided. The allusions and indirection of Solomon [26] lend that atmosphere of mystery dear to the heart of many an Old English poet. Though following the Christian practice of using the classical dialogue for didactic purposes, the author has infused his poem with the solemn and mysterious spirit proper to a contest between two mighty seers of the ancient world. Solomon and Saturn propound not merely the clever riddles that can be solved by intellectual ingenuity or esoteric erudition, but those age-old riddles of life and death to which only man's wisdom and faith can find an answer.

[22] *Heiðreks Saga*, ed. Jón Helgason (Copenhagen, 1924).

[23] Cf. above, p. 22.

[24] Cf. Tupper, *The Riddles of the Exeter Book*, p. xx, note §§.

[25] Cf. A. Heusler, 'Die altnordischen Rätsel,' *Zeitschrift des Vereins für Volkskunde*, XI (1901), 124–125, on the nature of these riddling contests, and below, pp. 62–66, for the Germanic elements in *Solomon and Saturn*.

[26] See lines 176ff., 216ff., 229ff., 331ff., 381ff.

3. The Oriental Elements

The Oriental elements in Poem II are much more important than those in Poem I. The introduction of Poem II describes the countries that Saturn has visited in search of knowledge, as does Saturn's speech in Poem I, but in greater detail (170–192). Saturn here, too, lives beyond the river *Cōfor* (196), and from time to time the poet reminds us of his descent from the Chaldeans, builders of the Tower of Babel (198–201, 318–322, 503), and of his association with the Philistines (421–426). In the previous section we have seen how the ultimate origin of the Solomon and Saturn dialogues in Solomon's riddle-contests with the Queen of Sheba and Hiram of Tyre is reflected in the character of the dialogue, notably in the propounding of 'hard questions' and the enigmatic tone that prevails throughout.[1] The second ultimate source of the Solomonic dialogues is the conversations of Solomon with the demons whom he brings under his power by means of his magic ring.[2] There can hardly be any doubt that the character of the second dialogue is influenced, however indirectly, by such Hebrew legends as that in which the chained demons Azza and Azzael are forced to reveal the heavenly mysteries to the King,[3] and by the Oriental stories preserved in Arabic, in which Solomon converses with Simurg about fate and prophecy and with the king of the djinns Shachruch, corresponding to the Hebrew Ashmedai, about fire, water, and air and the world-dragon who embraces the universe.[4] For the subjects discussed in Poem II, though greatly modified by Christian and Germanic conceptions of religion and nature, include similar mysteries of fate and the end of the world (314–330, 355–377, 416–466), and the power of the elements of water and fire (384–389, 390–415).

The most striking inheritance from the Jewish legends of Solomon and the king of the demons occurs in the Vasa Mortis passage (238–272), where we have, in little, a definite narration of the very story of Solomon's binding of the demon which contributed so largely to the development of the dialogue of Solomon with such a pagan prince of spiritual darkness as Saturn-Marcolf.[5] For in this speech, Solomon explains very clearly that the strange creature about whom Saturn

[1] See pp. 57ff., and especially pp. 21–24, where the origins of the Solomonic dialogues are traced.

[2] See pp. 23–24.

[3] See p. 23, note 10.

[4] See p. 23, note 12.

[5] See pp. 22–23, and the discussion of the origin of Saturn-Marcolf, pp. 26–35, and, for further details, my article, 'The *Vasa Mortis* Passage in the Old English *Salomon and Saturn*,' *Studies in Philology*, a Miscellany in honor of Frederick Klaeber (Minnesota, 1929), pp. 240–255; and the notes on lines 240–272.

asks is a monstrous demon guarded by the Philistines, whom Solomon himself discovered and commanded to be bound in chains (265–272):

> Nyste hine on ðǣre foldan fīra ǣnig
> eorðan cynnes ǣrðon ic hine āna onfand
> and hine ðā gebendan hēt ofer brād wæter,
> ðæt hine se mōdega hēht Mēlotes bearn,
> Filistīna fruma, fæste gebindan,
> lonnum belūcan wið lēodgryre.
> Đone fugel hātað feorbūende
> Filistīna fruman Vāsa Mortis.

In the Talmudic story Solomon ordered his chief man Benaiah to capture the demon Ashmedai and gave him a chain to accomplish his purpose.[6] The mountain about the demon in Poem II (255b–257a) likewise reflects Solomon's visiting of the fettered demons in the mountain of darkness.[7] Thus Poem II retains in this particular passage a story that goes straight back to the Hebrew legend of Solomon. When Saturn declares that he is consumed with curiosity (238–243) about this strange creature, he is inquiring, if he but knew it, about the very opponent of Solomon who has now, through centuries of transformation, become Saturn himself.

The Philistines, who guard Vasa Mortis, appear again and again in Poem II. Saturn has visited their land (183a), and debated with their princes on fate and foreknowledge (422); and the Wolf is known to them (204–205). The repeated references to the Philistines are a puzzling feature of the poem. It seems as if certain apocryphal stories had been attached in Jewish or early Christian tradition to these ancient enemies of the Jews. The beginnings of such a tradition might be found in the Old Testament passages where the Philistines are called giants or Anakim. They are said, for example, to be the remnant of the Anakim in Jeremiah XLVII, 5, according to the Septuagint.[8] In

[6] This version of the story appears in the *Tractate Gittin* (cf. above, p. 23, note 10), but similar legends are found elsewhere, cf. Ginzberg, *Jewish Ency.*, art. *Asmodeus*, 218b.

[7] Cf. [Klaeber] *Studies in Philology*, pp. 246–247, Ginzberg, *Legends of the Jews*, IV, 149, and note on line 255. It is noteworthy that in the *Testament of Solomon* Asmodeus worships a fish-god (ed. McCown, V, 9, pp. 23*–24*), and perhaps in this way became connected with the Dagon of the Philistines; cf. note on line 255 for Vasa Mortis as a fish-god.

[8] Cf. Joshua XI, 21–22, where the conquest of the Anakim is that of the land of the Philistines. On the Philistines in Jewish legend see the note on line 205a and Ginzberg, *Legends of the Jews*, I, 257–259, 270, 325, 364; IV, 62–63, 92, 94; VI, 223–224; and Index, s.v. *Philistines;* but there is no cycle of legends mentioned that seems related to the Saturn–Vasa-Mortis–Philistine connections of Poem II.

view of Saturn's familiarity with the Philistines and the connection between the Philistine god Vasa Mortis and Solomon's demonic opponent Ashmedai, it is not impossible that the antagonist of Solomon in debate was represented at an early stage in the development of the Solomonic dialogue as a pagan prince of the Philistines.[9] This early *contradictio* would thus have been one between Solomon upholding the Jewish tradition and a Philistine potentate, perhaps possessed of demonic powers.

Allusions to the Tower of Babel appear in two passages. In the first Solomon remarks that the Chaldeans were so proud that a warning befell them about the field of Shinar (198–201a). In the second Solomon alludes to the fact that Saturn's ancestors (the Chaldeans) strove against God's might but were unable to complete that work (318–322). Both of these passages were recognized by Vincenti as allusions to the building of the Tower in the plain of Shinar (Gen. XI).[10] The relation to the first of these passages of the difficult section on Nimrod and the *Weallende Wulf* (203–220) immediately following is somewhat obscure. Nimrod in Jewish legend and medieval Christian tradition is usually assumed to be the builder of the Tower of Babel,[11] because Nimrod, the mighty hunter (*γίγας* in the Septuagint) of Genesis X, 8–10, whose land was 'Babel, and Erech, and Accad, and Calneh, in the land of Shinar,' was directly connected with the builders of the Tower in the land of Shinar (Gen. XI). The sea-faring Wolf, friend (or father?) of Nimrod (205),[12] who killed twenty-five dragons only to be struck down by death himself, is the most mysterious figure in the poem. From the desolate scene of this dragon-combat, the land where no human foot may tread, proceed the poisonous exhalations that overrun the earth. Most of the elements of this passage are traceable to Oriental legends. The waste land has all the characteristics of the desert abode of demons in Hebrew literature; the scattering of the poisons [13] resembles the conclusion of the Jewish legend of the destruction of the Tower of Babel; and the struggle of dragons at dawn, in which the Wolf meets his death, may be a reflection of the myth of Gilgamish and Enkidu or of the primeval dragons of chaos and

[9] On this possibility cf. note on lines 265ff., and my article, *JEGP*, XXXVII (1938), 352–353.

[10] Pp. 68, 73; on the second passage, cf. O. F. Emerson, 'Legends of Cain, especially in Old and Middle English,' *PMLA*, XXI (1906), 909. Further discussion will be found in the notes on lines 198ff., 320ff.

[11] See notes on lines 203ff., and 'Nimrod and the Wolf in the Old English *Solomon and Saturn*,' *JEGP*, XXXVII (1938), 332–354.

[12] See the note on lines 204f.

[13] See the note on line 211a.

Bel, the slayer who is himself slain.[14] Poem II thus not only preserves in its general outline the ancient legend of Solomon's contests with princes and demons, an outward form that appears with less Oriental coloring in Poem I; it is also full of details directly traceable to its Oriental origin, the Philistines and their demon-god Vasa Mortis, the Tower of Babel and Nimrod, and even perhaps a dim reflection of the old story of the Babylonian myth of creation.[15]

4. The Germanic Elements

The central themes of the second dialogue are, as Vincenti rightly observed,[1] 'the last things,' Wyrd, Old Age, Death, and Doomsday. Of these it is Wyrd, the mythological personification of inexorable destiny, that most clearly reflects Germanic beliefs. This mighty power, 'Wyrd sēo swīðe' (434), accomplished the predetermined events of the whole world of nature, and governed the course of man's life, bringing him death and the end of earthly joys.[2] In a poem as late as *Solomon and Saturn* the heathen conception of Wyrd is naturally influenced by both classical and Christian views of Fate. Saturn's question about which is mightier, Wyrd or Providence (*wyrd ðe warnung*, 419), is almost Boethian, and his further characterization of Wyrd the mighty as the daughter of death and the source of all wickedness and woe, though ostensibly a pagan characterization, has been fundamentally influenced by Christian beliefs.[3] Solomon, replying to Saturn's question concerning why Wyrd torments us, tells the story of Satan's revolt and fall (441–466). But even Solomon, who, as the

[14] See the notes on lines 203ff. and my article on Nimrod and the Wolf, *JEGP*, XXXVII (1938), 332–354.

[15] The Jewish legends that have become a definite part of Christian tradition, such as the Fall of Lucifer, will be treated below, under Christian elements, pp. 66ff.

[1] P. 12.

[2] On Wyrd, see J. Grimm, *Teutonic Mythology*, trans. J. S. Stallybrass, I, 405, 417; IV, 1399; A. Wolf, *Die Bezeichnungen für Schicksal in der angelsächsischen Dichtersprache* (Breslau, 1919); R. Jente, *Die mythologischen Ausdrücke im altenglischen Wortschatz, Anglistische Forschungen*, LVI (Heidelberg, 1921), pp. 196–208; A. Brandl, 'Zur Vorgeschichte der Weird Sisters im *Macbeth*,' *Texte und Forschungen zur englischen Kulturgeschichte* [Liebermann-Festgabe] (Halle, 1921), pp. 252–270, reprinted in *Forschungen und Charakteristiken* (Berlin und Leipzig, 1936), pp. 82–97; for the relation to Roman and Christian beliefs, see especially G. Ehrismann, 'Religionsgeschichtliche Beiträge zum germanischen Früh-Christentum,' *Beiträge zur Geschichte der deutschen Sprache und Literatur*, XXXV (1909), 209–239; F. Kauffmann, 'Über den Schicksalsglauben der Germanen,' *Zeitschrift für deutsche Philologie*, L (1923/26), 361–408; Bertha S. Phillpotts, 'Wyrd and Providence in Anglo-Saxon Thought,' *Essays and Studies . . . of the English Association*, XIII (1928), 7–27; and the notes on lines 325a, 362ff., 385a, 419a, 427ff., 434ff.

[3] See the note on lines 434ff.

champion of Christianity, must be expected to give a Christian interpretation of Wyrd, shows the influence of the ancient Germanic belief when he says that Wyrd is hard to change (427). His declaration that the wise man may temper every blow of fate if he seeks aid of his friends and the divine spirit reminds us of the compromises of the Beowulf-poet.[4] The word *wyrd* is here used in the plural (*wyrda gehwylce*) and means 'a destined event,' 'a blow of fate,' as frequently.[5] A similar use occurs in the curious passage in which Solomon tells Saturn that *gewurdene wyrde*, 'accomplished fates,' are the ropes of the doomed man (323–326). This seems to refer to the Germanic belief in the fettering of the doomed warrior. The valkyrs and *dísir* had the power to bind with chains and fetters,[6] and the ancient Irish goddesses of war likewise had the 'ropes of their slaughter on their necks.' [7]

The Germanic belief that even man's defeat by Wyrd was offset by the hero's enduring fame and the greatness of human character, an heroic conception that made the heathen religion more than a despairing fatalism,[8] could not appear in *Solomon and Saturn*. Nevertheless, something of Wyrd's mysterious power over men's minds is inherited from heathen times. The poet's view of destiny 'hard to change' is not limited to the mention of Wyrd, but appears in many other references to fate that reveal the persistence of the heathen tradition. Man must endure his *orlegstunde* (366), his 'hour prescribed by ancient law,' 'hour of fate.' [9] The mother has no power over her children, but each must fare, one after another, to his destiny (*gebyrd*, 376), for 'ðæt is eald gesceaft' (377), 'the ancient condition of man's nature.' The laws of fate affect not only man but nature, and water must pursue its mysterious appointed course, 'drēogeð dēop gesceaft' (385), as fire must follow its natural destiny (*gecyndo*, 406). The speeches of both Solomon and Saturn thus pay respect to the deep-rooted Germanic belief in the power of Wyrd even while they modify it.

A theme very characteristic of Old English poetry and Germanic life is the brief elegy describing the young exile's plight (367–374). A mother cannot control her son's fate, but must grieve when he fares forth in wild mood as a young warrior. He may be destined, weary of heart, to live far from men as a wretched exile, because his lord's face

[4] See note on lines 427ff. and *Beow.* 2291, 2574 and 979; 2526-27; 1056.

[5] Cf. Wolf, p. 41.

[6] See the note on line 325a.

[7] W. Stokes, citing this passage from the *Bruden da Derga* in *Revue Celtique*, II (1873–75), 491–492, aptly compares the passage in *Solomon and Saturn*.

[8] Cf. Bertha S. Phillpotts, 'Wyrd and Providence,' p. 13.

[9] See the note on line 366.

is turned from him. Here the subject and tone are both reminiscent of the *Wanderer.* Another familiar theme, found in the *Wanderer* and the *Ruin*, the passing of earthly splendor and treasure, finds expression in Solomon's speech beginning 'Lȳtle hwīle lēaf bēoð grēne' (305), though this lament is given a Christian application. A more typically Germanic interpretation of the theme of time's devouring all things occurs in the riddle propounded by Saturn to Solomon (273–282). The wondrous thing that neither star nor stone nor bright gem can escape is recognized by Solomon as *Yldo*, Old Age (283–292). In the *Gylfaginning* even Thor is brought to his knee by the wrestling of the old woman Elli, Old Age personified.[10]

The Germanic and Oriental sources of the poem are blended in its riddles and 'hard questions.' Although riddles are the common property of many peoples and literatures, there is no doubt that the Germanic peoples, Germans, Scandinavians, and English, took a particular delight in them.[11] The English love of the riddle is attested by the great collection of Old English riddles in the Exeter Book,[12] and by the Latin riddles of Aldhelm, Tatwine, Eusebius, Alcuin, and Boniface.[13] The indirect mode of expression and the touch of mystery appealed to these Englishmen as much as it did to the author of Poem II.

The riddling element in Poem II has already been discussed in considering its general form and character as a dialogue and *Wettkampf*.[14] It may be noted here that even some of the formal elements of the Germanic riddle appear in Poem II. Saturn's most frequent question, it is true, is 'but why?' (*ac forhwon?*);[15] and this often savors less of the riddle than of the question that a pupil might ask his master in a dialogue of instruction.[16] But genuine stylistic formulas of the riddle remain, not only in the riddles of the Book and Old Age, but elsewhere. The riddle of the Book begins with the conventional 'Ac hwæt is' (221), which is paralleled by the opening 'Hvat er' of the Scandinavian riddles addressed to King Heiðrek, and the questions of

[10] *Edda Snorra Sturlusonar*, ed. F. Jónsson (Copenhagen, 1931), p. 58.

[11] On the Scandinavian parallels, see above, p. 58.

[12] Edited by Frederick Tupper, Jr. (Boston, 1910); Krapp-Dobbie III, 180–210, 229–243.

[13] The riddles of Aldhelm and Alcuin are influenced by the enigmas of Symphosius. On the relation of the literary riddle to the folk-riddle, see Tupper, *MLN*, XVIII (1905), 1–8.

[14] See section VII, 2: The Dialogue and the Riddle, pp. 53–58.

[15] Lines 293, 331, 339, 350, 378, 384; cf. 344.

[16] See above, p. 55.

the *Vafþrúðnismál* and *Alvísmál*,[17] and ends with the 'Saga hwæt ic mǣne' (228) that corresponds to the end of Riddle 62: 'Rǣd hwæt ic mǣne.'[18] The formula introducing the riddle of Old Age 'Ac hwæt is ðæt wundor' (273) is the characteristic formula of many of Odin's riddles in his contest with King Heiðrek: 'Hvat er þat undra?'[19] Finally, the 'Saga (ðū) mē' of Saturn's question is the conventional opening formula of the questions in the *Vafþrúðnismál* and *Alvísmál*: 'Seg mér (þat)' or 'Seg þat.'[20]

A second type of Germanic poetry especially cultivated by the Scandinavians and the English appears in Poem II in the gnomic passages. Gnomic verses, those sententious sayings concerning moral wisdom or observation of life, marked by their pregnant style and rhetorical balance, are found incidentally in Old English and Old Norse verse as well as in such collections as those of the Exeter and Cotton manuscripts and the *Hávamál*.[21] The type beginning with *ne mæg* is found twice in Solomon's answers:

> Ne mæg fȳres fēng nē forstes cile,
> snāw nē sunne somod eardian (346–347).
>
> Ne mæg mon forildan ǣnige hwīle
> ðone dēoran sīð, ac hē hine ādrēogan sceall (353–354).[22]

The mere statement with *bið* is illustrated by the fine long lines:

> Nieht bið wedera ðīestrost, nēd bið wyrda heardost,
> Sorg bið swārost byrðen, slǣp bið dēaðe gelīcost. (303–304)

A characteristic variant of this type is the verse beginning with an adjective, such as:

> Dol bið sē ðe gǣð on dēop wæter (216),

[17] *Heiðreks Saga* (*Hervarar Saga*), ed. Helgason (Copenhagen, 1924), pp. 58, 63, 83; *Vafþrúðnismál* 7; *Alvísmál* 2, 5.

[18] The usual formula of the riddle in which the object describes itself is of course 'Saga hwæt ic hātte,' *Exeter Riddles*, 11, 11; 20, 9; 24, 16; 63, 9; 67, 10; 80, 111; 83, 14; 86, 7.

[19] Each of a whole series of riddles begins: 'Hvat er þat undra / er ek uttí sa / firi Dellings durum?' (pp. 60–80, ed. Helgason).

[20] *Vafþrúðnismál*, 11, 13, 15, 17, 21, etc.; *Alvísmál*, 11, 13, 15, etc.

[21] On the gnomic verses, see Blanche C. Williams, *Gnomic Poetry in Anglo-Saxon*, New York, 1914, an edition of the Old English collections with a valuable introduction; and further, A. Heusler, *Die altgermanische Dichtung, Handbuch der Literaturwissenschaft* (Wildpark-Potsdam, 1926), pp. 64–72.

[22] Miss Williams mentions the second, p. 66, and cites also 172bf., 229ff., 303ff., 336ff., 342f., 427ff. The type most familiar to readers of *Beowulf*, that with *sceal*, does not occur in *Solomon and Saturn*.

which is strikingly paralleled by two gnomic verses in the *Seafarer* (106) and the *Exeter Gnomes* (35).[23] Similar are Solomon's 'Unlǣde bið and ormōd' (342)[24] of the man who mourns overmuch, and Saturn's gnomic utterance on books beginning:

Bald bið sē ðe onbyregeð bōca cræftes (234).

'Wyrd bið wended hearde' (427) is also reminiscent of the gnome. This, like the passages beginning 'dol bið' and 'unlǣde bið,' just cited, is given a Christian development, but the first three gnomic passages mentioned above may be considered just as pagan in sentiment as they are Germanic in expression.

The gnomic tradition and the riddle tradition are integral parts of the second dialogue. The condensed wisdom of the gnomic verses raises the poet's didacticism above the commonplace and the dark questions and mysterious allusions lend a dignity even to the lore that is merely curious. In noting the Germanic elements that affect both the matter and style of the poem, the most pervasive influence of Germanic antiquity must not be forgotten—the alliterative verse itself, which with its closely-knit structure and solemn cadence is well fitted to express the lofty thoughts of those two venerable sages, Solomon and Saturn.

5. The Christian Elements

Since the theme of the whole dialogue is the triumph of Christian religion over pagan ignorance, the Christian elements must be treated somewhat differently from the Oriental and Germanic. Pagan materials are often turned to Christian use. But, in spite of the theme, the Christian view of life is by no means all-pervasive, and much of the material, as we have seen, retains a distinctly pagan coloring. Christ himself is mentioned only three times (191, 327, 401) and rather incidentally, although it must be remembered that the missing portion of the text possibly contained more references to him. Yet certain reasons for this lack of definite references to Christianity may be suggested. The inclusion of much non-Christian material is permissible because the poem is a contest of wisdom, designed for entertainment as well as edification. Even the didactic element may be curious learning or homely wisdom rather than distinctive Christian teaching. Saturn, being a pagan, quite naturally utters thoughts and asks ques-

[23] See the note on line 216.

[24] Cf. 'Unlǣde bið on eorðan, unnit līfes' (21ff.), the only gnomic passage in Poem I; but even this, it should be noted, is developed rather too freely to have the characteristic gnomic condensation.

tions that have nothing to do with Christianity. Only once or twice does the poet, perhaps unconsciously, make him refer to Christian traditions of which he might be presumed to be ignorant (Doomsday, 314ff.; Wyrd as the daughter of death, 434ff.).[1] Finally, the poet may have felt that the rôle of Solomon, a patriarch of the Old Testament and a defender of Christianity only because of Christian symbolism, might easily become difficult and inconsistent if he were allowed to expound Christian doctrine too obviously and obtrusively. Whatever the reason, such crude insistence on the value of Christian practice as we find in Poem I is almost entirely absent in Poem II,[2] and Solomon's Christian interpretation of life is apt to be indirect and allusive.[3] In this section I shall discuss, first, the more important themes obviously considered part of Christian doctrine or tradition by the poet, and, secondly, the more incidental comments reflecting a Christian interpretation of human life or of natural phenomena.

The passages that are definitely part of Christian tradition are the story of the fall of Lucifer, the references to Doomsday, the allusions to the future life and the Heavenly Jerusalem, and the account of the Guardian Angel. The fall of the proud angel (441–466) is recounted by Solomon in answer to Saturn's question on the reason for the persecutions of mighty Wyrd, the daughter of death and source of evil. Without naming the offending angel, Solomon tells of his revolt with a tenth part of the angelic host (446), a tradition derived through Gregory the Great from the Book of Enoch, and explains that the fallen angels, bound in Hell, are the enemies who fight against man.[4] There is no reference to the temptation of Eve and the fall of man.

The Last Judgment is mentioned three times by name and is plainly in the poet's mind in several passages. The first reference to Doomsday is the incidental one in the description of the demon Vasa Mortis, who in his torment thinks it thrice thirty thousand years until he hears the din of Doomsday (264), and the second, Saturn's reference to the Flood that will cease only when the din of Doomsday is heard (314–317). Solomon takes the opportunity offered by this remark to prophesy woe at Doomsday to the proud who live wickedly in this transitory life, and to warn Saturn not to follow in the ways of his arrogant and wicked ancestors who vainly attempted to build the

[1] In other cases his references to Christian tradition are not departures from his rôle, for in 226ff. he may not know the full significance of the Heavenly Jerusalem of which he has heard, and in 327 he obviously betrays his ignorance; see p. 52.

[2] The only possible exception is the blessing of the morsel (396–399).

[3] Cf. above, p. 57.

[4] For detailed comment on this passage, see the notes on lines 443b, 446; and cf. above, p. 63.

Tower of Babel (318–322). The passage immediately following is that on the *wyrda* which are the ropes of the doomed man; and the fact that the fate of the man destined to die is connected in the poet's mind with Doomsday is shown by Saturn's next question, which contains the third mention of Doomsday: 'Who then will judge the Lord Christ at Doomsday, when he judges all created things?' (327–328), a rash question that is properly rebuked by Solomon. The allusion to the Last Judgment in the final passage (497–501) is plain enough, in spite of its fragmentary form. Sinful souls are to be thrust in Hell, and the High King will then command (*hāteð*) Hell to be enclosed. The phraseology of the passage on the Guardian Angel (484–496), though this section is likewise incomplete, seems to look forward to this judgment of the wicked soul.[5]

The references to the future life can hardly be dissociated from those to the Last Judgment. Solomon speaks of rewards and punishments in several passages, and the answer to Saturn's disturbing questions about the injustices and inequalities of this world, is, by implication, that these will be rectified in the world to come. The Heavenly Jerusalem is first mentioned in Saturn's riddle of the mysterious book of seven tongues, which is reported to lead man to this fair vision.[6] There is a plain warning of the future fate of the wicked who hoard their treasures for this life (308–313) in Solomon's remark that their miserliness will make the fiends rejoice and prevent God from 'listening' to such men. Similarly, Solomon's answer to Saturn's question on the longer life of the 'worse' man, is simply that no one can postpone the grievous journey (of death) (350–354), which seems to imply that mere length of life is insignificant in comparison with the lasting rewards and punishments of the life after death. The unequal distribution of shadow and sunshine and wealth and poverty leads Solomon to point out that the man who strives for good and yet has too little finds his reward among the blessed (331–338).

Belief in a guardian angel sent by God to watch over every man was inherited by the Christians from the Jews.[7] Though the guardian angel was not defined by the Church and his existence was not an article of faith, such an angel was often mentioned in patristic writings and became a familiar tradition in the Middle Ages. The existence of two spirits, one inciting a man to good, the other to evil, is a less common tradition, but this too is found in Jewish teaching and is plainly stated in Christian literature as early as the *Shepherd of Her-*

[5] Cf. above, p. 11.

[6] See the note on lines 221ff.

[7] See the notes on lines 472ff., 477b.

mas.[8] The poet's elaborate description of the attempts of the wicked spirit, the Devil's emissary, to seduce man and to thwart the influence of the good angel, is paralleled in Old English literature only by the description of the two angels in *Guthlac A*, though a briefer description occurs in the Vercelli Homilies.[9]

Some of the shorter passages that embody Christian concepts rather than expound Christian teachings have already been noticed in the discussion of allusions to the future life.[10] Similar references to the relation of God and man occur in the passages which may be called Christian gnomes,[11] where Solomon turns what might have been a purely pagan utterance to Christian uses. A notable example is the fine passage beginning 'Foolish is he who ventures into deep water,' which ends with the remark that such a man rashly tempts God's power (216–220).[12]

Just as the native gnomic wisdom is frequently given a Christian turn, so the observations on water and fire, which probably derive ultimately from the Greek and Roman philosophers, are interpreted in the light of Christianity. The passage on the power of water (384–389) is unfortunately cut short by the disappearance of a leaf of the manuscript; and Solomon's answer is entirely lacking. But the nature of the Christian application may be deduced from the hint in Saturn's own question, which asks why water 'christeneth and cleanseth a multitude of living men' (387). The cleansing power of water is to be applied to the rite of baptism. Light, considered identical with fire, is said to have the color of the Holy Ghost, with allusion to the Pentecostal tongues of fire, and the nature of Christ (400f.). As fire it seeks to return to its heavenly dwelling, as in the *Metres of Boethius*.[13] He who can share the Lord's torch will have a vision of light (409–410).

Thus Oriental legends, Germanic beliefs, and Stoic natural philosophy are mingled in Poem II, and interpreted in Christian fashion. It cannot be said that all these discrepant elements have been fused into a completely harmonious whole. But though here and there a story or observation may strike us, who know their origins, as merely curious, or crude, or inconsistent in tone with other parts of the poem, the diversity of the sources was not so obvious to the poet's contem-

[8] See the note on line 477b.

[9] See the note on lines 479–480.

[10] See above, p. 68.

[11] Discussed above, p. 65.

[12] Cf. also lines 342–343.

[13] XX, 152–160.

poraries as to us.[14] The convenience of discussing under three headings the various elements of which the dialogue is composed has exaggerated the differences of subject-matter. The reader of the poem itself will find in it a certain unifying dignity and solemnity. The figures of the contestants are conceived in the grand manner, and their conversation, if sometimes curious and learned, as befits two princely sages of antiquity, is never trivial. Drawing upon the Hebrew lore of the East and the native Germanic wisdom of the West, the Christian poet makes his characters talk not merely of strange demons and the legendary struggles of giants and dragons, but also of fate and providence, of sin and its punishment, of the passing of time and the coming of death.

[14] Little significant comment on the literary value of the dialogues is to be found in histories of literature. Notable exceptions are the important and interesting criticism of ten Brink and Schücking (*History of English Literature*, I, 88–90; H. Hecht and L. L. Schücking, *Die englische Literatur im Mittelalter*, pp. 31–32). For references to other comments, see Bibliography, pp. 73–76.

BIBLIOGRAPHY

The reader should consult the Introduction for bibliographical notes on special subjects, such as the Pater Noster and the dialogue. The order is alphabetical except in sections II (Manuscripts) and III (Editions and Selections). A list of abbreviations will be found on pp. 78 f. The bibliography does not pretend to be complete, although it is believed that all the studies now relevant are listed, except in section V, where it would be impossible to include all articles on the legend of Solomon.

I. Books Containing Bibliographical Lists

Assmann, B. In R. P. Wülker's revision of Grein's Bibliothek der angelsächsischen Poesie III.2. Leipzig, 1898. Pp. 57–58.

Benary, W. Salomon et Marcolphus, kritischer Text [of the Latin dialogue], Sammlung mittellateinischer Texte, ed. A. Hilka, 8. Heidelberg, 1914. Pp. v–vi.

Ehrismann, G. Geschichte der deutschen Literatur des Mittelalters II.1. Leipzig, 1922. P. 314, Anm. 2.

Heusinkveld, A. H., and Bashe, E. J. A Bibliographical Guide to Old English. University of Iowa Studies, Humanistic Studies IV, 5. Iowa City, 1931. P. 88.

Vincenti, A. R. von. Die altenglischen Dialoge von Salomon und Saturn, Erster Teil. Leipzig, 1904. Pp. ix–xxi. See V, Vincenti.

Wülker, R. P. Grundriss zur Geschichte der angelsächsischen Litteratur. Leipzig, 1885. Pp. 360–361.

II. Manuscripts

1. MS A: Corpus Christi College Cambridge 422. For full description see Introduction, pp. 1 ff.
2. MS B: Corpus Christi College Cambridge 41. For full description see Introduction, pp. 2 ff.
3. Descriptions of MSS
    a) Wanley, H. Antiquæ literaturæ septentrionalis liber alter, seu Humphredi Wanleii librorum vett. septentrionalium, qui in Angliæ bibliothecis extant . . . catalogus historico-criticus (Book ii or Vol. iii, of George Hickes's Thesaurus Linguæ Anglo-Saxonicæ). Oxford, 1705. P. 114a, b (MS B), p. 149a (MS A).
    b) James, Montague Rhodes. A Descriptive Catalogue of the Manuscripts in the Library of Corpus Christi College, Cambridge. 2 vols. Cambridge, 1912. II, 315–316 (MS A); I, 81, 83 (MS B).
4. For collations of the MSS see IV, Schipper, J.; Sweet, H.; Zupitza, J.

III. Editions and Selections

The order in this section is chronological.

Wanley, H. See II, Wanley, H. Lines 1–6 (from MS B), p. 114a.

Conybeare, J. J. Illustrations of Anglo-Saxon Poetry, ed. by W. D. Conybeare. London, 1826. Lines 1–6 (from Wanley); 305–313 (from the transcript of Mr. Shelford of Corpus Christi), with translation, pp. lxxxii–lxxxv.

Kemble, John M. 'On Anglo-Saxon Runes,' Archæologia XXVIII (1840), 327–372. Lines 158–163a (p. 336); lines 84–139 (pp. 367–370).

Kemble, John M. Salomon and Saturn. Without title-page. Probably printed before 1845. Bound page-proof of a proposed edition privately distributed and later, when the edition for the Ælfric Society [see next item] was prepared, called in except for twenty copies, one of which is in the British Museum. Lacks the Old English texts. See IV, Larsen, H., for a complete analysis of the differences between this edition and that of 1848.

Kemble, John M. The Dialogue of Salomon and Saturnus, with an historical introduction. London: printed for the Ælfric Society, 1848. This appeared in parts from 1845 to 1848 as publications 8, 13, and 14 of the Ælfric Society, with the cover-title: Anglo-Saxon Dialogues of Salomon and Saturn. No. 8 (pp. 1–112) bears the date 1845; No. 13 (pp. 113–220) 1847; No. 14 (pp. 221–326) 1848. Poetry and prose, with translation and invaluable introduction. The text is printed in half-lines, 1–59 [= lines 1–30] (to the word *lēofre*) from MS B, thereafter from MS A, with variants from MS B.

Ettmüller, L. Engla and Seaxna Scôpas and Bôceras. Quedlinburg and Leipzig, 1850. Lines 305–313 (based on Conybeare, see III, Conybeare), p. 239.

Bouterwek, K. W. Cædmon's des Angelsachsen biblische Dichtungen, Erster Teil. Gütersloh, 1854. Lines 416–496, based on Kemble, with German translation, pp. lxv–lxix.

Grein, C. W. M. Bibliothek der angelsächsischen Poesie II. Göttingen, 1858. Poetic dialogues, based on Kemble, pp. 354–368; cf. Druckfehler, p. 416.

Rieger, Max. Alt- und angelsächsisches Lesebuch. Giessen, 1861. Lines 1–20, 151–169, 273–292, pp. 139–142 (based on Kemble and Grein).

Schipper, J. See IV, Schipper, J.

Assmann, B. In R. P. Wülker's revision of Grein's Bibliothek der angelsächsischen Poesie III.2. Leipzig, 1898. Pp. 58–82. Poetic dialogues based on independent examination of the MSS, with careful recording of earlier readings. Lines 1–30 (to the word *lēofre*) are printed from MS B, the rest from MS A, with variants from MS B.

Wyatt, A. J. An Anglo-Saxon Reader. Cambridge, 1919. Lines 273–292, p. 198.

IV. Textual Criticism and Collations

Grein, C. W. M. 'Zur Textkritik der angelsächsischen Dichter,' Germania X (1865), 428. Comment on lines 18, 22, 42b, 47, 52, 107, 198, 222, 225, 241, 278–279, 282, 288, 298, 325, 354.

Holthausen, F. 'Zu alt- und mittelenglischen Dichtungen XII,' Anglia XXIII (1901), 123–125. Comment on lines 11, 34, 107–108, 163–164, 167, 171, 205, 227, 243, 268, 278, 302, 330, 332, 386, 455, 468–470, 472–473.

Holthausen, F. 'Zur altenglischen Literatur, XI,' Anglia Beiblatt XXI (1910), 175–176. Comment on lines 449–450.

Holthausen, F. 'Zu Salomo und Saturn,' Anglia Beiblatt XXVII (1916), 351–357. Comment on lines 5–9, 18, 43, 98, 101, 105, 107–108, 112, 132, 136–137, 138, 141–142, 158–159, 172, 177, 181, 184–185, 193–194, 227, 260, 268, 291, 330, 374, 386, 393, 443–444, 446–447, 455, 463, 468, 479.

Holthausen, F. 'Zur Textkritik altenglischer Dichtungen,' Englische Studien XXXVII (1914), 205. Comment on lines 289–290, 358–359.

Kock, E. A. 'Interpretations and Emendations of Early English Texts, IV,' Anglia XLII (1918), 122–123. Comment on lines 129–131.

Kock, E. A. Jubilee Jaunts and Jottings. Lunds Universitets Årsskrift, N. F., Avd. 1, XIV (1918), no. 26, 67–69. Comment on lines 138–140, 148–152, 158–159, 254–256, 385–386.

Schipper, J. 'Salomo und Saturn,' Germania XXII (1877), 50–70. Complete text of poems and prose from MS A.

Sievers, E. 'Zur Rhythmik des germanischen Alliterationsverses. III. Der angelsächsische Schwellvers,' Beiträge zur Geschichte der deutschen Sprache und Literatur XII (1887), 480. Comment on lines 325f., 327–328.

Sweet, H. 'Collation of the Poetical Salomon and Saturn with the MS.,' Anglia I (1878), 150–154. Collation of text and comment on lines 249–250, 254–257, 299.

Zupitza, J. 'Zu Salomon und Saturn,' Anglia III (1880), 527–531. Collation of MS A with Schipper's text.

V. Literary and Historical Criticism [1]

Björkman, E. Archiv für das Studium der neueren Sprachen CXVI (1906), 392–396. Review of Vincenti, see V, Vincenti.

Börnemann, D. F. A. 'Das Testament des Salomo,' Zeitschrift fur die historische Theologie XIV (1844), 9–56. German translation of the Greek Testament of Solomon, see V, McCown.

Brandl, A. Englische Literatur, *in* Hermann Paul, Grundriss der germanischen Philologie, 2nd ed., II.1. Strassburg, 1908. P. 1092.

Brooke, S. A. English Literature from the Beginning to the Norman Conquest. London, 1898. Pp. 210–211.

[1] The most important studies of the legend of Solomon are included.

[Brunet, G.] Dictionnaire des Apocryphes. J. P. Migne's Encyclopédie Théologique, III Ser., vols. 23, 24. Paris, 1856–58. Article on Solomon, 24, 839–886. French translation of prose dialogues, cols. 875–879.

Burdach, K. 'Zum Ursprung der Salomosage,' Archiv für das Studium der neueren Sprachen CVIII (1902), 131–132.

Cambridge History of English Literature I. Cambridge [Eng.] and New York, 1907. Pp. 11–12 (Paues), p. 69 (M. Bentinck-Smith), p. 85 (M. R. James).

Conybeare, F. C. 'The Testament of Solomon,' Jewish Quarterly Review XI (1899), 1–45. English translation and introductory remarks. See V, McCown.

Cosquin, E. 'Le Conte du chat et de la chandelle dans l'Europe du moyen âge et en Orient,' Romania XL (1911) 371–430, 480–531. French versions of Solomon and Marcol, pp. 374–377.

Crapelet, G. A. Proverbes et Dictons Populaires. Paris, 1831. Pp. 189–200, Proverbes de Marcoul et de Salemon.

Dictionnaire des Apocryphes. See Brunet.

Dobschütz, E. von. Das Decretum Gelasianum, *in* Harnack's Texte und Untersuchungen zur altchristlichen Literatur XXXVIII.4. Leipzig, 1912. Contains a reference to the *Contradictio* (*Interdictio*) *Salomonis*. Pp. 8, 13, 57, 315.

Duff, E. G. The Dialogue or Communing between the Wise King Salomon and Marcolphus. London, 1892. Facsimile of the English translation printed by Gerard Leeu (Antwerp, ca. 1492) of the Latin dialogue.

Earle, J. Anglo-Saxon Literature. London, 1884. Pp. 210–212.

Ebert. A. Allgemeine Geschichte der Literatur des Mittelalters im Abendlande. 3 vols. Leipzig, 1874–1887. III, 91–96.

Ehrismann, G. See I, Ehrismann, G.

Faral, E. 'Pour l'histoire de *Berte au Grand Pied* et de *Marcoul et Salomon*,' Romania XL (1911), 93–96.

Förster, M. 'Das lateinisch-altenglische Fragment der Apokryphe von Jamnes und Mambres,' Archiv für das Studium der neueren Sprachen CVIII (1902), 15–28.

Förster, M. 'Zu Adrian und Ritheus,' Englische Studien XXIII (1897), 431–436.

Gaster, M. Literatura Populară Română. Bucharest, 1883. Pp. 78–91, 324–339.

Ginzberg, Louis. The Legends of the Jews. 7 vols. Philadelphia, 1909–38. Vol. IV, ch. 5 'Solomon,' with notes VI, 277–303.

Grein, C. W. M. Kurzgefasste angelsächsische Grammatik. Kassel, 1880. P. 9.

Grimm, J. Kleinere Schriften IV.1 (Berlin, 1869), 22–56. Review of von der Hagen, see V, Hagen. Reprinted from Heidelberger Jahrbücher II (1809).

Hagen, F. H. von der. Salomon und Marolf, *in* F. H. von der Hagen and J. G. Büsching, Deutsche Gedichte des Mittelalters I. Berlin, 1808.

Hammerich, F. De Episk-kristelige Oldkvad hos de gotiske Folk. Copenhagen, 1873. Pp. 80–81. Translation by A. Michelsen, Aelteste christliche Epik (Gütersloh, 1874), pp. 111–113.

Hartmann, W. Die deutschen Dichtungen von Salomon und Markolf, II Band: Salomon und Markolf, Das Spruchgedicht. Halle, 1934. See V, Vogt.

Hecht, H., and Schücking, L. L. Die englische Literatur im Mittelalter, *in series* Handbuch der Literaturwissenschaft, ed. O. Walzel. Wildpark-Potsdam, 1930. Pp. 30–32 (Schücking).

Herford, C. H. Studies in the Literary Relations of England and Germany in the Sixteenth Century. Cambridge, 1886. Pp. 253–271. Solomon and Markolf.

Hertz, W. 'Die Rätsel der Königin von Saba,' Zeitschrift für deutsches Altertum XXVII (1883), 1–33. Also in Gesammelte Aufsätze (Stuttgart-Berlin, 1905), pp. 413–455.

Hofmann, K. 'Über Jourdain de Blaivies, Apollonius von Tyrus, Salomon und Marcolf,' Sitzungsberichte der k. b. Akademie der Wissenschaften zu München, phil.-hist. Classe, I (1871), 415–448.

Jagić, V. 'Die christlich-mythologische Schicht in der russischen Volksepik,' Archiv für slavische Philologie I (1876), 82–133.

James, Montague Rhodes. The Lost Apocrypha of The Old Testament. London, 1920. Pp. 40–42, 51–53.

James, Montague Rhodes. 'Irish Apocrypha,' Journal of Theological Studies XX (1919), 9–16.

[Klaeber] Studies in Philology. See Menner, R. J. 'The *Vasa Mortis* Passage,' etc.

Kemble, John M. See III, Kemble, John M., The Dialogue of Salomon and Saturnus.

Larsen, H. 'Kemble's *Salomon and Saturn*,' Modern Philology XXVI (1929), 445–450.

Lehmann, Paul. Die Parodie im Mittelalter. Munich, 1922. Pp. 235–240.

McCown, C. C. The Testament of Solomon. Leipzig, 1922. Chicago dissertation. Edition of the Greek text, with valuable introduction.

Menner, R. J. 'Nimrod and the Wolf in the Old English *Solomon and Saturn*,' Journal of English and Germanic Philology XXXVII (1938), 332–354.

Menner, R. J. 'The *Vasa Mortis* Passage in the Old English *Salomon and Saturn*,' *in* Studies in English Philology, A Miscellany in Honor of Frederick Klaeber, edited by K. Malone and M. B. Ruud. Minneapolis, 1929. Pp. 240–253.

Merrill, E. The Dialogue in English Literature. Yale Studies in English XLII. New York, 1911. Pp. 18–20, 24–25.

Morley, H. English Writers. London, 1867. I, 328. Unchanged in 2nd ed. 1888, II, 205.

Murko, M. Geschichte der älteren südslawischen Literatur. Leipzig, 1908. Pp. 88, 91, 99f., 131f., 212f., Anm. 70.

Pagani, G. C. 'Il Bertoldo di Giulio Cesare Croce ed i suoi fonti' (I. La Leggenda di Salomone e Marcolfo; II. Il Bertoldo di Giulio Cesare Croce), Studi Medievali III (1908–1911), 533–587.

Richter, C. Chronologische Studien zur angelsächsischen Literatur auf Grund sprachlich-metrischer Kriterien, [Morsbach's] Studien zur englischen Philologie XXXIII. Halle, 1909. P. 98.

Salzberger, G. Die Salomosage in der semitischen Literatur, I. Teil: Salomo bis zur Höhe seines Ruhmes. Berlin, 1907.

Schaumberg, W. 'Untersuchungen über das deutsche Spruchgedicht Salomo und Marolf,' Beiträge zur Geschichte der deutschen Sprache und Literatur II (1876), 1–63. Important study.

Seymour, St. John D. Tales of King Solomon. London, 1924.

Ten Brink, B. Geschichte der englischen Litteratur I. Berlin, 1877. Pp. 112–114. 2nd ed. revised by A. Brandl (Strassburg, 1899), I, 105–106 (unchanged). Translation of first edition by Horace M. Kennedy, History of English Literature (New York, 1884), I, 88–89.

Thomas, P. G. English Literature Before Chaucer. London, 1924. Pp. 36–37.

Thorpe, Benjamin. A Dialogue between Saturn and Solomon, *in* Analecta Anglo-Saxonica (London, 1834), pp. 95–100. Edition of 1846, pp. 110–115. Edition of the prose dialogue in Cotton Vitellius A XV.

Vincenti, A. R. von. Die altenglischen Dialoge von Salomon und Saturn, Erster Teil. Münchener Beiträge zur romanischen und englischen Philologie XXXI. Leipzig, 1904 Invaluable.

Vogt, F. Die deutschen Dichtungen von Salomon und Markolf, I Band, Salomon und Marolf. Halle, 1880. II Band, see V, Hartmann. Important introduction.

Wardale, E. E. Chapters on Old English Literature. London, 1935. Pp. 232–233.

Wattenbach, W. 'Die Apologie des Guido von Bazoches,' Sitzungsberichte der kgl. pr. Akad. der Wissenschaften, Jahrgang 1893, I, 395–420.

Weil, G. Biblische Legenden der Musselmänner. Frankfurt a. M., 1845.

Wesselofsky, A. 'Neue Beiträge zur Geschichte der Salomonssage,' Archiv für slavische Philologie VI (1882), 393–411, 548–590.

Wesselofsky, A. Slavianskiia skazaniia o Solomonie i Kitrovasie [Slavic Tales of Solomon and Kitovras]. St. Petersburg, 1872.

Wülker, R. Geschichte der englischen Literatur. 2nd ed. Leipzig and Vienna, 1906–07. I, 51, 71.

Wülker, R. Grundriss. See I, Wülker, R. Grundriss. Pp. 361–367. Important comment.

TABLE OF ABBREVIATIONS

Full titles are given only when the works are not listed in the Bibliography; if listed in the Bibliography, the section follows in parenthesis, thus: (Bibl. V).

As. B. Assmann, in Grein-Wülker (Bibl. III, Assmann).

Angl. Anglia, Zeitschrift für Englische Philologie, Halle, 1877ff.

Angl. Beibl. Beiblatt zur Anglia, Halle, 1890ff.

Benary. W. Benary, Salomon et Marcolfus (Bibl. I).

Bouterwek, or Bout. K. W. Bouterwek, Cædmon's des Angelsachsen biblische Dichtungen (Bibl. III).

B-T. J. Bosworth and T. N. Toller, An Anglo-Saxon Dictionary, Oxford, 1892–98. Suppl. Supplement by Toller, Oxford, 1908–21.

Bülbring. K. D. Bülbring, Altenglisches Elementarbuch, Heidelberg, 1902.

Cath. Hom. B. Thorpe, ed., The Homilies of the Anglo-Saxon Church: the first part, containing the Sermones Catholici, or Homilies of Ælfric . . . 2 vols. London, 1844–46.

D. Elliot van Kirk Dobbie. Some readings of MS A sent to the editor in 1939.

EETS. Early English Text Society, London, 1864ff. (Original Series); 1867ff. (Extra Series).

Edd. Editors of Solomon and Saturn: Kemble, Grein, Assmann.

ESt. Englische Studien, Leipzig, 1877ff.

Gr. C. W. M. Grein, in his Bibliothek der angelsächsischen Poesie, unless otherwise noted (Bibl. III, Grein).

Gr. Spr. C. W. M. Grein in his Sprachschatz der angelsächsischen Dichter, Göttingen, 1861–64. Cf. Sprachschatz.

Grein-Wülker. R. P. Wülker's revision of C. W. M. Grein's Bibliothek des angelsächsischen Poesie, 3 vols., Cassel and Leipzig, 1883–98.

Holt. Ferdinand Holthausen (Bibl. IV).

JEGP. Journal of (English and) Germanic Philology, Urbana, Ill., 1897ff.

JJJ. E. A. Kock, Jubilee Jaunts and Jottings (Bibl. IV).

K. or Kemble. John M. Kemble, The Dialogue of Salomon and Saturnus, London, 1848 (Bibl. III).

Krapp-Dobbie. George P. Krapp and (beginning with Vol. III) Elliot van Kirk Dobbie, Anglo-Saxon Poetic Records, New York, 1931ff.

Luick. Karl Luick, Historische Grammatik der englischen Sprache, Leipzig, 1914ff.

MLN. Modern Language Notes, Baltimore, 1886ff.

Mod. Phil. Modern Philology, Chicago, 1903ff.

NED. A New English Dictionary, Oxford, 1888ff.

P. John C. Pope, transcription of MS A made in 1933.

PBB. Beiträge zur Geschichte der deutschen Sprache und Literatur, ed. Hermann Paul and W. Braune, Halle, 1874ff.

PMLA. Publications of the Modern Language Association (of America).

R. Max Rieger, Alt- und angelsächsisches Lesebuch (Bibl. III).

Sch. J. Schipper (Bibl. IV).

Sievers-Cook. Ed. Sievers (transl. and ed. A. S. Cook), Old English Grammar, 3rd ed., Boston, 1903.

Sk. W. W. Skeat, cited in Schipper's collation (Bibl. IV).

Spr. or Sprachschatz, see Gr. Spr.

Spr.[2] or Sprachschatz[2]. Grein's Sprachschatz der angelsächsischen Dichter, rev. by F. Holthausen and J. J. Köhler, Heidelberg, 1912.

Sw. Henry Sweet (Bibl. IV).

Vincenti. A. R. von Vincenti, Die altenglischen Dialoge von Salomon und Saturn (Bibl. V).

Z. J. Zupitza (Bibl. IV).

ZfdA. Zeitschrift für deutsches Altertum und deutsche Literatur, Leipzig-Berlin, 1841ff.

ZfdPh. Zeitschrift für deutsche Philologie, Halle, 1869ff.

THE TEXT

Italics indicate emendation by altering the letters of the MSS. Square brackets indicate emendation by adding letters omitted by the scribes. Parentheses are used when letters written by the scribes are now illegible because of the damaged condition of the MSS. Expansion of abbreviations is not marked in the text, but unusual abbreviations are recorded in the apparatus of variant readings. The capitalization and punctuation of the MSS are disregarded in the text, but recorded in the apparatus when they might possibly be significant. The accents of the MSS are not recorded. In the text extensive omissions or probable omissions are indicated by dots; in the apparatus the illegible letters of the MSS are indicated by colons.

Only a selection of early readings and emendations of the MSS has been given. A more complete record will be found in Assmann's apparatus in Grein-Wülker's *Bibliothek*. It is hoped, nevertheless, that all important suggestions for the possible improvement of the text have been included. As explained in the Preface, the text of the poems depends on photostats of the MSS, and, for the badly damaged portions, on Pope's careful examination of MS A. The earlier collations of Sweet, Schipper, Zupitza, and Assmann are cited when their readings of obscure words seemed significant or differ markedly from Pope's. It seemed unnecessary to cite all of Kemble's mistaken readings, since his text is often very inaccurate, and his habit of silent emendation sometimes makes it impossible to distinguish attempted readings of the MSS from emendations. Grein's text depended on Kemble's edition, not on the MSS, and many of his emendations, like those of Bouterwek, are manifestly irreconcilable with the MS readings. Grein's readings, when dependent on Kemble's, are indicated by (Gr.). Abbreviations in the apparatus, which follow a different system, in order to save space, from those of the Introduction and Notes, will be found in the Table of Abbreviations.

SOLOMON AND SATURN I

MS B

Sāturnus cwæð:

Hwæt, ic īglanda eallra hæbbe
bōca onbyrged þurh gebregdstafas,
lārcræftas onlocen Libia and Grēca,
swylce ēac istoriam Indēa rīces.
5 Mē þā treahteras tala wīsedon
on þām micelan bēc . . . . . .
M.ces heardum, swylce ic nǣfre on eallum
þām fyrngewrytum findan ne mihte
sōðe sam[n]ode. Ic sōhte þā gīt
10 hwylc wǣre mōdes oððe mægenþrymmes,
elnes oððe ǣhte [oððe] eorlscipes,
se gepalmtwigoda Pāter Noster.
*S*ille ic þē ealle, sunu Dāuides,
þēoden I[s]raēla, ðrītig punda
15 smǣtes goldes and mīne suna twelfe,
gif þū mec gebringest þæt ic sī gebrydded
ðurh þæs cantices cwyde, Crīstes līnan,
gesēmesð mec mid sōðe, and ic mec gesund fa[re],
wende mec on willan on wæteres hri*cg*
20 ofer Cōferflōd Caldēas sēcan.

MS B, p. 196, margin, begins with heading preceding 1; MS A, p. 1, is largely illegible (cf. Introduction, p. 2), but all the letters and words read by Pope on p. 1 are recorded. Heading MS A S:::RN. 1a *MS A* :WÆT *of* hwæt *partly legible.* 3a *MS A* on. 3b and, *MS B* ⁊ (*not noted hereafter*). 4a *MS B* Swylce *with period after* greca. 5a *MS B* þa; *K.* ða, *changing* þ *to* ð, *as often; MS A* hter *of* treahteras *legible.* 6b *MS B leaves a space for eleven or twelve letters blank between* bēc *and* M:ces (*note*). 7a *MS B* M:ces; *Holt. Angl. Beibl.* 27.351 mōdes (*note*); heardum, a *inserted above the line.* 7b *MS A* fre *of* nǣfre *visible; MS B* Swylce *with period after* heardum (*note*). 8a *MS B* fyrngewrytum, u *corrected from* e. 9a *MS B* samode, *Spr.*[2] samnode; *MS A* git. 10a *MS A* h:::: wær:. 11 *MS B* oððe æhte eorlscipes; *K.* (*Gr.*), *R.* iehte; *MS A* oððe æh:a oððe eor:. 12b *MS B* pater nr̄. 13a Sille, *MS B* Wille. 14a I[s]-raēla, *MS B* iraela. 14b *MS B* xxx; *MS A* pun::. 16b *MS B* gebrydded; *Gr. sugg.* gebryrded (*note*); *R.*, *Holt. Angl.* 23.124 gebrydded sī. 17a *MS A* cantices *visible.* 18a *MS B* gesemesð, *K.* (*Gr.*), *R.*, *Sch.* em. gesemest. 18b *MS B* mec gesund, *MS A* sund *visible; MS B* fa, *K.* fa[re]; *Holt. Angl. Beibl.* 27.352 fa[die] (*note*). 19b *K.* (*Gr.*), *R.*, *Sch.* hricg, *MS B* hrigc, *MS A* ryc *visible.*

MS B

Salomon cwæð:

Unlǣde bið on eorþan, un[n]it līfes,
wēsðe wīsdōmes, wealla̓ð swā nīeten,
feldgongende feoh būtan gewitte,
sē þurh ðone cantic ne can Crīst geherian,
25 warað windes full; worpað hine dēofol
on dōmdæge, draca, egeslīce,
bismorlīce, of blacere liðran
īrenum aplum— ealle bēoð āweaxen
of edwittes īða hēafdum.

Heading prec. 21 *MS B* SALOM̃. 21b *MS A* eorðan unnit; *MS B* eorþan unit. 22a *MS B* wesðe, *MS A*, *K.* weste; *MS A* wis *visible.* 23b *MS A* butan gewitte *visible.* 24a *MS B* Se, *period after* gewitte; *MS A* Se, ðone *visible, with space for* [ðe ðurh] *between.* 25a *MS A* worað he windes. 26 *MS A* on domdæge draca egeslice. 27a *MS A* bismor *visible.* 28a *MS B* aplum, p *faint, mistakenly read* aflum (*Sch.*); *K. em.* afelum 'strength'; *MS A apparently* irenum æpplum, *but letters only partly visible.* 29a *MS A* of edwi *visible.*

MS B

30 þonne him bið lēofre ðonne eall þēos lēohte gesceaft
gegoten fram ðām grunde goldes and silofres,
feðerscētte full fyrngestrēona,
gif hē ǣfre þæs organes ōwiht cūðe.
Fracoð hē bið þonne and fremde frēan ælmihtigum,
35 englum ungesibb āna hwarfað.

Sāturnus cwæð:

Ac hwā mæg ēaðusð eallra gesceafta
ðā hāligan duru heofna rīces
torhte ontȳnan on getales rīme?

Salomon cwæð:

þæt gepalmtwigude Pāter Noster
40 heofnas ontȳneð, hālie geblissað,
Metod gemiltsað, morðor gefilleð,
ādwǣsceð dēofles fȳr, Dryhtnes onǣleð.
Swilce ðū miht mid beorhtan gebede blōd onhǣtan,
þæs dēofles drȳ, þæt him dropan stīgað
45 swāte geswīðed sefan intingan,
egesfullīcra þane sēo ǣrene gripo,
þonne for twelf fȳra tȳdernessum
ofer glēda gripe gīfrost weallað.
Forðan hafað se cantic ofer ealle Crīstes bēc
50 wīdmǣrost word: hē gewritu lǣreð,
stefnum stēreð and him stede healdeð
heofonrīces, heregeatowe wegeð.

Sāturnus cwæð:

Ac hūlīc is se organan ingemyndum
tō begangenne þām þe his gǣst wile

---

30 *From here on MSS B and A are printed side by side (note).* 30a *MS B* þōn; 30b ðōn (*abbreviation not noted hereafter*). 34b frēan *begins, p.* 197, *MS B. Heading preceding* 39, *MS B* SALOM̄. 39a *MS B* ge palm twigude, l *inserted above the line.* 39b *MS B* pater nr̄. 40a *MS B* ontyneð, *so K.* (*Gr.*), *Sch.; As. mistakenly read* untyneð. 42b *MS B* dryħ (*end of line*) nes. 43a *MS B* Swilce; mid, *d corrected from a letter partly erased and followed by another erasure.* 45a *MS B* swatege (*end of line*) swiðed.

MS A

30 [Đonne him bið] lēofre ðonne eall ðēos lęohte gesceaft
geg(ote)n fram ðām grunde goldes and seolfres,
feðersceātum full feohgestrēona,
gif hē ǣfre ðæs organes ōwiht cūðe.
Fracoð hē bið ðonne and fremede frēan ælmihtigum,
35 englum ungelīc āna hwearfað.

Sāturnus cwæð:

Ac hwā mæg ēaðost ealra gesc(ea)fta
ðā hālgan duru heofona rīcės
torhte ontȳnan on getælrīme?

Salomon cwæð:

Đæt gepalmtwigede Pāter Noster
40 heofonas ontȳneð, hālige geblissað,
Metod gemiltsað, morðor ge*f*ylleð,
ādwǣsceð dēofles fȳr, Dryhtnes onǣleð.
Swylce ðū miht mid ðȳ be(o)rhtan gebede blōd onhǣtan,
ðæs dēofles drē*or*, (ðæ)t him dropan stīgað,
45 swāte geswīðed seofan intingum,
egesfullīcran ðonne sēo ǣrene gripu,
ðonne hēo for twelf (f)ȳra tȳdernessum
ofer glēda gripe gīfrust wealleð.
Forðon hafað se cantic ofer ealle Crīstes bēc
50 wīdmǣrost word: hē gewritu lǣreð,
stefnum stēoreð and h(im) stede healdeð
heofona rīces, heregeatewa wigeð.

Sāturnus cwæð:

Ac hūlīc is se organ ingemyndum
tō begonganne ðām ðe his gāst wile

30a lēofre *begins p. 2, MS A, see the note on this line. MS A* ðōn (*not noted hereafter*). 31a *MS A* gegoten, *only fragments of* ote *remaining; Sch. read* gegeoten. 34b *Holt. Angl.* 23.123 ælmihtgum, *metri causa.* 36b *MS A* gesceafta, ea *blurred.* 38b *MS A* getæl, t *obscure; As. read only* g::æl. 39b *MS A* pat̄ noster. 41b *MS A probably* gesylleð (*so K., Sch., P.*), *cross-bar of* f *being apparently omitted; As. read* gefylleð; *K. em.* gefylleð. 43a *K., Holt. Angl. Beibl.* 27.352 swylce ðu miht *considered unfinished line; MS A* be:rhtan, o *not legible.* 44a *MS A, Gr., As.* dream; *Gr. sugg.* drēor. 44b ðæt, *MS A, only* t *remains.* 47a *MS A* xii :yra, *hole before* yra; *K. em.* fyra; *Gr. Germania* 10.428 twel-fȳra, twēl-fȳra, *or* twelf fȳra? 51b *MS A* h:n, *hole after* h *to second minim of* m. 52b *MS A* wigeð, *K. em.* wǣgeð 'wieldeth', *adapting MS B's* wegeð; *Gr.* wīgeð (= wīheð?); *Gr. Germania* 10.428, *As.* wigeð.

MS B

55 miltan wið morðre, merian of sorge,
āscēad*an* of scyldum? Hūru him Sceppend geaf
wundorlīcne wlite. Mec þæs on worulde full oft
fyrwet frīneð, fūs gewīteð,
mōd geondmengeð. Nǣnig monna wāt,
60 hæleða under heofnum, hū mīn hige drēogeð
bisi æfter bōcum. Hwȳlum mē bryne stīgeð,
hige heortan [nēah] hearde wealleð.

Salomon cwæð:

Gylden is se Godes cwide, gymmum āstǣned,
hafað seolofren [lēaf]. Sundor mæg ǣghwylc
65 þurh gǣstæs gife godspellian.
Hē bið sefan snytero and sāwle hunig
and mōdes meolc, mǣrþa gesǣlgost.
Hē mæg þā sāwle of synnihte
gefetian under foldan, nǣfre hī se fēond tō ðæs niðer
70 feterum gefæstnað; þēah hē hī mid fīftigum
clausum beclemme, hē þane cræft briceð
and þā orþancas ealle tōslīteð.
Hungor hē gehīdeð, helle gestrūdeð,
wylm tōworpeð, wuldor getymbreð.
75 Hē is mōdigra middangeardes
staðole, hē is strengra þone ealle stāna gripe.
Lamana hē is lǣce, lēoht winciendra,
swilce hē his dēafra duru, dēadra tunge,
scildigra scild, Scippendes seld,
80 flōdes feriend, folces neriend,
ȳþa yrfeweard, earma fixa,
wyrma wlenco, wildēora holt,
wēstenes weard, weorðmynta geard.
And sē ðe wile geornlīce þon*e* Godes cwide
85 singan smēalīce and hine symle

56a *MS B* Asceaden. *Heading preceding* 63 SALOM̄. c̄. 63a godes *begins p. 198, MS B.* 64a lēaf *om. in MS B.* 68a *MS B* He, *period preceding.* 70a *MS B* gefæstnað, t *inserted later.* 70b *MS B* Þeah. 73a *MS B* hungor, n *inserted above the line;* hege hege hideð, *with first* hege *underlined for deletion.* 75a *MS B* He, *period preceding.* 76b *MS B clearly* þone (*so Z.*), *not* þonne (*As.*). 77b *MS B* winciendra, e *inserted above the line.* 79a *MS B* scildigra, c *incompletely corrected from* w, e *erased after* d, *the scribe apparently having first written* swilce; *two letters erased after* ra. 82a *MS B* wlenco; *K.* (*Gr.*) wlence. 84b *MS B* þono.

MS A

55 meltan wið morðre, mergan of sorge,
āscēadan of scyldigum? Hūru him Scippend geaf
wuldorlīcne wlite. (M)ec ðæs on worolde full oft
fyrwit frīneð, fūs gewīteð,
mōd gemengeð. Nǣ(nig) manna wāt,
60 hæleða under hefenum, hū mīn hige drēoseð
bysig æfter bōcum. Hwīlum mē bryne stīgeð,
hige heortan nēah hædre wealleð.

Salomon cwæð:

Gylden is se Godes cwide, gimmum (āst)ǣned,
hafað sylfren lēaf. Sundor mæg ǣghwylc
65 ðurh gāstes gife godspel secgan.
Hē bið seofan snytro and sāule hunig
. . . .
Hē mæg ðā sāule of siennihte
gefeccan under foldan, nǣfre hīe se fēond tō ðæs niðer
70 feterum gefæstnað; ðēah hē hīe mid fīftigum
clūsum beclemme, hē ðone cræft briceð
and ðā orðancas ealle tōslīteð.
Hungor hē āhīeðeð, helle gestrūdeð,
wylm tōweorpeð, wuldor getimbreð.
75 Hē (i)s mōdigra middangearde,
staðole strengra ðonne ealra stāna gripe.
Lamena hē is lǣce, lēoht wince(ndr)a,
swilce hē is dēafra duru, dumbra tunge,
scyldigra scyld, Scyppendes seld,
80 flōdes ferigend, folces nerigend,
ȳða yrfeweard, earmra fisca
and wyrma welm, wildēora holt,
on wēstenne weard, weorðmyn(d)a geard.
And sē ðe wile geornlīce ðone Godes cwide
85 singan sōðlīce and hine siemle wile

56a *MS A* scyldigum, *K.* (*Gr.*), *Sch. emend to* scyldum *following MS B;* 56b geaf, *prev. read* gaf. 59b Nǣnig, *MS A shows only* næ *and faint traces of second* n. 60a under *begins p. 3, MS A.* 63b āstǣned, *only fragments of* ast *in MS A.* 67 *omitted in MS A.* 75a He is, i *illegible, and* e *and* s *faint in MS A.* 77a Lamena, la *obscure in MS A.* 77b wincendra, *second stroke of second* n *to* a *illegible because of hole in MS A.* 82a welm, w *obscure in MS A; K. em.* helm. 83b weorðmynda, n *obscure,* d *illegible in MS A.*

MS B

lu[f]ian wile būtan leahtrum, hē mæg þone lāþan gesīð,
feohte*n*ne fēond, flēonde gebringan,
gyf þū him ǣrest ufan yorn gebringe[s]ð
prologo prīm, þām is ·**P**· nama:
90 hafað gūðmāga gyrde lange,
gyldene gāde, and þone grymman fēond
swīðmōd swāpeð; and on swaðe filgið
·**Ā**· ofermægene and hine ēac ofslehð.
·**T**· . . . .

86a *MS B* luian; *K. read* liuan. 87a *MS B* feohterne. 88a *MS B* Gyf. 88b *MS B* gebringeð. 89a *MS B* ꝓlogo prim, *with dot after* prim; 89b *MS B* ·P·. 92b *MS B* filgið *written over deleted* læteð. 93a *MS B* A·. 94 *MS B ends at the bottom of p. 198, margin, with* ·T·.

MS A

lufian būtan leahtrum, hē mæg ðone lāðan gǣst,
feohtende fēond, flēonde gebrengan,
gif ðū him ǣrest on ufan ierne gebrengest
prologa prīma ðām is ·ᛈ·P· nama:
90 hafað gūðmæcga gierde lange,
gyldene gāde, and ā ðone g(rim)man fēond
swīðmōd sweopað; and him on swaðe fylgeð
·ᚪ·Ā· ofermægene and hine ēac ofslihð.
·ᛏ·T· hine teswað and hine on ðā tungan sticað,
95 wrǣsteð him ðæt woddor, and him ðā wongan brieceð.
·ᛖ·Ē· hiene yflað, swā hē ā wile
ealra fēonda gehwane fæste gestondan.
Ðonne hiene on unðanc ·ᚱ·R· ieorrenga gesēceð,
bōcstafa brego, bregdeð sōna
100 fēond be ðām feaxe, lǣteð flint brecan
scin[n]es sconcan; hē ne bescēawað nō
his leomona lið, nē bið him lǣce gōd.
Wendeð hē hiene ðonne under wolcnum, wīgsteall sēceð
heolstre behelmed; hūru him bið æt heartan wā
105 ðonne [h]ē hangiende helle wīsceð,
ðæs engestan ēðelrīces.
Ðonne hine forcinnað ðā cirican getuinnas
N, [Ō] s(am)od. Ǣghwæðer brengeð

89a *MS A, K.* prologa prima; *Gr., As. em.* prologum primum; *large runic letter and capital* P *followed by period.* 90a gūðmæcga, *a later hand has inserted* o *after* guð, *which is at the end of a line in MS A.* 91b grimman, rim *illegible in MS A;* fēond *begins p. 4, MS A.* 93a *MS large runic* A *and small* á, *periods preceding both.* 94a *MS large runic* T *and small* t (*larger than usual*), *periods before and after.* 95b *MS* brieceð; *K.* (*Gr.*) briceð, *without comment.* 96a *MS large runic* E *and small* e (*larger than usual*), *periods before each and after* e. 98a *MS large runic* R *and small* r (*larger than usual*), *periods before and after.* 98b *Holt. Angl. Beibl.* 27.352 gesēceð ieorrenga (*type C*); *K.* (*Gr.*) eorringa, *without comment.* 101a *MS* scines, *Holt. Angl. Beibl.* 27.352 scin[n]es, *metri causa.* 105a hē, h *illegible in MS;* hangiende, *Holt. Angl. Beibl.* 27.352 hangende (*note*). 107a *MS, K.* (*Gr.*), *As.* forcinnað; *Gr.* forcirrað?; *Gr. Germania* 10.428 forcumað. 107b *MS, edd.* cirican, *Holt. Angl.* 23.123, cinlican, *but cf. Angl. Beibl.* 27.352; *MS* getuinnas, *K. em.* ge tūnas 'and houses,' *Gr.* getwinnas. 108a *MS obscure small* n (*larger than usual*), *set off by periods, followed by a straight line* (*so Z., P.*) *mistakenly taken as* 7 'and' *by Sch.* (*note*); *K. Archaeologia* 28 (1840). 388 N. O *with bracketed runes preceding each letter; K.* (*ed.*) *printed runes for* U *and* I, *but translated* N and O; *Gr. guessed* N 7 O (O *for K.'s* od); *As.* N 7 [O]; *Holt. Angl.* 23.123 O, N, *Angl. Beibl.* 27.352 N, O; *MS* s::od, *with hole between* s *and* o, *K.* [som]od, *Gr. om., Sch.* s[am]od, *As.* sa[m]od, *P. fragment of second letter perh. resembles beginning of* a *rather than* o.

MS A

sweopan of sīðe; sārg*a*ð hwīle
110 fremdne flǣschoman, feorh ne bemurneð.
Ðonne ·ᛋ·S· cymeð, engla gerǣswa,
wuldores stæf, wrāðne gegrīpeð
fēond be ðām fōtum, lǣteð foreweard hlēor
on strangne stān, and stregdað tōðas
115 geond helle hēap. Hȳdeð hine ǣghwylc
æfter sceades sciman; sceaða bið gebisigod,
Sātanes ðegn swīðe gestilled.
Swilce hiene ·ᛢ·Q· and ·ᚢ·Ū· cwealme gehnǣgað,
frome folctogan farað him tōgegnes,
120 habbað lēoht speru, lange sceaftas,
swīðmōde sweopan, swenga ne wyrnað,
dēorra dynta; him bið ðæt dēofol lāð.
Ðonne hine [Ī and] ·ᛚ·L· and se yrra ·ᚳ·C·
gūðe begyrdað, gēap stæf wigeð
125 biterne brōgan; bīgað sōna
helle hæftli[n]g ðæt hē on hinder gǣð.
Ðonne hiene ·ᚠ·F· and ·ᛗ·M· ūtan ymbðringað
scyldigne sceaðan, habbað scearp speru,
atole earhfare, ǣled lǣtað
130 on ðæs fēondes feax flāna stregdan
biterne brōgan; banan heardlīce,
grimme ongieldað ðæs hīe oft gilp brecað.
Ðonne hine æt nīehstan nearwe stilleð
·ᛄ·G· se gēapa, ðone God sendeð
135 frēondum on fultum; færeð æfter ·ᛞ·D·
fīfmægnum full— f[ȳ]r bið se ðridda;
stæf strǣte nēah stille bīdeð.
·H· ōnetteð; engel hine scierpeð,

109b *MS, edd.* sargiað. 110b *MS, K.* bemurneð; *Gr., As. em.* bemurnað. 111a *Large runic letter and capital* S, *periods before each and after* S. 112a *Holt. Angl. Beibl.* 27.353 [weorð] wuldọres, *metri causa.* 114b *MS* 7 stregdað, 7 s *obscure,* 7 *written into* s *acc. to As.*, d *above line; Gr.* stregdeð? 118a *Large runic* Q *and capital* Q, *separated by period, large* 7, *large runic letter and capital* V (*for* U), *period before and after* V. 122a dēorra *begins p. 5, MS A.* 123a *MS Runic* L *and small* l (*larger than usual*), *periods before each and after* l; *Gr. inserted* [J and] (*note*). 123b *Runic* C *and small* c (*larger than usual*), *periods before each and at end.* 126a *MS* hæftlig, *K. em.* hæftling. 132b *MS* brecað, *Gr.* sprecað?, *Holt. Angl. Beibl.* 27.353 wrecað. 134a *Large* J-*rune and capital* G, *periods before each and at end.* 136a *MS, edd.* fifmægnum (*note*), *Holt. Angl. Beibl.* 27.353 fīfl-. 136b f:r, *with hole between letters, but part of* y *visible; K. semi-colon after* ðridda; *Gr., As. connect* ðridda *with* stæf (137); *for* ðridda, *Holt. Angl. Beibl.* 27.353 *sugg.* ōðer (*note*).

MS A

Crīstes cempan, on cwicum wǣdum,
140 Godes spyrigend*e*, geonges hrægles.
Đonne hine on lyfte līfgetwinnan
under tungla getrumum tuigena ordum,
sweopum seolfrynum, swīðe wǣlað,
oððæt him bān blīcað, blēdað ǣdran;
145 gārtorn gēotað gīfrum dēofle.
Mæg simle se Godes cwide gumena gehwylcum
ealra fēonda gehwane flēondne gebrengan
ðurh mannes mūð, mānfulra hēap
sweartne geswencan, nǣfre hīe ðæs syllīce
150 blēoum bregdað, æfter bāncofan
feðerhoman onfōð. Hwīlum flotan grīpað;
hwīlum hīe gewendað in wyrmes līc
str[o]nges and sticoles, stingeð nīeten,
feldgongende feoh gestrūdeð;
155 hwīlum hē on wætere wicg gehnǣgeð,
hornum gehēaweð, oððæt him heortan blōd
fāmig flōdes bæð, foldan gesēceð;
hwīlum hē gefeterað fǣges mannes
handa gehefegað, ðonne hē æt hilde sceall
160 wið lāð werud līfes tiligan.
Āwrīteð hē on his wǣpne wællnōta hēap,
bealwe bōcstafas, bill forscrīfeð,
mēces mǣrðo. Forðon nǣnig man scile
oft orðances ūt ābrēdan
165 wǣpnes ecgge, ðēah ðe him se wlite cwēme;
ac symle hē sceal singan, ðonne hē his sweord getēo,
Pāter Noster, and ðæt Palmtrēow
biddan mid blisse, ðæt him bū gife
feorh and folme, ðonne his fēond cyme.

140a *MS, edd.* spyrigendes, *Kock JJJ. p. 67* spyrigende (*note*). 143b *MS, edd.* weallað, *Gr.* wælað?. 146a *MS* Mæg, *period preceding.* 149a *K.*, *R. semi-colon after* geswencan, *Gr.*, *As. period.* 149b *MS* Næfre, *period preceding.* 153a stronges: *MS* str:nges, *all obscure with only faint traces of* o. *first read by Sk.* (*see Sch.'s note*), *K.* [scearpes], *Gr.* [styrnes]; and (*MS* 7) *begins p. 6, MS A.* 153b *MS*, *Gr.*, *As.* stingeð, *K. em.* stingað (*note*). 154b *K. em.* gestrūdað. 155a *MS* Hwilum, *period preceding; K. em.* hīe. 155b *K. em.* gehnǣgað. 156a *MS* hornum, n *above the line; K. em.* gehēawað. 158a *MS* Hwilum, *period preceding; K. em.* hīe; *MS* gefeterað, ge *above the line, Gr.*, *R.*, *As.* [folme] gefeterað. 161a *MS* Awriteð, *three dots preceding; K. em.* āwrītað hīe. 162b *K. em.* forscrīfað. 163b *R.* man nǣnig; scile, *edd.* (*exc. Gr.*) *take with* 164a. 166a *MS* Ac, *three dots preceding.* 167a *MS* paт̄ noster. 167b *MS, edd.* palmtreow, *Holt. Angl.* 23.124 gepalmtwigede. 169b cyme (*see note*).

SOLOMON AND SATURN II

MS A

170 Hwæt, ic flītan gefrægn on fyrndagum
(180) mōdglēawe men, middangeardes rǣsw*an*,
gewesan ymbe hira wīsdom. Wyrs dēð sē ðe līehð
oððe ðæs sōðes ansæceð. Saloman was brēmra,
ðēah ðe S(ātu)rnus sumra hæfde,
175 bald brēosttoga, bōca c(ǣ)g(a),
(le)ornenga locan. Land eall geondhwearf:
Ind(ēa) mer(e), (Ēa)st-Corsias,
Persēa rīce, Palestinion,
Niniuen ceastre, and Norð-Predan,
180 Mēda maððumselas, Marculfes eard;
Saulus rīce, swā hē sūð ligeð
ymbe Geallbōe and ymb Geador norð,
Filistīna flet, fæsten Crēca,
wudu Ēgipta, wæter Māthea[n]
185 cl*ū*das Coreffes, Caldēa rīce,
Crēca cræftas, cynn Arabia,
lāre Libia, lond Syria
*B*itðinia, Buðanasan,
Pam*ph*ilia, Pōres gemǣre,
190 Macedonia, Mesopotamie,
(200) Cappadocia; Crīstes [ēþel]:
Hiery*ch*o, Galilēa, Hiērusā[lem].

---

170 *Line 8, p. 13, MS A:* HWÆT.IC.FLI.TAN.GEFRÆGN, *large capitals covering two lines,* H *covering nearly five.* 171b *MS, As.* ræswum, *K.* (*Gr.*) ræswan *without comment; Holt. Angl.* 23.124 ræswum *part of a missing verse* (*note*). 173b Saloman, *large capital* S *in margin covering two lines.* 174a Sāturnus, *only fragments of* atu *visible.* 175b cǣga, c *clear,* g *barely legible, only faint traces of* æ *and* a, *not legible as these letters.* 176a leornenga, *K.* (*Gr.*) [leorn]inga, *Sw.* :::nenga, *Sch., Z., P.* ::ornenga. 177a *MS* Indea mere, *acc. to Z; P.* ea *obscure,* mere *possibly* merc; *K.* [Indea eard], *Gr.* [India eard], *Sch.* Indea [eard]. 177b Ēast-, ea *illegible, K.* [ea]st, *Gr.* [and ēa]st, *Holt. Angl. Beibl.* 27.354 Ēast-Corsias (*note*). 179b *MS* norð predan, *Holt. Angl. Beibl.* 27.354 Norð-Prēdan, *or* Pearðan? (*note*). 181a *MS* Saulus, *capital in margin, three dots at end of* eard. *which concludes preceding line; Holt. Angl. Beibl.* 27.354 Saules. 183b *MS* creca, *edd.* Creca, *Gr.* Creta? 184b *MS* wæt, w *resembling* p; *MS, edd.* mathea, *Holt. Angl. Beibl.* 27.354 Matheanes (*note*). 185a *MS, edd.* claudas, *Holt. Angl. Beibl.* 27.354 clūdas (*note*); *MS* coreffes, *edd.* Coreffes, *Holt. Angl. Beibl.* 27.354, *em.* cōferes. 188a *MS, K.* pitðinia, *Gr., As.* Bitðinia. 189a *MS* pam hpilia, *K., As.* Pamphilia. 191b *MS* cristes *no space bef.* hieryhco, *so K.; Gr., As.* [ēðel]. 192a *MS* hieryhco, *K.* Hierycho. 192b *MS* hierusa *ends p. 13; p. 14 is erased and a Latin text is written over it; cf. Introd., p. 2.*

MS A

[Salomon cwæð:]

. . . . oððe ic swīgie,
nyttes hycgge, ðēah ic nō spr(e)c(e).
195 Wāt ic ðonne, gif ðū gewītest on Wendelsǣ
ofer Cōforflōd cȳððe seccan,
ðæt ðū wille gilpan ðæt ðū hæbbe g(um)ena bearn
forcumen and forcȳððed. Wāt ic ðæt wǣron Caldēas
gūðe ðæs gielpne and ðæs goldwlonce,
200 mǣrða ðæs mōdige, ðǣr tō ðām moning gelomp
sūð ymbe Sanere feld. Sæge mē from ðām lande
ðǣr nǣnig fȳra ne mæg fōtum gestæppan.

Sāturnus cuæð:

Se mǣra was hāten *mere*līðende
Weallende Wulf, w(e)rðēodum cūð
205 Filistīna, frēond Nebrondes.
Hē on ðām felda ofslōg fīf and twēntig
dracena on dægrēd, and hine *ðā* dēað offēoll.
Forðan ðā foldan ne mæg fīra ǣnig,
ðone mercstede, mon gesēcan,
210 fugol geflēogan nē ðon mā foldan n(ēat).
Ðanon ātercynn ǣrest gewurdon
(220) wīde onwæcned, ðā ðe nū weallende
ðurh attres oroð ingang rȳmað.
Gīt his sweord scīn*e*ð swīðe gescǣned,
215 and ofer ðā byrgenna blīcað ðā hieltas.

193b oððe *begins p. 15, MS A, the first line difficult to read; MS* swigie (*note*), *acc. to P. and D.; K., Sch., As.* stigie, *Gr. em.* wīg-, *Holt. Angl. Beibl.* 27.354 s[w]īgie. 194a *MS* hycgge, *acc. to P. and D.; K.* bicge, *Gr.* bycge, *Sch., As.* [b]ycgge; *Holt. proposed* [h]ycgge *Angl. Beibl.* 27.354. 194b ic nō spr[e]c[e], *MS obscure, vellum wrinkled; acc. to P. probably* ic nó spr:c:, *K.* . . . . , *Sch.* :::ic:::, *Z.* [:::] ic spr:::?, *As.* ::: ic s[pr]:::; *Holt. proposed* [nāht], '*indem* ic *der rest von* ht *sein wird.*' 195a *MS* Wát. 196b *MS, Sk., As., P., D.* seccan; *K.* (*Gr.*), *Sch.* secean. 197b gumena, *K.* ::::ena, *Gr.* [gum]ena, *Sch., As., P.* g[um]ena. 201b *MS* Sæge. 202a *MS plainly* fyra (*Sw., P., D.*), *not* fyre (*Sch., As.*). *Heading preceding line* 203: SATVRNVS CVÆÐ, S *large capital two lines high in margin, in this and later headings.* 203a was, *MS probably has* a (*P.*), *previously read* æ. 203b *MS, edd.* sæliðende, *Gr.* merelīðende? 204b werðēodum, *first* e *illegible.* 206a felda (*P., D.*), *MS* a *obscure, previously read* e. 206b fīf and twēntig, *MS* xxv. 207b ðā dēað offēoll, *MS, edd.* ða of deað offeoll (*note*); *Gr. proposed* þā dēað onfēoll. 208a *MS* ða (*P., D.*), *previously read* ðas. 210b n(ēat), *only* n *now legible; K.* (*Gr.*) nēat *without comment.* 213a attres *obscure, perh.* atres (*P.*). 214a scineð (*Gr. em.*); *MS, K.* scinað.

MS A

Salomon cwæð:

Dol bið sē ðe gǣð on dēop wæter
sē ðe sund nafað nē gesegled scip,
nē fugles flyht, nē hē mid fōtum ne mæg
grund gerǣcan. Hūru sē Godes cunnað
220 full dyslīce, Dryhtnes meahta.

Sāturnus cuæð:

Ac hwæt is se dumba sē ðe on sumre dene resteð?
Swȳðe snyttrað, hafað seofon tungan,
hafað tungena gehwylc twēntig orda,
hafað orda gehwylc engles snytro,
225 ðāra ðe wile ānra hwylc uppe bringan,
ðæt ðū ðǣre gyldnan gesiehst Hiērusālem
weallas blīcan and hiera winrōd līxan,
sōðfæstra segn. Saga hwæt ic mǣne!

Salomon cuæð:

Bēc sindon brēme, bodiað geneahhe
230 weotodne willan ðām ðe wiht hygeð,
gestrangað hīe and gestaðeliað staðolfæstne geðōht,
(240) āmyrgað mōdsefan manna gehwylces
of ðrēa*nī*edlan ðisses līfes.

Sāturnus cwæð:

Bald bið sē ðe onbyregeð bōca cræftes,
235 symle bið ðē wīsra ðē hira geweald hafað.

Salomon cuæð:

Sige hiē onsendað sōðfaestra gehwām,
hǣlo hȳðe, ðām ðe hīe lufað.

Sāturnus cwæð:

Ān wīse is on woruldrīce
ymb ðā mē fyrwet bræc fīftig wintra

Heading preceding 216: SALOMON cwæð, S *large capital two lines high in margin in this and all other headings;* æ *of* cwæð *resembles* a *and was so read by As. Heading preceding* 221 *begins p. 16, MS A:* SATVRNVS CVÆÐ. 223b twēntig. *MS* xx. 227b *MS, edd.* winrod (*note*); *Holt. Angl.* 23.124 wuldǫr, *Holt. Angl. Beibl.* 27.355 wundǫr. *Heading preceding* 229: SALOMON CVÆÐ. 230b *MS, edd.* wiht, *Gr.* wīse? 233a ðrēanīedlan (*cf.* 420), *MS, As., Sch.* ðreamedlan, *K.* (*Gr.*) ðrēanȳdlan, *without comment. Heading preceding* 236: SALOMON CVÆÐ. 238a *MS, P., D.* wise, *edd., Sch. mistakenly* wisa. 239b fīftig, *MS* L.

MS A

240 dæges and niehtes ðurh dēop gesceaft,
geōmrende gāst, dēð (n)ū gēna swā,
ǣrðon mē geunne ēce Dryhten
ðæt mē gesēme snoterra monn.

Salomon cwæð:

Sōð is ðæt ðū sagast, sēme ic ðē recene
245 ymb ðā wrǣtlīcan wiht. Wilt ðū ðæt ic ðē secgge?
Ān fugel siteð on Fili[s]tīna
middelgemǣrum; munt is hine ymbūtan,
gēap gylden weall. Georne hine healdað
witan Filistīna, wēnað ðæs ðe nāht is,
250 ðæt hiene him scyle eall ðēod on genǣman
wǣpna ecggum. Hīe ðæs wǣre cunnon:
(260) healdað hine niehta gehwylce norðan and sūðan
on twā healfe tū hund wearda.
Se fugel hafað fēower hēafdu
255 medumra manna and hē is on middan hwælen;
gēowes hē hafað fiðeru and griffus fēt.
Ligeð lonnum fæst, lōcað unhīere,
swīðe swingeð and his searo hringeð,
gilleð geōmorlīce and his gyrn sefað,
260 wylleð hine on ðām wīte, wunað unlustum,
singgeð syllīce; seldum ǣfre
his leoma licggað. Longað hine hearde,
ðynceð him ðæt sīe ðria ðrītig ðūsend wintra
ǣr hē dōmdæges dynn gehȳre.
265 Nyste hine on ðǣre foldan fīra ǣnig
eorðan cynnes ǣrðon ic hine āna onfand,
and hine ðā gebendan hēt ofer brād wæter,

241b nū, *MS read* iu *by K., Gr., Sch., As., but Sk.* nu, *and P. rather fragmentary* n, *of which first stroke has disappeared, than* i, *Gr. em.* nū? 243b *Sievers PBB.* 10.508 snotterra, *metri causa, approved by Holt. Angl.* 23.124. *Heading preceding* 244: SALOMON C̄ð. 244b ðē *begins p. 17, MS A.* 246b Fili[s]tina, *MS* filitina. 249b *K. (Gr.) omits* wēnað . . . genǣman (250), *printing three half-lines of asterisks, though MS is perfectly clear.* 252a *MS* healdeð; *K. (Gr.) em.* healdað, *without comment.* 254b fēower, *MS* iiii. 255b *MS, As.* hwælen; *Kock JJJ, p. 68* swǣ lēon; *K. added* hwælan (*sic*) *to next half-line, reading* hiwes *for* gēowes, *and assuming half-line omission after* fēt; *Sweet Angl.* 1.153 *gave correct* arrangement. 256b *Gr. fol. K.'s text, but supplied* se grimma fugel *after* fēt. 258b searo, *MS* e *with faint cross-line resembles* c, *Sch. doubtful, Sw., As.* scaro. 260a *Holt. Angl. Beibl.* 27.355, *ESt.* 51.182 wylteð? 262b longað, o *ill-formed, previously read* e, *but cf.* o *of* lēoma. 263a ðrītig, *MS* xxx. 267a gebendan, *MS resembles* gebeindan *with high* e *acc. to P., possibly a correction from* gebundan *or* gebandan; *prev. read* gebændan.

MS A

ðæt hine se mōdega heht   Mēlotes bearn,
Filistīna fruma,   fæste gebindan,
270 lonnum belūcan   wið lēodgryre.
Ðone fugel hātað   feorbūende
(280) Filistīna fruma[n]   Vāsa Mortis.

Sāturnus cwæð:

Ac hwæt is ðæt wundor   ðē geond ðās worold færeð,
styrnenga gǣð,   staðolas bēateð,
275 āweceð wōpdropan,   winneð oft hider?
Ne mæg hit steorra nē stān   nē se stēapa gimm,
wæter nē wildēor   wihte beswīcan;
ac him on hand gǣð   heardes and hnesces,
micles, mǣtes;   him tō mōse sceall
280 gegangan gēara gehwelce   grundbūendra,
lyftflēogendra,   laguswemmendra,
ðria ðrēotēno   ðūsendgerīmes.

Salomon cuæð:

Yldo bēoð on eorðan   ǣghwæs cræftig:
mid hīðendre   hildewrǣsne,
285 rūmre racentēage   rǣceð wīde,
langre līnan,   lisseð eall ðæt hēo wile.
Bēam hēo ābrēoteð   and bebriceð telgum,
āstyreð standen[dn]e   stefn on sīðe,
āfilleð hine on foldan,   friteð æfter ðām.
290 Wulf hēo oferwīgeð,   wildne fugol;
hīo oferbīdeð stānas,   hēo oferstīgeð stȳle,
(300) hīo ābīteð īren mid ōme,   dēð ūsic swā.

268a *K.* [oð]ðæt; *Holt. Angl.* 23.124 mōdga. 272a *K.* (*Gr.*), *Sch.* (*without comment*) fruman, *MS* fruma. 272b Vāsa Mortis (*note*), *MS* úasa mórtis. 273b ðās *begins p. 18, MS A.* 278 *R.* ac him heardes and hnæsces on hand gǣð; *R. ZfdPh.* 7.11 *sugg.* gangeð, *Holt. Angl.* 23.124 gangeð *or* gǣeð. 279a *MS* micles mætes; *K.* mycles metes; *Gr.*, *R.* mycles [and] mētes (*Gr.* mētes = mǣtes); *As.* micles mǣtes, *Wy.* micles, mǣtes. 281b *MS*, *As.* laguswemmendra; *K.* (*Gr.*), *R.* (*without comment*), *Wy. em.* laguswimmendra. *Heading preceding* 283: SALOMON CVÆÐ. 285b *MS* ręceð. 288a standen[dn]e, *em. Gr.*, *As.*, *Wy.*; *MS*, *K.*, *R.*, *Sch.* standene, *K.* 'in the stony nest.' 288b sīðe, *R. em.* sīde. 289b *K.*, *Gr.*, *As.*, *Wy. no period after* ðām, *R. semi-colon after* ðām, *Holt. ESt.* 37.205 *period after* ðām. 290 *MS* wildne fugol heo oferwigeð wulf, *so K.* (*Gr.*), *As. with period after* fugol; *R.* wulf hēo oferwigeð, wildne fugol; *Holt. ESt.* 37.205 *follows R. but adds* [ond] *before* wildne, *metri causa* (*note*). 291 *R.* hēo oferstíceð (*em.*) stȳle, stānas hēo oferbīdeð, *which Holt. Angl. Beibl.* 27.355 *approves* (*note*).

MS A

Sāturnus cwæð:

Ac forhwon fealleð se snāw, foldan behȳdeð,
bewrīhð wyrta cīð, wæstmas getīgeð,
295 geðȳð hīe and geðrēatað ðæt hīe ðrāge bēoð
cealde geclungne? Full oft hē gecostað ēac
wildēora worn, wǣtum hē oferbricgeð,
gebryceð burga geat, baldlīce fēreð,
rēafað . . . .

[Salomon cwæð:]

300 swīðor micle ðonne se swipra nīð
sē hine gelǣdeð on ðā lāðan wīc
mid ðā frǣcnan [fyrd] fēonde tō willan.

Sāturnus cwæð:

Nieht bið wedera ðīestrost, nēd bið wyrda heardost,
sorg bið swārost byrðen, slǣp bið dēaðe gelīcost.

Salomon cwæð:

305 Lȳtle hwīle lēaf bēoð grēne;
ðonne hīe eft fealewiað, feallað on eorðan,
and forweorniað, weorðað tō dūste.
Swā ðonne gefeallað ðā ðe fyrena ǣr
lange lǣstað, lifiað him in māne,
310 hȳdað hēahgestrēon, healdað georne
on fæstenne fēondum tō willan,
and wēnað wanhogan ðæt hīe wille Wuldorcining,
(320) ælmihtig God ēce gehīran.

Sāturnus cwæð:

Sōna bið gesīene siððan flōwan mōt
315 ȳð ofer eall lond, nē wile hēo āwa ðæs
sīðes geswīcan sioððan hire se sǣl cymeð
ðæt hēo dōmes dæges dyn gehīere.

Heading preceding 293: SATURNUS C̄. 296b *MS* hie, *K.* (*Gr.*), *Sch.* he, *without comment.* 297b *MS* ófer bricgeð, eð *obscure* (*P.'s reading*); *K.*, *Gr.*, *Sch.*, *As. read* oferhrægeð, *but Z. noted* æ *not quite certain.* 299a rēafað *attached to next line by edd.* 300a swīðor *begins p. 19, MS A, a leaf having disappeared between p. 18 and p. 19, see Introd. p. 2, and note.* 300b swipra, *K.* (*Gr.*) swiðra, *Sw. Angl.* 1.154 swipra. 301b lāðan, *MS* an *above the line.* 302a *K.* ðām fǣcnan (*a silent emendation?*), *Holt. Angl.* 23.124 ðā frēcnan [fyrd]. *Heading preceding* 305: SALOMON. 310b *MS* Healdað, *period preceding.* 315b *K.*, *Sch. took* ðæs *with next line.*

MS A

Salomon cwæð:

*W*ā bið ðonne ðissum mōdgum monnum ðām ðe hēr nū mid māne lengest
lifiað on ðisse lǣnan gesceafte! Iēo ðæt ðīne lēode gecȳðdon:
320 wunnon hīe wið Dryhtnes miehtum; forðan hīe ðæt worc ne gedēgdon.
Ne sceall ic ðē hwæðre, brōðor, ābelgan; ðū eart swīðe bittres cynnes,
eorre eormenstrȳnde. Ne beyrn ðū in ðā inwitgecyndo!

Sāturnus cwæð:

Saga ðū mē, Salomon cyning, sunu Dāuides,
hwæt bēoð ðā fēowere fǣgæs rāpas?

Salomon cuæð:

325 Gewurdene wyrda
ðæt bēoð ðā fēowere fǣges rāpas.

Sāturnus cwæð:

Ac hwā dēmeð ðonne Dryhtne Crīste
on dōmes dæge ðonne hē dēmeð eallum gesceaftum?

Salomon cwæð:

Hwā dear ðonne Dryhtne dēman ðē ūs of dūste geworhte,
330 Nergend of niehtes wunde? Ac sæge mē hwæt nǣren *ðē* wǣron.

Sāturnus cwæð:

Ac forhwon ne mōt sēo sunne sīde gesceafte
scīre geondscīnan? Forhwām besceadeð hēo
(340) muntas and mōras and monige ēc
wēste stōwa? Hū geweorðeð ðæt?

Heading preceding 318: SALOMON C̄. 318a Wā, *MS* swa, *K.* (*Gr.*) *em. without comment.* 322b in (*P.*), *previously read* on: *this word begins p. 20, MS A.* 324b fǣgæs, *previously read* fǣges. *Heading preceding* 325: SALOMON CVÆÐ. 325a *MS, edd.* gewurdene, *Gr. Germania* 10.428 gewundene?, *Sievers PBB* 12.480 gewund(e)ne (*note*). 326a ðæt, *obscured by fold* (*P.*); *K.* (*Gr.*) ða *without comment, Sch., As.* ðæ; *edd. made* ða (ðæ) beoð *end of preceding line. Heading preceding* 329: SALOMON. 329b *MS erasure after* ūs. 330a niehtes, *Holt. Angl. Beibl.* 27.355 nīðes; *MS* wunde (*so Z., P., D.*); *K.* (*Gr.*), *Sch. read* sunde (*note*). 330b nǣren ðē (*note*), *MS, edd.* nærende, *Holt. Angl.* 23.125 nearwende?, *Angl. Beibl.* 27.355 neriende? neosende? nǣtende? nǣgende? 332b *MS, edd.* besceadeð, *Sievers PBB* 10.506 besceadweð, *metri causa.* 333b *MS* ⁊ monige ec, *K.* (*Gr.*) and ēac monige, *without comment.*

MS A

Salomon cuæð:

335 Ac forhwām nǣron eorð[we]lan ealle gedǣled
lēodum gelīce? Sum tō lȳt hafað
gōdes grǣdig. Hine God seteð
ðurh geearnunga ēadgum tō ræste.

Sāturnus cwæð:

Ac forhwan bēoð ðā gesīðas somod ætgædre,
340 wōp and hleahtor? Full oft hīe weorðgeornra
sǣlða tōslītað. Hū gesǣleð ðæt?

Salomon cuæð:

Unlǣde bið and ormōd sē ðe ā wile
geōmrian on gihðe: sē bið Gode fracoðast.

Sāturnus cwæð:

Forhwon ne mōton wē ðonne ealle mid onmēdlan
345 gegnum gangan in Godes rīce?

Salomon cwæð:

Ne mæg fȳres fēng nē forstes cile,
snāw nē sunne somod eardian,
aldor geæfnan, ac hira sceal ānra gehwylc
onlūtan and onlīðigan ðē hafað lǣsse mæg*n*.

Sāturnus cwæð:

350 Ac forhwon ðonne leofað se wyrsa leng?
Se wyrsa ne wāt in woruldrīce
on his mǣgwinum māran āre.

Salomon cwæð:

(360) Ne mæg mon forild*a*[n] ǣnige hwīle
ðone dēoran sīð, ac hē hine ādrēogan sceall.

Heading preceding 335: SALOMON CVÆÐ. 335a eorð[we]lan (*K.*), *MS* eorð *end of line, then scratches,* lan *beginning next line;* 335b gedǣled (*K. without comment*), MS gode led. 338b *MS* eadgum (*P.*, *D.*) *previously read* endgum (*K.* [*Gr.*], *Sch.*, *As.*), *Gr. em.* ēadgum? *Heading preceding* 342: SALOMON CVÆÐ. 343a *MS* gihðe (*P.*, *D.*), *previously read* gihða. *Heading preceding* 344: SatvRNUS c̄, *begins p.* 21, *MS A*. *Heading preceding* 346: SALOMON C̄. 349b *MS* mægnn. 350b *Gr.* leng se wyrsa? *Heading preceding* 353: SALOMON C̄. 353a forilda[n], *MS* for ildo. *K.* (*Gr.*) foryldan, *without comment.* 354a dēoran, *Gr.* dēopan?, *Gr. Germania* 10.428 deorcan?

MS A

Sāturnus cwæð:

355 Ac hū gegangeð ðæt gōde oððe yfle?
Đonne hīe bēoð ðurh āne idese ācende,
twēgen getwinnas, ne bið hira tīr gelīc:
ōðer bið unlǣde on eorðan, ōðer bið ēadig swīðe,
lēoftǣle mid lēoda duguðum; ōðer leofað lȳtle hwīle,
360 swīceð on ðisse sīdan gesceafte and ðonne eft mid sorgum gewīteð.
Fricge ic ðec, hlāford Salomon, hwæðres bið hira folgoð betra?

Salomon cu(æ)ð:

Mōdor ne rǣdeð ðonne hēo magan cenneð,
hū him weorðe geond worold wīdsīð sceapen.
Oft hēo tō bealwe bearn āfēdeð,
365 seolfre tō sorge, siððan drēogeð
his earfoðu, orlegstunde.
Hēo ðæs afran sceall oft and gelōme
grimme grēotan, ðonne hē geong færeð,
hafað wilde mōd, wērige heortan,
370 sefan sorgfullne; slīdeð geneahhe
wērig, wilna lēas, wuldres bedǣled.
(380) Hwīlum higegeōmor healle weardað,
leofað lēodum feor; lōcað geneahhe
fram ðām unlǣdan ǣng*a* hlāford.
375 Forðan nāh sēo mōdor geweald, ðonne hēo magan cenneð,
bearnes blǣdes, ac sceall on gebyrd faran
ān æfter ānum: ðæt is eald ges[c]eaft.

Sāturnus cwæð:

Ac forhwan nele monn him on giogoðe georne gewyrcean
dēores dryhtscipes and dǣdfruman,
380 wadan on wīsdom, winnan æfter snytro?

---

358 *Edd., Holt. ESt.* 37.205 *made three normal lines of 358–359* (*see note*), *but Holt. transferred* on eorðan *to his third line, and transposed* bið ēadig. 359 *Holt. ESt.* 37.205 ōðer lȳtle hwīle leofað on eorðan (*cf. 358 and note*). 361a hlāford, *Gr.* frēa? *Heading preceding* 362: SALOMON CV(Æ)ð, *Æ obscure*, ð *a large letter not of capital form.* 363b wīdsīð, wid *at end of line, three letters erased before* sið *of next line.* 366b orlegstunde *begins p.* 22, *MS A.* 372a *MS* Hwilum, *three dots preceding.* 374b ǣnga, *MS* ængan (*note*); *MS, edd.* hlāford, *B-T., Spr.*[2] hlāforde, *s.v.* ǣnga; *Holt. Angl. Beibl.* 27.355 frēgan? 377b *MS* geseaft. *Heading preceding* 378: S *of* Saturnus *drawn with straight lines here and before* 434. 379b dǣdfruman (*note*), *K.* (*Gr.*) dǣd fremman *without comment.*

MS A

Salomon cwæð:

Hwæt, him mæg ēadig eorl ēaðe gecēosan
on his mōdsefan mildne hlāford,
ānne æðeling; ne mæg dōn unlǣde swā.

Sāturnus cwæð:

Ac forhwām winneð ðis wæter geond woroldrīce,
385 drēogeð dēop gesceaft? Ne mōt on dæg restan,
neahtes nēð*e*ð, [nearo]cræfte tȳð,
crīstnað and clǣnsað cwicra manigo,
wuldre gewlitigað. Ic wihte ne cann
forhwan se strēam ne mōt stillan neahtes.

[Salomon cwæð:]

. . . .

390 his līfes fæðme. Simle hit bið his lārēowum hȳrsum.
Full oft hit ēac ðæs dēofles dugoð gehnǣgeð
(400) ðǣr weotena bið worn gesamnod,
ðonne snottrum men snǣd oððglīdeð,
ðā hē be lēohte gesihð, lūteð æfter,
395 gesegnað and gesyfleð, and him sylf friteð.
Swilc bið sēo ān snǣd ǣghwylcum men
sēlre micle, gif hēo gesegnod bið,
tō ðycgganne, gif hē hit geðencan cann,
ðonne him sīe seofon daga symbelgereordu.
400 Lēoht hafað hēow and hād hāliges gāstes,
Crīstes gecyndo: hit ðæt gecȳðeð full oft.
Gif hit unwitan ǣnige hwīle
healdað būtan hæftum, hit ðurh hrōf wædeð,
bryceð and bærneð boldgetimbru,
405 seomað stēap and gēap, stīgeð on lenge,
clymmeð on gecyndo; cunnað hwænne mōte
fȳr on his frumsceaft, on fæder geardas,

386a *K.* [nē] nihtes, *preceded by* restan *from* 385b, *Gr.* nihtes [stillan]; nēð*e*ð (see note), *MS, Sch.*, neðyð; *K.* (*Gr.*) nȳdað; *Kock JJJ, p.* 69, nēðyð, *As.* ne ðyð, *Holt. Angl.* 23.125 ne ðȳ[e]ð, *Angl. Beibl.* 27.356 nȳdeð 'strebt'? 386b *MS* cræfte (*no space*), *Holt. Angl. Beibl.* 27.356 [nearo]cræfte; *Kock JJJ*, p. 69 [nēod]cræfte. 390 his *begins p.* 23, *MS A*. *As. printed continuously, though K. had noted that a leaf or more had been cut before p.* 23, *see note, and Introd. p.* 2. 391b gehnǣgeð, *K.* (*Gr.*) gemætgeð. 393a ðonne, *MS* ðōn, *large* ð *in margin, three dots at end of previous line.* 394a *K.* (*Gr.*) ða *for MS* be. 394b *As. mistakenly read* æftær. 401b *Sch. began next line with* full oft. 405a *MS, edd.* seomað, *Gr.* samod?

MS A

eft tō his ēðle, ðanon hit ǣror cuōm.
Hit bið eallenga eorl[e] tō gesihðe
410 ðām ðe gedǣlan can Dryhtnes ðecelan.
Forðon nis nǣnegu gecynd cuiclifigende,
(420) nē fugel nē fisc, nē foldan stān,
nē wæteres wylm, nē wudutelga,
nē munt nē mōr, nē ðes middangeard,
415 ðæt hē forð ne sīe fȳrenes cynnes.

Sāturnus cwæð:

Full oft ic frōde menn fyrn gehȳrde
secggan and swerian ymb sume wīsan:
hwæðer wǣre twēgra būtan twēon stren[g]ra,
wyrd ðe warnung, ðonne hīe winnað oft
420 mid hira ðrēa*nī*edlan hwæðerne āðrēōteð ǣr.
Ic tō sōðon wāt, sægdon mē geāra
Filistīna witan, ðonne wē on geflitum sǣton,
bōcum tōbrǣddon and on bearm legdon,
meðelcwidas mengdon, moniges fēngon,
425 ðæt nǣre nǣnig manna middangeardes
ðæt meahte ðāra twēga tuīon āspyrian.

Salomon cwæð:

Wyrd bið wended hearde, wealleð swīðe geneahhe;
hēo wōp weceð, hēo wēan hladeð,
hēo gāst scyð[eð], hēo gēr byreð;
430 and hwæðre him mæg wīssefa wyrda gehwylce
gemetigian, gif hē bið mōdes glēaw,
(440) and tō his frēondum wile fultum sēcan,
ðēhhwæðre godcundes gǣstes brūcan.

409b *MS* eorlto, *K.* eorlum, *Gr.* eorlum [on], *Sch.* eorlu*m*, *As.* eorl[e] to. 416b gehȳrde *begins p.* 24, *MS A.* 417a *MS, edd.* swerian *exc. Bout.* syrwan. 418b *MS* strenra, *K.* strengra *without comment.* 419a *Bout. em.* ðe *to* oððe. 420a ðrēanīedlan (*cf.* 233a); MS, *Sch., As.* ðreamedlan, *K.* (*Gr., Bout.*) ðrēanȳdlan (*without comment*). 420b *MS, K., Bout., Sch.* hwæðer ne; *Gr., As.* hwæðerne. 421a *MS* soðon, *fold covering* on, *K.* (*Gr., Bout.*) sōðum, *without comment.* 426b tuīon, *Bout.* [būton] twēon. *Heading preceding* 427: SALOMON C̄. 427a *MS, edd.* wended, *Bout. em.* wēdend. 429a *MS, As.* scyð, *K.* (*Gr., Bout.*) scȳt, *without comment, Sievers PBB* 10.475 scȳeð. 429b *MS, As.* ger, *K.* (*Gr., Bout.*) gār *without comment.*

MS A

Sāturnus cwæð:

Ac hwæt wīteð ūs wyrd sēo swīðe,
435 eallra fyrena fruma, fǣhðo mōdor,
wēana wyrtwela, wōpes hēafod,
frumscylda gehwæs fæder and mōdor,
dēaðes dohtor? Ac tō hwon drohtað hēo mid ūs?
Hwæt, hīe wile lifigende late āðrēotan
440 ðæt hēo ðurh fyrena geflitu fǣhðo ne tȳdre.

Salomon cwæð:

Nolde gæd geador in Godes rīce
ēadiges engles and ðæs ofermōdan.
Ōðer his Dryhtne hīerde, ōðer him ongan wyrcan ðurh dier[n]e cræftas
segn and sīde byrnan, cwæð ðæt hē mid his gesīðum wolde
445 hīðan eall heofona rīce and him ðonne on healfum sittan,
(t)ȳ(d)ran him mid ðȳ tēoðan dǣle oððæt hē his (to)r(nes) (ne) (c)ūðe
ende ðurh insceafte. Đā wearð se æðel(a) (ð)ēoden
gedrēfed ðurh ðæs dēofles gehygdo, forlēt hine ðā of dūne gehrēosan,
āfielde hine ðā under foldan scēatas, heht hine ðǣr fæste gebindan.

Heading preceding 434: SATVRNVS C̄. 438b hwon (*Sw.*, *P.*), *though* o *resembles* a (*Z.*, *Sch.*, *As.*). 439b *MS*, *edd.* late, *Bout. em.* lāðe. 440b *MS*, *edd.* tydre, *Bout. em.* tydrie '*schwach werden.*' *Heading preceding* 441: SALOMON. 443a ne *of* dryhtne *begins p.* 25, *MS A.* *K. placed* ðurh dyrne cræftas *after* hyrde, *without comment, assuming omission after* wyrcan; *Gr. fol. K. but supplied* wæpenþræge *after* wyrcan, *making two normal verses; Bout. similarly two normal verses, second beginning* [wīg] him; *Holt. Angl. Beibl.* 27.356 *long line:* ōðer his dryhtne hīerde, ōðer him ðurh dierne cræftas, *with* ongan wyrcan *beginning an incomplete line* (*note*). 443b MS diere, *K.* (*Gr.*, *Bout.*) dyrne, *without comment, Sch.*, *As. em.* dierne. 445b ðonne, *MS* ðōn *P.'s reading, obscured by fold, previously read* ðær; sittan (*Z.*, *P.*), *MS obscure*, *As.* sitta[n], *K.* [sittan], *Gr.* [rīxian]. 446a (t)ȳ(d)ran, *MS obscure, letters probably* tydran *acc. to P.* (*note*); *Z. read* cyrran, *finding* ran *certain,* cy *less certain, first* r *uncertain; Sch.*, *As. read nothing; Gr.* [tihhian]. 446b (to)r(nes) (ne c)ūðe, *P.'s reading, the letters in parenthesis obscure* (*note*); *K.* [āgenne cūðe], *Gr.* [tēonan ongeald], *Sch.*, *As. read nothing, Z. only* cūðe, *Holt. Angl. Beibl.* 27.356 [getrumes] cūðe. 447a *K.* [ende], *Gr.* [egeslīce], *Sch.*, *As.*, *P.* ende; *MS* insceafte *acc. to Sch.*, *As.*, *P.*; *K.* [metod]sceafte, *Gr.* [orleg]sceafte. 447b *MS probably* æðela ðéoden, *P.'s reading,* a *and* ð *of* ðéoden *obscure*, *K.* (*Gr.*), *As.* seo æðele gedryht, *Sch. read* se. 449 *Gr.*, *As. end this line with* scēatas, *adding* heht *to* gebindan *to next* (*long*) *line* (*note*); *Holt. Angl.Beibl.* 21.175 *as in text* (*note*).

MS A

450 Ðæt sindon [ðā fēondas] ðā ūsic feohtað on:
forðon is witena gehwām wōpes ēaca.
Ðā ðæt ēadig onfand engla Dryhten
ðæt hēo leng mid hine lāre ne nāmon,
āweorp hine ðā of ðām wuldre and wīde tōdrāf,
455 and him bebēad bearn heofonwara
ðæt hīe ēc scoldon ā ðenden hīe lifdon
wunian in wylme, wōp ðrōwian,
hēaf under hefonum; and him helle gescōp,
wælcealde wīc wintre beðeahte,
460 wæter in sende and wyrmgeardas,
atol dēor monig īrenum hornum,
blōdige earnas and blace nǣdran,
ðurst and hungor and ðearle gewin,
ēgna egesan, unrōtnesse;
465 and ǣghwylc him ðissa earfeða ēce stondeð
būtan edwende ā ðenden hīe lifigað.

Sāturnus cwæð:

Is ðonne on ðisse foldan fīra ǣnig
eorðan cynnes ðāra ðe *ā* man*i*ge
dēað ābǣde, ǣr se dæg cyme
470 ðæt sīe his cālendcwide [clǣne] ārunnen
and hine mon ānnunga ūt ābanne?

Salomon cwæð:

(480) Ǣghwylc(um men) engel onsendeð

---

450 (*cf.* 449) *MS, edd.* sindon ða usic, *Holt. Angl. Beibl.* 21.175 sindon [ðā fēondas] ðā ūsic. 454a *Bout.* hī *for* hine. 455a *Holt. Angl. Beibl.* 23.125 [bealu] (*adj. acc. pl. n.*) bebēad; *Holt. Angl. Beibl.* 27.356 [beorhta] bebēad. 455b *Holt. ibid.* brego *for MS* bearn. 460a *Edd.* insende, *MS small space between* in *and* sende, *Gr. Spr.*[1] in sende. 464a *MS, As.* egna, *K.* (*Gr.*, *Bout.*) ēacne (*see note*). *Heading preceding* 467: SATVRNVS. 467b fīra *begins p.* 26, *MS A*. 468a *MS, edd.* eorðan, *Holt. Angl. Beibl.* 27.357 [mǣran], *but cf. Angl.* 23.125. 468b *MS* ðara ðe man man áge, *K.* (*Gr.*) ðara ðe * * ān age, *Bout. sugg.* þāra þe þǣron æðm āge; *Holt. Angl.* 23.125 ǣðm *or* oroð *for* man, *but retracted Angl. Beibl.* 27.357 (mægn āge?) *cf.* 468a. *Kock, Angl.* 44.113 endemān. 469a dēað; *Holt. Angl.* 23.125, *cf. Angl. Beibl.* 27.357 [ðe] dēað. 470b *Holt. Angl.* 23.125 [clāne] ārunnen. *Heading preceding* 472: SALOMON Č. 472a Ǣghwylc(um men), h *obscure*, um men *only fragmentary* (*P.*), *Sk.* (*in Sch.*) æghwel[cum men]; *K.*, *Sch. read nothing*, *Z.* æghwylc[um men]. 472b engel, *first* e *obscure*.

MS A

Dryhten heo(fona   ðonne dæg styr)eð;
sē sceall behealdan   hū his hyge (wille)
475 (grǣ)dig grōwan   in Godes willan,
murnan Metodes ðrym,   mid ðȳ ðe hit dæg bið.
Ðonne hine ymbegangað   gāstas twēgen:
ōðer bið golde glædra,   ōðer bið grundum sweartra;
ōðer cymeð . . . .
480 . . . . ofer ðǣre stȳlenan helle;
ōðer him lǣreð   ðæt hē lufan healde
Metodes miltse   and his mǣga rǣd;
ōðer hine tyhteð   and on tæso lǣreð,
ȳweð him and yppeð   earmra manna
485 misgemynda,   and ðurh ðæt his mōd hweteð,
lǣdeð hine and lǣceð   and hine geond land spaneð,
oððæt his ēge bið   æfðancum full,
ðurh earmra scyld   yrre geworden.
Swā ðonne feohteð se fēond   on fēower gecynd
490 oððæt hē gewendeð   on ðā wyrsan hand
dēofles dǣdum   dæglongne fyrst,
(500) and ðæs willan wyrcð   ðē hine on wōh spaneð.
Gewīteð ðonne wēpende   on weg faran
engel tō his earde   and ðæt eall sagað:
495 'Ne meahte ic of ðǣre heortan   heardne āðringan
stȳlenne stān,   sticað him tōmiddes.'

. . . .

(170) . . . . swīce,   ǣr hē sōð wite,

---

473 *Gr.*, *Sch.*, *As. put* dryhten *at end of* 472b; *MS acc. to P. probably* heo(fona ðōn dæg styr)eð, *as in text, enclosed letters fragmentary; only* he:::::::::::eð (*Sch.*) *read previously* (*see note*). 473–474 *For earlier division of these lines because of incomplete MS readings, see note.* 474b (wille) *P.'s guess at almost illegible MS, Gr. supplied* [mōte], *Sch.*, *As. apparently read* g *for* w *immediately after* hyge. 475a *MS* :::dig, *acc. to P. fragments of* gr *visible*, æ *illegible; K.*, *Sch.*, *As. read only* -dig; *Gr.* [gōdspē]dig. 475b willan, *P.'s reading, D.* will::, *mistakenly read* sibbe *by K.*, *Sch.*, *As.* 476b *MS* mid, *K.* (*Gr.*) and; *Gr.*, *As. assumed lacuna after* 475a *and made* and (mid) *to* bið *the second half of another line of which first half is lost.* 479a *K. put* ōðer cymeð *with next line supplying* sūsle *after* ofer, *Gr. substituted* of [stēame] *for* ofer *and assumed omission of a preceding line* [ōðer cymeð of hēahþrymme heofona rīces], *As. assumed omission of line before* ōðer cymeð, *making one line of these words and* 480b, *Holt. Angl. Beibl.* 27.357 ōðer cymeð [of stēame] (*see note*). 490a gewendeð, w *imperfect, resembling* s. 496b middes *ends p.* 26, *MS A.* 497b swīce *begins p.* 13, *MS A*, *see Introd.*, *p. 10.*

MS A

ðæt ðā sienfullan   sāula sticien
(172) mid hettendum   helle tōmiddes.
500 Hāteð ðonne Hēahcining   helle betȳnan
fȳres fulle   and ðā fēondas mid.

(175) Hæfde ðā se snotra   sunu Dāuides
forcumen and forcȳðed   Caldēa eorl.
Hwæðre was on sǣlum   sē ðe of sīðe cwōm
505 feorran gefered;   nǣfre ǣr his ferhð āhlōg.

502a *MS* Hæfde, *three dots preceding.* 505b *MS* áhlog, *followed by three dots in middle of line 7, p. 13;* Hwæt ic flītan gefrægn, *beginning of Poem II follows immediately, see line* 170 *and Introd., pp. 8 ff.*

NOTES

1.* Sāturnus cwæð. Saturn appears as Solomon's opponent in the two poetic dialogues and in two prose dialogues; cf. Introduction, pp. 5ff. and 55ff. On the character of Saturn as a prince of the Chaldeans see note on line 20b, and on the relation of Saturn to Marcolf and to earlier opponents of Solomon see Introduction, pp. 26ff., pp. 31ff.

3b. Grēca. The earlier and normal Old English form *Crēca* appears in Poem II, 183, 186, and elsewhere in the poetry.

4a. istoriam. The Latin ending shows that the borrowed word was still felt to be foreign, though *istoria* is used as an accusative without ending in Alfred's *Orosius* (ed. Sweet, *EETS*, LXXIX, p. 160). The pronunciation was evidently *ístòri̯am*, since the alliteration is vocalic, and the half-line is a C-type: x x x ´ | ` x; cf. O. Funke, *Die gelehrten lateinischen Lehn- und Fremdwörter in der altenglischen Literatur* (Halle a. S., 1914), p. 62.

6a. on þām micelan bēc. On the possible significance of the neuter declension of the usually feminine *bōc* as indicating a Northumbrian original see Introduction, p. 20.

6bff. Between *bēc* and *M.ces* in MS B there is a blank space sufficient for eleven or twelve average letters, although there is no trace of erasure. There is also a blank space for a single letter between the following *M* and *ces*. Nothing at all is visible in MS A, p. 1, at this point, but line 4 of MS A shows [*trea*]*hter*[*as*] (5) at the end, and line 6 shows [*nǣ*]*fre* (7) one-third of the way from the end, according to Pope. A calculation based on the average number of the scribe's letters per line (44, including spaces between words) shows that line 5 had only some thirty-one letter-spaces to the end of *bēc*, and since what corresponded to *M.ces heardum* would have begun the scribe's line 6, there must have been about thirteen letter spaces after *bēc*, though it is impossible to say whether these were blank as in B—which seems unlikely—or contained the lost words. This comparison with MS A therefore shows that the space in B was not left by mere caprice of the scribe, but that something has been omitted, yet not more than a few words and probably a half-line. That more than a mere omission is involved is plain from the lack of alliteration in line 7 of the text.

7a. M.ces heardum. The lack of alliteration in this line shows that the passage is corrupt. It is tempting, at first sight, to transfer the phrase to line 6b, since we should then have *m*-alliteration for line 6. But, apart from the evidence of MS B, where the omission precedes *M.ces*, *heardum* cannot be conveniently translated 'difficult to understand' since 'hard' acquired this meaning only in the fourteenth century. Even if one should translate 'in the great stern book of M,' the word-order of the Old English still remains awkward. Holthausen would emend *M.ces* to *mōdes*, and connecting *heardum* with *mē* of line 6, translate 'bold of spirit' (*Angl. Beibl.*, XXVII, 351); but this ignores the position of the blank space in the manuscript, apart from the fact that one would expect some mention of the nature of the 'great book.' Vincenti, p. 55, suggested that this great book *M.ces* referred to the books of Moses. This is not impossible, since between the books of the Greeks, Libyans, and Indians, on the one hand, and the Pater Noster on the other, Saturn might have mentioned the Old Testament; but it is not easy to see how *Moyses* could become *M.ces* or why so common a name should be corrupted at all. *Marces* would be another possibility, but only guesses are possible in view of the state of the manuscripts.

7b. swylce. The editors, except Kemble and Rieger, begin a new sentence with *swylce*, but in spite of the scribe's preceding period, it seems stylistically preferable to connect *swylce* directly with *tala* of line 5: 'tales . . . such as I could never find truly collected in all the ancient writings.' *Swylce* cannot, in any case, be adverbial, since there would then be no object for *findan*.—**ic nǣfre.** To fill out the line Holthausen, who had transferred *m[ōd]es* (MS *M.ces*) *heardum* to 6b, added *nēode* 'mit Eifer,' between *ic* and *nǣfre*; but this seems unnatural with the negative.

11. oððe ǣhte oððe eorlscipes. MS A has *oððe æh(t)a oððe eor(lscipes)*. B's omission of the second *oððe*, fortunately preserved by A, spoils the sense and the metre.

12. On the palm-branched Pater Noster see Introduction, pp. 35ff. *Pāter*, as the metre shows, has long *ā*, not the short *a* of classical Latin. Ælfric tells us in his *Grammar* (ed. J. Zupitza, p. 2) that the prose pronunciation differed from that required by [Latin] metre. The long *ā* was borrowed from the school pronunciation of Latin, which had long vowels in the penultimate syllables (cf. OE *grād* < *grădus*, and Luick, *Hist. Gram.*, § 218.1); *Pāter Noster*, which occurs in the poetry only here and in lines 39, 167, is often found in tenth-century prose.

13ff. On Saturn's promise of payment as an inheritance of the original wager of Solomon and Hiram see Introduction, p. 45.

15b. suna twelfe. I do not find this number elsewhere, but Saturn's whole character and history in this poem are so different from those of the classical traditions that this is hardly surprising. The number of children in Hesiod is six (*Theognis* 453ff.). There may be a confusion with the traditional number of the Titans, which is twelve (*Theognis* 132ff.).

16b. gebrydded. This *hapax legomenon*, defined 'terrified' by the dictionaries, is perhaps justified by OHG. *gebrutten*, 'perterrere,' 'tremefacere,' and OE. *brogdettan*, *broddettan*, 'shake,' 'tremble.' But the parallel phrase in 18a, 'reconcilest me with truth,' makes it somewhat doubtful that Saturn is saying 'if thou bringest me to the point that I am terrified by the Pater Noster.' 'Shaken,' 'overawed' would be more in keeping with the context and etymologically possible if the word is related to *brygd*, *bregdan* and those mentioned above, as Holthausen suggests (*Altenglisches Etymologisches Wörterbuch*). But Grein's suggestion that *gebrydded* is an error for *gebryrded* from *bryrdan*, 'incite,' 'inspire' may be right after all.

17a. cantices. *Cantic* is used of the Lord's prayer again in lines 24, 49, and twice in the prose dialogue (Appendix, p. 170, line 3; p. 170, line 34). This late loan-word appears elsewhere in the poetry only in the *Paris Psalter* 143, 10, and is not found in the prose before the tenth century. Cf. the note on *organ* 53a.

18b. mec gesund fa[re]. One would expect the dative *mē*, not accusative *mec* (cf. Grein, *Germania*, x, 428), and Holthausen (*Angl. Beibl.*, XXVII, 352) to avoid emendation to *mē* suggested *fa[die]* 'guide,' which does not occur in the poetry. *Gesund faran* is a common idiom (*B-T. Suppl.*, s.v. *gesund* iv a), and *mec* is either an error or survives from a Northumbrian original; cf. Introduction, p. 19.

20a. ofer Cōferflōd. Cf. *ofer Cōforflōd*, 196a. This is probably the Biblical Chebar, which appears in the Vulgate as Chobar and in the Septuagint as Χοβάρ. Chebar and Chaldea are mentioned together in Ezech. I, 3: 'in terra Chaldaeorum, secus flumen Chobar.' The Chebar is now identified with the great canal sixty miles long which ran from the Euphrates north of Babylon through Nippur, and was called *nâru kabari*, 'the great river'; cf. G. A. Cooke, *The Book of Ezekiel* (New York, 1937), p. 4. It was often confused in early Christian times and indeed until recently with the Chabur, a tributary of the Euphrates, called Chabōras by Greeks and Romans, the Biblical Habor (II Kings XVII, 6). Jerome translating the *Onomasticon* of Eusebius writes 'Chobar [Eusebius has Χωβάρ], flumen Babylonium, sicut in Iezechiel' (ed. E. Klostermann, III, 175), but in his *Commentary* on Ezechiel he explains that Chobar either is the name of a river or signifies, according to its interpretation, which is *grave*, the Tigris and Euphrates 'et omnia magna et gravissima flumina quae in terra Chaldaeorum esse perhibentur' (*Pat. Lat.*, XXV.18). The fact that Saturn's home, the land of the Chaldeans, lies beyond the *Cōforflōd*, which seems to be a kind of boundary, might point rather to the geographical position of the Chabur, which flows into the Euphrates from the Northeast, than to that of the Chebar; but the Christian commentators who connected the Chobar (Greek Χοβάρ, Χωβάρ) with Chaldea probably had no precise knowledge of Mesopotamian geography.

20b. Caldēas. This connection of Saturn with the Chaldeans is not, of course, the poet's, but goes back to his source. The reason for representing the Roman god Saturn as a Chaldean ruler is the Greek and medieval identification of Saturn-Kronos with Nimrod or Ninus. Nimrod's kingdom was 'Babel, and Erech, and Accad, and Calneh, in the land of Shinar' (Gen. X, 10), and Ninus, with whom he was often identified, was founder of Niniveh in Greek mythology (*Clementine Recognitions*, *Pat. Gr.*, I, 1327; *Chronicon Paschale*, *Pat. Gr.*, XCII, 126). According to Isidore of Seville, Ninus, the first king of the Assyrians, was called Saturn by some (*Etymologiae*, VIII, 11.23), and the eleventh-century Cedrenus identifies Nimrod with the planet Kronos (*Pat. Gr.*, CXXI, 56). Thus Saturn-Kronos, the oldest and wisest of the gods, was equated with both Nimrod and Ninus, whom the Hebrews and Greeks respectively considered the founders of

Babylon and Assyria. The real reason for this equation is obscure. If the Biblical Nimrod were a reflection of the Babylonian god Ninurta or Nimurta (earlier deciphered as Ninib), as some scholars hold (cf. S. D. H. Langdon, *Mythology of All Races: Semitic* [Boston, 1931], p. 55), the connection of Nimrod with Saturn-Kronos would be easy to understand, since the planet Saturn-Kronos was the planet Ninurta in Babylonian astronomy (A. Bouché-Leclercq, *L'Astrologie Grecque*, pp. 69, 93; B. Meissner, *Babylonien und Assyrien*, II, 9; Bezold-Boll, *Sternglaube und Sterndeutung*, 3d ed., pp. 10–11). Saturn would thus have become a prince of Chaldea because the Greeks applied the name of the God Kronos to the planet called by the Babylonians Ninurta, whom the Greeks identified rightly or wrongly with Nimrod. Cf. further the notes on lines 198b–202, 320b; and Vincenti, pp. 98–101, who attempts to connect Saturn with the Chaldeans on the basis of an older identification of the planet with El-Moloch.

It should be noted that Saturn is represented as a prince of the Chaldeans only in the two poetic dialogues. When Saturn is mentioned elsewhere in Old English it is either as a god or as a planet; see *Metres of Boethius*, XXVI, 43ff., cf. XXIV, 17ff. (Saturn as a star); Ælfric, *De Falsis Deis*, in *Wulfstan*, ed. Napier, p. 106; *Lives of the Saints*, ed. Skeat, I, 126 (devourer of children); *Catholic Homilies*, II, 260 (day of the week); cf. Vincenti, pp. 92–95. Kemble, pp. 84–88, thought there was an independent allusion to the Solomon-Saturn legend in a homily in Cotton Tiberius A 3, fol. 85ff. (reprinted by Vincenti, pp. 103–105), which mentions Solomon's (the text has an obvious mistake in *Samsones*) beauty and wisdom, and within a few lines Saturn's daughter; but the collocation of Solomon and Saturn here may well be accidental.

21.* Salomon. On Solomon in dialogue and legend see Introduction, pp. 21–35, and on Solomon as a symbolic representative of Christianity, pp. 47–48.

22a. wēsðe. Cf. *ēaðusð* 36aB. These are typical Early West Saxon back-spellings resulting from the change of *sþ* to *st*; cf. Sievers-Cook, § 196.1, § 201.6, § 356. n. 1; Bülbring, § 472; Luick, § 674.3. The spelling of *gesēmesð* (18a) might be a genuine etymological spelling, since the usual *-st* is from *-sþ(ū)*. On the importance of the *sð* spellings for the provenience of the manuscript and the date of the poem, see Introduction, pp. 3, 16f.

23. feldgongende feoh. Cf. 154 and *Soul and Body* 76 (81): 'feldgongende feoh būtan snyttro.'

25a. warað. MS A (see textual variants) has *wōrað*, 'wanders,' which is probably correct, being a good variation of *weallað* (22). *Warað* would have to mean 'remains,' not 'inhabits,' an intransitive use of the verb unparalleled in Old English except for the very doubtful case of *Paris Psalter* 134, 19, adduced by Bosworth-Toller. Kemble, it is true, translated *warað windes full* 'he shall inhabit the void expanse,' explaining *windes full* as *poculum venti* (p. 176); but this is improbable. 'Full of wind' means simply 'empty,' 'devoid of wisdom,' and is parallel to *wēsðe wīsdōmes* (22a).

26b. draca. For this epithet of the Devil cf. *Elene* 766, *Panther* 57. It comes from Rev. XII, 9: 'Et projectus est draco ille magnus, serpens antiquus, qui vocatur diabolus et Satanas.'

28ff. īrenum aplum. There is nothing unusual in the use of *æppel* in the general sense of ball; cf. Wright-Wülker, *Anglo-Saxon and Old English Vocabularies*, I, 502.20; '*Spere* (*sphaerae*) æpples.' The following figure, 'all are grown from the heads of the waves of scorn (or disgrace)' (28b–29), is curious and smacks of the Irish Latin of Aldhelm's school. The comparison of the temptations of the Devil to weapons, usually javelins or arrows (cf. *Christ* 762, *Beow.* 1743ff.), is a commonplace of medieval literature, and the thought underlying the figure here may be that the Devil's weapons, his 'iron apples' spring from man's disgraceful or shameful sins; cf. *Beow.* 1742–47, where Klaeber points out that the Devil's *biteran strǣle* is equated with his sinister suggestions *wōm wundorbebodum;* Gregory, *Moralia*, XIII, 16: 'sancta ecclesia . . . tentationum jaculis impetitur' (*Pat. Lat.*, LXXV, 1026); F. J. Mone, *Hymni Latini Medii Aevi*, I, 388.13: 'doleo multis peccatorum jaculis'; and Klaeber, *Anglia*, XXXV, 129.

30. The second page of MS A begins with *lēofre*, and the texts of the two manuscripts are printed side by side. The reader should first follow the text of MS A, which is much superior. The text of MS B has been left with a minimum of correction to facilitate comparison of the manuscripts. On the illegibility of MS A, p. 1, see Introduction, p. 2.

39ff. The personification of the Pater Noster is fantastic, but not quite so extravagant as that of the prose dialogue, in which the various parts of its body and even its apparel are described; see Introduction, p. 8, Appendix, and note on lines 66ff.

44a. drēor. There can be no doubt that both *drēam* (MS A) and *drȳ* (MS B) are wrong, both scribes probably being misled by an earlier error (cf. Introduction, p. 3), which may have been the result in part of the unfamiliarity of the poetic word *drēor*. Cf. *Gen.* 1030–31, *drēor . . . blōd*, and *Christ* 1085–87, where *blōde . . . drēore . . . swāte* are all used, as here.

45a. swāte geswīðed. B actually wrote *swatege* [end of line] *swiðed*, in which case the first word might be an adjective *swātege* modifying *dropan*, and *swīðed* an error for postpositive *swīðe*. The usual meaning of (*ge*)*swīðan* is 'strengthen,' 'support,' and the meaning here may be that the Devil's blood is so heated that 'drops rise reinforced with blood' or perhaps 'forced out' in view of the possible meaning of *swīðan*, intr., 'press against' suggested by Klaeber, *Angl.*, XXXVI, 66, for Ælfric's *Preface to the Old Testament*, p. 11, l. 23. The *seofan intingum* (B *sefan intingan*, perhaps with LWS. *-an* for *-um*) is also obscure, Kemble's 'in the thoughts of his breast' being unwarranted by any recorded sense of *intinga*, which means 'matter,' 'happiness,' 'cause,' 'sake.' Possibly the phrase means 'because of the mind' or even 'by pressure on the heart'; cf. the related *getingan*, 'to press against'; *getenge*, 'resting on,' 'oppressing,' and Holthausen, *Angl. Beibl.*, XXXIV, 351–352, who believes the primary meaning of *intinga* is 'Anliegen.'

The physical effect of the Pater Noster on the Devil would then be supposed to work through his mind or heart. More remote possibilities are (1) that *sefan intingan* (B's reading) is parallel to *swāte*, and *intingan* is used mechanically to translate a Latin *cordis materia* not in the ordinary sense of 'matter,' but rather 'material,' 'substance'; (2) that, in view of the following comparative, *egesfullīcran seofan* is an error for *seofon* and the phrase means something like 'seven times more dreadful' or 'for seven causes (referring possibly to the seven petitions of the Pater Noster?) more dreadful.'

46ff. The brazen kettle that boils for twelve generations of men is probably a relic of heathendom, since the cauldron played a large part in the cults of ancient peoples, being used for sacrifice and prophecy; cf. J. J. Jones, 'The Cauldron in Ritual and Myth,' *Aberystwyth Studies*, v (1923), 75–82; Grimm, *Teutonic Mythology*, trans. Stallybrass, I, 55–57; E. H. Meyer, *Germanische Mythologie* (Berlin, 1891), § 234, p. 173; *Handbuch des deutschen Aberglaubens*, s.v. *Kessel*. Strabo (VII.2) gives an account of the priestesses of the Cimbri who slit the throats of prisoners over a huge cauldron and prophesied over their blood. In the Welsh poem called the *Harrying of Hades* (*Book of Taliessin*, XXX, ed. J. G. Evans) the invaders found the continuously boiling cauldron of the Head of Hades, from which voices arose (cf. J. Rhys, *Celtic Heathendom*, pp. 256–257). In Christian times hot springs became associated with Hell and were called *Hellekessel* (cf. OE. *helle sēað*, *Jul.* 422). In the *Grimnismál* 26, *Hvergelmir*, 'roaring cauldron,' is said to be a spring in Niflheim under one of the roots of Yggdrasil; cf. *Gylfaginning* 4, 15, 16, 39.

51–52. 'It guides the peoples and keeps a place for them in the kingdom of heaven, it wears armor.' Kemble translated: 'with voice it directeth, and its place holdeth, heaven-kingdom's arms it wieldeth' (emending to *wǣgeð*), and similarly Vincenti, p. 56: 'lenkt mit der Stimme, hält (behauptet) die (Wal)statt, trägt des Himmelreiches Heeresrüstung.' But *stefn* is evidently 'stock,' 'race,' 'people' here, as in *lēodstefn*, *þēodstefn* (so the *Sprachschatz*[2]). For the Pater Noster's armor, compare the prose dialogue (Appendix).

53a. organ A, **organan** B, 'song.' B's reading is probably an error, perhaps the result of the scribe's acquaintance with *organa*, pl. *organan*, in the sense of 'organ'; cf. *organes* 33A, B, and *se gyldena organ*, likewise referring to the Pater Noster, in the prose dialogue (Appendix, p. 170, line 34). The *Sprachschatz*[2] suggested *organ an* (= *ān*).

56a. scyldum B, **scyldigum** A. B's reading is almost certainly correct, corresponding to the other abstract nouns *morðre*, *sorge* (55), but since a modicum of sense may be made from A's *scyldigum*, this has been left in the text.

57b–59a. 'Full often curiosity asks me concerning this, eagerly coming disturbs my mind.'

63. The reference is to the ornamentation of the Pater Noster, cf. Introduction, p. 43, and note on 143a.

66ff. The extraordinary series of figures applied to the Pater Noster is unparalleled. The prayer is given attributes and epithets that are ordinarily reserved for Christ or the Virgin. *Snytro* (66), *lǣce* (77), *lēoht* (77), *weard* (83) are all used of God or Christ in Old English poetry; cf. *snyttro* (Sapientia), *Christ* 239; *hālig lǣce, Lord's Prayer,* III, 63 (Grein-Wülker, II, 235); *lēoht, Elene* 7, 486; and *weard* in such combinations as *heofonrīces weard, Gen.* 1363 etc., *middangeardes weard, And.* 82, 227. *Folces nerigend* (80) is paralleled by *folca nergend, Christ* 426. *Hunig* and *meolc* (66) are reminiscent of the *mel* and *lac* often applied to the Virgin (A. Salzer, *Die Sinnbilder und Beiworte Mariens* [Linz, 1893], pp. 488, 496); and *scyppendes seld* (79) certainly reflects the use of *aula* as a symbol for the Virgin: *aula aeterni regis,* F. J. Mone, *Hymni Latini Medii Aevi,* II, 260, 31; *aula coelestis speciosa regis,* Mone, II, 62, 13; *aula summi regis,* Mone, II, 278, 221; cf. Salzer, pp. 37–39. The Pater Noster becomes not only the means of entrance to heaven and the savior of men from the Devil, but the refuge and protector of fish and wild beasts (82–83).

Close parallels to this hypostasis of a prayer are hard to find. Somewhat comparable is the description of an Irish prayer called the *Litany of Creation,* in *Irish Litanies,* ed. C. Plummer, *Henry Bradshaw Society* LXII (London, 1925), pp. 104–105: 'This is in brief the wise "besom of devotion." Though it be brief in words, it is a pure brightly ordered strain; it is full of devotion, it is perfect in clerkship. It is a summons to saints, it is a . . . to elements, it is an entreaty to angels, . . . breast-plate. It is a breast-plate to my soul, it is a protection to me, body and heart, it is a pleasant ready nurture, it is a praising of the King of heaven. It is a sanctification to men who recite it continually; it is a judgment of him who recites it, it is (ascetic) devotion, it is suffering. It is a partaking of the Body of Christ, and it is a hard conflict; it is fair perfect faith, it is converse with angels.' The tone of the English passage reminds one, in its extravagant use of figure, of the Old Irish prayers (cf. Plummer, *Irish Litanies,* pp. 6–7, pp. 75–85), and in its general inclusiveness, of the famous *loricae* of St. Patrick and Gildas (*The Irish Liber Hymnorum,* ed. J. H. Bernard and R. Atkinson, *Henry Bradshaw Society* XIII, XIV [London, 1898], I, 133–135; 206–210; II, 49–51). Cf. further Introduction, p. 42, and note on line 89b.

69b. nǣfre . . . tō ðaes niðer. 'Though the fiend fastens it never so far down.' Cf. 149, and Kock's analysis of the construction in 'Jubilee Jaunts and Jottings,' *Lunds Univ. Årsskrift,* N.F. Avd. 1, XIV (1918), 67, and *Anglia,* XLVI (1922), 83–84. Assmann wrongly connects both *nǣfre*-clauses (69, 149) with what follows, despite Kemble's correct translation.

71a. clūsum A; **clausum** B. B's spelling does not occur elsewhere, but may be directly imitated from the Latin *clausa,* which existed side by side with Med. Lat. (from VL.) *clūsa;* cf. the similar variations in *claustrum,* Med. Lat. *clūstrum,* which gave LOE. *clauster,* 'cloister,' 'lock,' and OE. *clūstor,* 'lock,' 'cell,' respectively. The *ū/au* variation is common in *clūdo,* *claudŏ*, cf. *occlūdo;* and in *clausum*, *clūsum;* see C. H. Grandgent, *Vulgar Latin*, § 211, note 2.

79. scyld . . . seld. The rhyme would be exact, as in the following line, if *scyld* had the Anglian form *sceld*, which always appears in the *Vespasian Psalter*. *Seld* with *ld* (< *sedl* < *seðl* < **seþl*) is itself peculiar to Anglian, see Luick, § 638.1 and Anm. 4. Cf. further Introduction, p. 7 and note on 107a.

88–90. 'If thou first bringest down on him from above the wrathful prime prologue, whose name is P.' A's *ierne*, strangely distorted to *yorn* in B, is acc. masc. sg. agreeing with *prologa prima*. Grein and Assmann correct A's reading to *prologum primum*, but this is probably unnecessary in view of the variety of forms that such loan-words take; cf. *cristalla* (Ælfric, Numbers XI, 7), *cristallan* (*Lives of Saints* V, 252), beside *cristallum* (*Paris Psalter* 146, 6) and *cristal* (*Engl. Stud.*, XIII, 475); see Funke, *Die gelehrten lateinischen Lehn- und Fremdwörter in der altenglischen Literatur*, pp. 61–62.

89b. The letters of the Pater Noster appear in order, except for a few transpositions, but with no repetitions, as explained in the Introduction, pp. 35–45. O, I, and B are omitted by accident in MS A. MS B stops with the third letter T at the beginning of line 94. In MS A runic letters precede all the Latin letters included by the scribe except N and H. On the importance of runes and alphabetic magic, see Introduction, pp. 45–49.

90. The belief that the Pater Noster is a weapon wherewith to fight the Devil is paralleled in the Irish homily on the Pater Noster in the *Leabhar Breac*, where it is said that the Pater Noster 'is the iron hammer by which the power of the devil is broken, as saith Job in the person of the Lord:— "I will break thy power, O devil, saith the Lord, with an iron hammer," viz: with the Pater Noster' (*The Passion and Homilies from Leabhar Breac*, ed. R. Atkinson, *Royal Irish Acad. Todd Lectures* II (Dublin, 1887), p. 501; Irish, p. 264; Latin comment, pp. 505–506). This is later than *Solomon and Saturn*, but may go back to an earlier Latin source. The reference to Job seems incorrect, the only *malleus* being in Job XLI, 20 (Vulg.): 'quasi stipulam aestimabit malleum.' Jer. XXIII, 29 seems more to the point: 'Numquid non verba mea sunt quasi ignis, dicit Dominus, et quasi malleus conterens petram?' The whole homily is an interesting commentary on the Pater Noster.

93a. Ā ofermægene. D-type. It is plain that the names of the letters of the alphabet were pronounced with long vowels; cf. 96, 108, 118.

94a. MS B ends with T at the bottom of the page in the margin of p. 198.

98b. ieorrenga. Kemble prints *eorrenga* without comment. The form *ieorrenga* may be a confusion of the scribe's WS. *ierrenga* with *eorrenga*.

99a. bōcstafa brego. Ebert suggested that R is called 'prince of letters' because of the important place of the letter in the Greek monogram of Christ, XHR (*Allgemeine Geschichte der Literatur des Mittelalters im Abendlande* III, 93, note 2). He thought this pointed to an ultimate Greek source behind the immediate Latin source (cf. III, 91). Although an ultimate Greek source is probable in itself, too much significance should not be attached to the epithets applied to the warrior-letters; cf. 107b note and 111b note.

101b–102a. 'He [T] does not consider the joints of his (the Devil's) limbs nor is he a good leech to him.' *Lið* for normal acc. pl. neut. *liðu, leoþu* is unexampled elsewhere and similar monosyllabic forms are very rare even in Late Northumbrian (cf. H. C. A. Carpenter, *Die Deklination in der Northumbrischen Evangelienübersetzung*, pp. 129–130). The curious monosyllabic *leoþ* of *Andreas* 1404 is emended by the latest editor, Krapp, *Anglo-Saxon Poetic Records* II.

105a. hangiende. The metre requires the Anglian *hangende*, as Holthausen notes (*Angl. Beibl.*, XXVII, 352). The clause means that the Devil who is 'hanging' by the hair from the hands of T (cf. 99–100) must indeed be suffering if he longs for hell.

107a. forcinnað. Since the meaning of this word is unknown, it is tempting to adopt Grein's suggested emendation (*Germania*, X, 428) to *forcumað*, 'destroy' (cf. lines 198, 503); but this is metrically difficult, and the existence of an unexplained *cinnið* in the *Rhyming Poem* 52, and the possibility of internal rhyme with *getuinnas* (as in 80, 83) make emendation venturesome; cf. Holthausen, *Angl. Beibl.*, XXVII, 352. It may be noted that the rhyme would be exact if *forcinnað* had been originally a Northumbrian *forcinnas;* cf. 79 note.

107b. ðā ciricān getuinnas. The letters N and O seem to be so called simply because they occur together in the Pater Noster; cf. 141 *līfgetwinnan*. Kemble, with characteristic rashness, emends to *ðā cyrican ge tūnas*, translating the line 'when him shall repudiate both churches and houses'!

108a. N, [Ō] s(am)od. For earlier reconstructions see the textual notes. It is obvious that O must be supplied because it is the next letter of *noster* and because *getuinnas* presupposes two letters. Following the dot after N is a straight line (so K., Z., P.) not ⁊ (Sch., Ass.), which may possibly represent what in an earlier text was the first stroke of a runic O. The emended half-line is a D-type with vocalic alliteration, the N being pronounced *en*, since it is one of the six letters (*f, l, m, n, r, s*) which Ælfric in his *Grammar* (ed. J. Zupitza, p. 6) says: 'ongynnað of ðām stæfe *e* and geendjað on him sylfum.' Cf. Holthausen, *Angl. Beibl.*, XXVII, 352.

110b. Cf. *And.* 154: 'Feorh ne bemurndan.'

111b. engla gerǣswa. It was suggested by Holthausen (*Angl. Beibl.*, XXVII, 353, note 1) that S is called 'leader of the angels' because it begins Σωτήρ or *salvator*, as applied to Christ, or possibly even because of Seraph. But see note on 99a.

114b. stregdað. As it stands this must be intransitive and *tōðas* subject, but Grein's suggested emendation to *stregdeð* would be stylistically preferable, S remaining the subject throughout the sentence. For other apparent confusions of singular and plural see 132, 153ff., and notes, and Introduction, p. 20.

116a. æfter sceades sciman. Cf. the similar description of hell in *Christ and Satan* 105–106: 'Nē hēr dæg lȳhteð / for scedes sciman.'

118a. The shape of the rune for Q is similar to that in Cotton Galba A 2, as indicated by O. von Friesen, *Runorna* (Stockholm, 1933), p. 60, but differs considerably from the *cweorð*-runes in Cotton Otho B 10 and Domitian A 9, both of which resemble the *ēa*-rune. It is probable that the *q*-rune is a late modification of the *p*-rune, as its name *cweorð* was of the name *peorð*.

123a. I, supplied by Grein, may have been omitted by the scribe because of its similarity to L. In this line the order of letters in the Pater Noster (qu*i* es in *cael*is) is not followed, L and C being transposed in order to bring the two alliterating letters (see note on 108a) in the first half-line.

124b. gēap stæf, 'curved letter.' This refers to only one of the letters in the previous line, and most naturally, from the point of view of style, to C, the last. *Gēap* has many meanings, 'crooked,' 'curved,' 'bulging' (translating *pandus, curvus* in the glosses), 'broad,' 'vaulted,' 'cunning,' 'bold' (?) (cf. J. Hoops' excellent analysis, *Engl. Stud.*, LXIV, 201–211), and has been variously rendered here 'crooked' (Kemble, *B-T.*), 'patulus,' 'amplus' (*Sprachschatz*[2]), 'bauchig' (?) (Hoops, p. 203). Since the same adjective is used of G (*sē gēapa*, 134), there can hardly be any doubt that it refers primarily to the curved shape of the letters, though perhaps the meaning 'cunning' is present secondarily. On another probable reference to the shape of the letters, cf. 136 note.

126a. helle hæftling. Cf. *Jul.* 246, *And.* 1342; and *helle hæfton* describing Grendel, *Beow.* 788. This is a translation of the Latin *captivus inferni* (Klaeber, *Angl.*, XXXV, 254). The names applied to the Devil elsewhere in the poem are not so striking; cf. *draca* 26 note; *lāðan gǣst* 86; *sceaða* 116, 128; *scinn*, 101.

130b. flāna. Kock would take this, not as gen. pl. masc., but as acc. pl. fem., a variation of *ǣled*, 129a (*Angl.*, XLII, 122–123).

131b–132. 'The devils severely and cruelly pay for the fact that they break into (?) boasting.' For the construction, cf. *Dan.* 597: 'hē ðæs hearde ongeald.' *Brecan* occurs nowhere else in this meaning, which seems doubtful. *B-T. Suppl.*, s.v. *brecan* I, 2a, gives a definition 'fail to perform,' with this line the only instance, an extension of the meaning 'violate' in such phrases as *brecan ǣwe, bebodu*, a *gilp* being considered a kind of promise to perform certain deeds. Holthausen may be right in emending to *wrecað* 'utter' (*Angl. Beibl.*, XXVII, 353). The change from the singular (Devil) in 127, 128, 130 to the plural here is curious, and the original may have read *bana, ongieldeð, breceð;* but cf. the similar shift in lines 152ff. For *bana*, 'slayer,' 'destroyer,' applied to the Devil, cf. *Beow.* 743, *And.* 1293, *Whale* 41, *Sat.* 640.

134a. The rune used here is not the *gifu*-rune, as we might expect, but the *gēar*-rune, the rune for *j*. The rune has the same shape that is found in the Salzburg Codex and is similar to that of the *Runic Poem* of Cotton Otho B 10, which has a circle instead of a diamond crossing the vertical line (Bruce Dickins, *Runic and Heroic Poems*, Table 1; O. von Friesen, art. *Runenschrift* in Hoops' *Reallexikon*, IV, Table 3, 13; 4, 14). Because of the falling together of *j* and palatal *g* in sound, the *gifu*-rune came to be regularly used for words which originally had Germanic *j* (Dickins, p. 16); and the *gēar*-rune is consequently rare in Old English outside of the runic alphabets. In this line the usual procedure is reversed: the *gēar*-rune has been substituted for the *gifu*-rune. The similar use of a *gēar*-rune, differently shaped, is found in the inscriptions of Thornhill (*Gilsuiþ*) and Dover (*Gislheard*); see Dickins, *Leeds Studies in English*, I (1932), 16, and the plates in George Stephens, *Old-Northern Runic Monuments of Scandinavia and England*, I, 415–416 (Thornhill); III, 465 (Dover).

136. 'Full of quintuple powers—fire is the third.' Similarly Kemble, though 'fire' (*fȳr*) is misprinted 'five.' Assmann, following Grein, omitted punctuation after *ðridda*, evidently interpreting *fyr* as 'further,' as does the *Sprachschatz*[2]: 'further shall the third letter be near the street.' Holthausen suggested *fīf[l]mægnum*, 'Riesenkräfte,' and *se ōðer*, referring to the missing letter B, the second letter of the alphabet, for *se ðridda* (*Angl. Beibl.*, XXVII, 353). *Fīflmægnum* is improbable because *fīfl* in Old English means 'monster' with an implication of wickedness, and *fīfmægnum* is perfectly intelligible when one remembers the importance attached to the number five by Pythagoreans, Zoroastrians, Neo-Platonists, and Gnostics, and particularly the mystic and magic use of the pentagram and pentacle. The quintuple powers of the spirit are mentioned in a Byzantine tract: *πέντε εἰσὶ τῆς ψυχῆς αἱ δυνάμεις* (C. F. Georg Henrici, 'Griechisch-Byzantinische Gesprächsbücher,' *Abhandlungen der kgl. sächs. Gesellschaft der Wissenschaften, philol.-hist. Kl.*, XXVIII [1911], 98); cf., further, V. F. Hopper, *Medieval Number Symbolism* (Columbia Univ. Press, 1938), pp. 123–124, and Sir Thomas Browne's *Garden of Cyrus*, with its observations on the quincunx. The magic pentagram plays a large part in the *Clavicula Salomonis* (cf. Introduction, pp. 46f.), and appears on Gawain's shield in *Sir Gawain and the Green Knight* 625, where the significance of the number five applied to Gawain is elaborated in great detail, as well as in *Faust* 1395–96; it is often supposed to be Solomon's seal in western literature (*Jewish Ency.*, art. *Solomon, Seal of;* Ginzberg, *Legends of the Jews*, IV, 150; VI, 292; Perdrizet, *Revue des Études Grecques*, XVI [1903], 56–57, note 3). It would have been more in keeping with ancient magic to have the fifth letter E full of quintuple powers, rather than D; cf. Plutarch's *De E apud Delphos* iv. The Greek Δ, as the fourth letter, was the symbol of the four elements in a fifth-century work on mysteries of the Greek alphabet (F. Dornseiff, *Das Alphabet in Mystik und Magie*, p. 22) and some similar tradition may account for the element *fire* being mentioned here, just as it is in the *Metres of Boethius* XX, 61: 'and fȳr is ðridde and fēowerðe lyft.' If the interpretation suggested here is accepted, it must be assumed that a line or so containing a reference to the letter B is omitted after 137.

The omission of the letter B is certainly not to be ascribed to the poet. The order of the letters in the Pater Noster is D G B H, but the poet has transposed D and G; B would therefore be expected after D and before H (cf. Introduction, pp. 36–37). Assuming no scribal omission in the text, one might suppose a hidden reference to B, in 'se ðridda/stæf strǣte nēah,' 'the third letter (of the group G, D, B), a letter near the street' (with reference to the shape of B). But apart from the objection that such a cryptic reference would be a total departure from the poet's custom of naming the letters definitely, line 41, which speaks of the *līfgetwinnan* (after H) seems to imply that B has been coupled with H (cf. Holthausen, *Angl. Beibl.*, XXVII, 353) rather than connected with G and D. It is tempting to consider *bið* an error for B, 'further, B, the third letter near the street waits quietly;' but the objection that B is then dissociated from its 'twin' H still remains, and it is improbable besides that *fyr*, 'further,' would receive the alliterating stress and B be unstressed, since in all other cases the letters have stress even when they do not alliterate. A scribal omission after 137, which may be regarded as the beginning of a description of B, is thus, on the whole, most probable.

140a. spyrigend*e*, MS *spyrigendes*. The emendation was suggested by Kock (*Jubilee Jaunts and Jottings*, p. 67), who translates: 'an angel clothes him, the champion of Christ, in living garments, when he is seeking for good [*gōdes*] fresh attire.' But apart from the curious word-order of line 140 with this interpretation, it seems more likely that the warrior is 'seeking God' *quaerere Dominum* in the common Scriptural phrase (Deut. IV, 29, I Chron. XVI, 10, 11, etc.): 'in living garments—the seeker after God—of fresh attire.' It would be natural to read *on cwicum wǣdum / Godes spyrigendes, geongum hrægle*, 'in the living garments of a seeker of God, in fresh attire,' but I have not ventured to make the emendations in the text. With *scierpeð . . . cwicum wǣdum* one may compare such a Biblical expression as Is. LXI, 10: 'Quia induit me vestimentis salutis.'

141b. līfgetwinnan. Cf. note on 136.

143a. sweopum seolfrynum. This refers to the *tuigena ordum* of 142, which are said to be silver because the palm-branches adorning the Pater Noster are silver (63–64). Cf. Holthausen, *Angl. Beibl.*, XXVII, 353.

143b. wǣlað, MS *weallað*. There can hardly be any doubt that *weallað*, 'rolls,' 'turns,' which would be the only case of this verb used transitively in Old English (*B-T.*, s.v. *weallan* VIII), is wrong, and an error for *wǣlað*, 'scourge,' 'torment,' a meaning plainly required by the context. The West Saxon scribe was unfamiliar with the rare Anglian verb *wǣlan*, for which see R. Jordan, *Eigentümlichkeiten des anglischen Wortschatzes*, p. 57, and Introduction, p. 21.

149b–151. 'Though they change their hues never so strangely, take a covering of feathers over their bodies.' For this construction cf. 69 note.

151a. feðerhoman onfōð. A characteristic appearance of the Devil; cf. Ælfric, *Cath. Hom.*, I, 466: 'hē wæs egeslīce gefiðerhamod.' For the appearance of the Devil as a bird, a dragon, a wolf, cf. the prose dialogue, Appendix, p. 168.

151b. Hwīlum flotan grīpað. 'Sometimes they seize the sailor.' This begins the series of clauses describing the appearance of demons in various forms and their sudden attacks on men and beasts. For a similar *hwīlum*-passage describing the shape-shifting of demons, cf. *Guth.* 907–912. The mention of the sailor implies their activity on sea as well as land; cf. Bede's story of the storm which the *inimica vis dæmonum* aroused when Germanus and Lupus came to England (*Hist. Eccl.*, I, 17). Kock, *Jubilee Jaunts and Jottings*, pp. 67–68, would read *flot angrīpað*, 'take to swimming (floating),' which makes excellent sense; but *flot* is not recorded in this sense in Old English, nor *ongrīpan* in any sense.

152b. in wyrmes līc. It was natural that the Devil should often appear in the original disguise in which the *fāh wyrm* (*Gen.* 899) tempted Eve; cf. *Guth.* 910b–911: 'hwīlum brugdon eft / āwyrgde wǣrlogan on wyrmes blēo.'

153b. stingeð nīeten. Kemble changed to *stingað* without comment, as he does all singular verbs in 153–156, 161–162, likewise printing *hīe* for *hē* in 155, 158, 161. Grein pointed out that this is unnecessary, the activity of the individual devils being referred to. The change from plural to singular is perhaps induced by the introduction of *in wyrmes līc* (152b). On other confusions of singular and plural, see Introduction, p. 20. For attacks by the Devil and demons on cattle, see the prose dialogue, Appendix, p. 169.

156b–157. 'Until his heart's blood seeks out the foamy bath of the stream, the ground (bottom).' The *Sprachschatz*[2], following Kemble, takes *fāmig blōdes bæð* (s.v. *bæð*) to refer to *blōd*, but more probably it refers to the water (155) in which the horse is attacked, this being pictured as a swirling stream.

158. Grein's [*folme*] after *gefeterað* is unnecessary, since *handa* (159a) is to be taken as object of both the preceding and following verb, the construction ἀπὸ κοινοῦ; cf. Holthausen, *Angl. Beibl.*, XXVII, 353; Kock, *Jubilee Jaunts and Jottings*, p. 30, and especially, H. D. Meritt, *The Construction ἀπὸ κοινοῦ in the Germanic Languages*, *Stanford Univ. Publ., Lang. and Lit.* VI (1938), Chap. II, p. 44.

161ff. Weapons were usually inscribed with runes to bring victory, as in the *Sigrdrifumál* 6, but enemies might use runes for evil purposes, as the compounds *heterūn*, *wælrūn* attest. The warrior's blade might be dulled by the charms and incantations of an enemy; cf. *Hávamál* 149: 'Eggjar deyfik minna andskota, / bítat þeim vǫpn né velir'; and Saxo IV (Gunholmus) VII (Haquinus), pp. 119, 219 (ed. Holder). The 'deadly marks' *wællnōta* of heathen times are ingeniously attributed to the Devil, and the Pater Noster commended as a means of nullifying the effect of his evil runes.

167b. Palmtrēow. Holthausen suggested (*Angl.*, XXIII, 124) substituting *gepalmtwigede* (cf. 39), considering the half-line senseless and metrically false as it stands. It seems possible that *palmtrēow* is another name for the palm-adorned Pater Noster.

169. The prose dialogue, printed in the Appendix, follows immediately after *cyme* in the middle of line 12, p. 6, of MS A. See Introduction, pp. 8–10.

170. Hwæt. This word clearly indicates the beginning of a new poem, as indeed does the whole sentence. To emphasize this the scribe has written HWÆT.IC.FLITAN.GEFRÆGN in capitals covering two lines, the initial H being unusually large and extending over five lines in the margin; cf. Introduction, p. 1.

171b. middangeardes rǣswan (MS *ræswum*). The half-line is obviously too long, and Holthausen assumes that *rǣswum* belongs to a line omitted (*Angl.*, XXIII, 124). In this case the verb *rǣswan*, 'meditate,' which would be parallel to *gewesan* (172a), is perhaps involved, and *middangeardes* goes with *mōdglēawe men*.

172a. gewesan. On this verb and its Northumbrian parallels see Introduction, pp. 20f.

172b. līehð. Holthausen, assuming an Anglian original, objects to *līehð*, 'lies,' from *lēogan*, on the ground that in a critical text Anglian *lēgeð* or *līgeð* would make an impossible E-line (*Angl. Beibl.*, XXVII, 353). He proposes *liehð*, Angl. *lehið* from *lēan*, 'blame.' This is relying too heavily on metrical regularity, for 'lie' not 'blame' is plainly the sense required, as the next half-line shows. At this late period 172b might be scanned as A-type (with Angl. *lēgeð*) rather than E-type.

174a. ðēah ðe Sāt(urn)us. The pronunciation of the Latin form of Saturn was *Sāturnus*, as the metre here (C-type) shows; cf. *Metres of Boethius* XXIV, 21: 'ðone Sāturnus' (C-type); XXVI, 48: 'Sāturnus ðone' (E-type).

177b. (Ēa)st-Corsias. *Corsias* is almost certainly an error for *Cossias*, the *Cossaei* or Κοσσαῖοι of classical writers (so Holthausen, *Angl. Beibl.*, XXVII, 354), who overran Babylonia about 1260 B.C. and founded a dynasty which lasted for 576 years (B. Meissner, *Babylonien und Assyrien* I, 28–29). Strabo XI, 13.3, 6, said they were neighbors of the Medes. It is not certain that *ēast* and *Corsias* should be compounded, and the same applies to *Norð-Predan* (179b). For the form *Corsias* for *Cossias*, compare the snakes called *corsias*, translating an equally curious Latin *corsias*, in the Old English *Wonders of the East*, ed. S. Rypins, *EETS*, CLVI, 55.

178b. Palestinion. This is a curious form for Palestine, Lat. *Palaestīna*, Gr. Παλαιστίνη.

179b. Norð-Predan. *Predan* perhaps equals *Perðan* for *Pearðan*, 'Parthians'; cf. Holthausen, *Anglia Beiblatt*, XXVII, 354. One would expect to find the Parthians mentioned with the Medes and Persians.

180b. Marculfes eard. This is the earliest mention of the Marcolf, Latin Marcolfus, who is Solomon's opponent in the non-English medieval dialogues of Solomon, notably in the Latin *Salomon et Marcolfus* (see Introduction, pp. 26–35). The presence of the name here shows that the poet or his source was familiar with Solomonic literature in which the figure of Marcolf appeared either beside that of Saturn or as an alternate to Saturn.

'Marculf's country' probably refers to Chaldea, since his *alter ego* Saturn is represented in our poem as a prince of the Chaldeans (see note on line 20b). In the Latin dialogue he is said to come *a parte orientis* when discoursing with Solomon on his throne.

The name Marculf is Germanic, and Latin Marculfus and Marcolfus are normal Latinizations of the Germanic name. The native Germanic name is in origin a combination of *mark*, 'borderland,' and *wulf;* cf. *JEGP*, xxxvii (1918), 352, and M. Schönfeld, *Wörterbuch der altgermanischen Personen- und Völkernamen*, pp. 161–162. It appears frequently in Frankish territory on the continent, and its rare and late appearance in England (*Domesday Book*, Suffolk, 373b, 450) may show that it is borrowed from either Old Danish or the continent (T. Forssner, *Continental-Germanic Personal Names in England* [Uppsala, 1916], p. 287; O. von Feilitzen, *The Pre-Conquest Personal Names of the Domesday Book* [Uppsala, 1937], p. 325). The origin of the Germanic name Marculf is not of great importance in the case of the legendary Marculf of 180b and the Latin dialogues, since there can hardly be any doubt that both Marculf and Marcolfus are equivalents and substitutes for *Marc(h)olus* (Morcholus), the deity identified with Saturn by Aethicus. Marcolus in turn is Hebrew Markolis, itself derived from Latin Mercurius (for details, see Introduction, pp. 31–32). Marculf-Marcolfus-Marcolus-Markolis-Mercurius, as a legendary semi-demonic figure, is to be equated with the opponent or rival of Solomon who appears in Solomonic literature as Saturn, Kitovras, or Ashmedai (for details, see Introduction, pp. 22–23, 31–33). On the possible connection with the *Weallende Wulf*, 204, see the note on lines 203ff.

182. Geallbōe is the Vulgate *Gelboa*, Mount Gilboa, the scene of Saul's death (i Sam. xxxi, 1). *Geador* is probably Gadara to the northeast of Gilboa on the other side of the Jordan. One would expect a long syllable in *Geador* for a proper B-type half-line.

183b. fæsten Crēca. One of the two *Crēca* (cf. 186b) was probably *Crēta* 'Cretans' (so Holthausen in *Sprachschatz*^{2}, s.v. *Crēcas*).

184b. wæter Māthea[n] (MS *Mathea*). Holthausen suggested *Matheanes*, correctly equating the word with the Vulgate Madian, the country of the Midianites. The *a* of *Máthèan* may have been lengthened in Old English, since the length of the antipenultimate vowel varies in Biblical trisyllables (Luick, § 219; Hüttenbrenner, *Angl. Beibl.*, xxviii [1917], 47–51). *Māthean* or *Matheana* 'of the Midianites' (see the Latin forms below) seems a more likely emendation paleographically than *Matheanes*. The land of the Midianites, now assumed to be in northwest Arabia, was considered in patristic tradition to be in southern Arabia, near the Red Sea, and hence is fittingly paired with *wudu Ēgipta;* cf. Eusebius-Jerome, *Onomasticon*, ed. Klostermann, p. 125.6: 'Madiam urbs . . . est autem trans Arabiam ad meridiem in deserto Saracenorum contra orientem maris rubri, unde vocantur Madianaei et Madianaea regio.'

185a. clūdas (MS *claudas*) **Coreffes,** 'the rocky cliffs of Horeb.' The emendation to *clūdas*, suggested by Holthausen (*Angl. Beibl.*, xxvii, 354), must be correct, in view of the two lines preceding, and two following, all of which have common nouns with proper names in each half-line. On the spelling *au* for *ū*, cf. the note on *clausum-clūsum*, 71. *Coreffes* is genitive of OE. *Choreb*, Vulgate *Choreb*, not, as Holthausen suggests, a perversion of *Cōferes* (cf. 20, 204). Midian and Horeb are mentioned together in Exodus III, 1, and the *Onomasticon* (p. 173.1) definitely places Horeb near Midian: 'Choreb mons dei in regione Madian iuxta montem Sina super Arabiam in deserto.' *Choreb* occurs in the Old English *Paris Psalter* 105, 17. A genitive *C(h)orebes* might easily give rise to *Corefes* (*Coreffes*) through the pronunciation of medial Latin *b* as *v*.

186b. cynn Arabia. This is a D-type with resolution of *Arab-*. *Arabia* had the chief stress on the first syllable, for the Latin stress is not followed in the anglicization of such names. In the *Paris Psalter* 71, 10, 15 *Arabia* alliterates with vowels.

188b. Buðanasan. This has not been identified and is certainly corrupt. It seems unlikely that it could represent *Byzantium* (Vincenti, p. 66). Perhaps it is a corruption of Lat. *Batanaea*, Gr. *Βαταναία*, the district of Palestine known in the Old Testament as Bashan; cf. Eusebius-Jerome, *Onomasticon*, ed. Klostermann, pp. 6.6, 12.12, 18.6, 44.11, 52.24, etc.

189b. Pōres. The reference is presumably to Porus, the Indian prince who was ruler of the region between the Hydaspes and the Acesines at the time of the invasion of Alexander the Great. Vincenti, p. 66, suggested *Pontus*.

191b. Crīstes [ēþel]. There is no space in the manuscript, but Grein's emendation seems necessary, both because the poet never uses a person's name directly with another proper name but always with some general word (*Marculfes eard* 180b, *Saulus rīce* 181a, *Pōres gemǣre* 189b), and because if *Hierycho* followed directly after *Crīstes* as part of 192b, *Galilēa* would be too short for a half-line by itself (cf. *Christ and Satan* 522, 525, 529), and too long if combined with *Hiērusālem* as a half-line.

192a. An extended D-type.

192b. Hiērusā[lem]. One may compare 226b, where *Hiērusālem* likewise forms a half-line by itself, and *Paris Psalter* 121, 3; elsewhere it is usually accompanied by a preposition, e.g. *Elene* 273, 1055; *Paris Psalter* 164, 1, etc., and the first syllable then is short. On the stress and length of vowel see Sievers, *Zum angelsächsischen Vokalismus*, pp. 6–7; Hüttenbrenner, *Angl. Beibl.*, XXVIII, 53–54. *Hiērusālem* alliterates with both *Hierycho* and *Galilēa;* cf. 226, *Christ* 533, *Paris Psalter* 164, 1.

193b–194. oððe ic swīgie / nyttes hycgge, ðēah ic nō spr(e)c(e). The page immediately preceding (p. 14) has been erased and written over, and the first line of p. 15, which has been chemically treated, is almost illegible. The text represents Pope's reading, though MS *nó* might be *ne*, and only *spr.c.* of *sprece* is visible. The difficulty of reading the first line of p. 15 is attested by the attempts of editors and collators. Kemble: 'oððe ic stigie, nyttes bicge, ðeah . . .'; Schipper: 'oððe ic stigie nyttes bycgge ðeah . . . ic . . .'; Assmann: 'oððe ic stigie, nyttes [b]ycgge: ðeah . . . ic s[pr] . . .' Vincenti's translation (p. 67) shows that he had apparently read *swīgie* and *hycgge*, which Holthausen also suggests by emendation in the following arrangement (*Angl. Beibl.*, XXVII, 354): oððe ic swīgie, / nyttes [h]ycgge, ðēah [nāht] ic spr[ece]. It is to be noted that Pope reads *nó* where Schipper, Zupitza, and Assmann read *ic*, but sees *ic* immediately between *ðeah* and *nó*. The meaning is evidently that Solomon will answer Saturn's riddling question if he can, or 'keep silent, think of something useful, though I speak not at all.' But if he fails to answer (*ðonne*, 195) he is well aware that Saturn will return home to boast of his victory (195–198a).

196b. seccan. Kemble and Schipper read *sēcean*. For the form *seccan*, see Luick, § 669.

198a. forcumen and forcȳððed. Cf. 503a, and Introduction, p. 11, on the rarity of the Anglian *forcuman*.

198b–202. The reference here is to the pride and insolence of the Chaldeans in erecting the Tower of Babel on the field of Shinar (Gen. XI, 1–9), for which, the poet tells us with typical *litotes*, an admonition (*moning*, 200) befell them; cf. lines 318–322. Since the builder of the Tower was generally reputed to be Nimrod in medieval tradition, a connection having been made in Jewish legend between the mighty man Nimrod (Gen. X, 9–10), and the builders of the Tower (Gen. XI, 1–9), Solomon's question about the land which no man may tread (209b–210) was really suggested by his reference to the Tower of Babel; for Saturn's answer shows that Nimrod has a connection with the waste land. See note on 203ff.

199a. gūðe ðæs gielpne. The meaning must be that the Chaldeans, Saturn's ancestors, were 'thus boastful in warfare' (that is, boastful in the same manner or to the same degree as Saturn, at the place) where the warning befell them to the south on the field of Shinar (that is, where they tried to build the Tower of Babel). For somewhat comparable uses of *ðæs* with backward reference, cf. *Jul.* 513, *Beow.* 968, 1509, *Gifts of Men* 17; but in all these cases a following *ðæt*-clause seems to be implied, and since in the overwhelming majority of cases *ðæs*, 'so, to such a degree,' is followed by *ðæt* (twenty instances in the *Sprachschatz*[2], s.v. *ðæt*, gen. sg. *ðæs*) it may be that *ðǣr* (200) is an error for *ðæt;* cf. *Gen.* 823–833, *Beow.* 1366, *Seafarer* 39–41.

203ff. This passage is the most obscure in the poem. Textual difficulties will be discussed in notes on the lines in which they occur. To account for the waste land Saturn tells of a dragon-combat in which a famous hero called raging (or wandering) Wolf, known to the Philistines, and a friend of Nimrod, slew twenty-five dragons at dawn only to die himself. The site of this battle is the deserted land that men and cattle cannot visit nor even the birds fly over. From it all kinds of poisons, or poisonous creatures, spread over the earth.

Accepting line 205 (see note, below) as textually correct, one might adduce as a parallel to the story of Nimrod and his friend the Wolf the Babylonian epic of the mighty hunter Gilgamesh and his friend Enkidu, a strange *Tiermensch,* who abandons his life with animals and conquers various demonic creatures, only to die himself; (see A. Schott, *Das Gilgamesch-Epos* (Leipzig, 1934). No extant version of the Nimrod legend seems to reflect this particular legend, but it is quite possible that the Gilgamesh-Enkidu theme appeared in some lost story of the Nimrod cycle, since Nimrod, the mighty hunter of Genesis x, 8–9, bears a close resemblance to Gilgamesh and has actually been equated with him mythologically by modern students (A. Jeremias, *The Old Testament in the light of the Ancient East* [New York, 1911], I, 288–290; S. D. H. Langdon, *Mythology of All Races: Semitic,* p. 55).

The connection of Nimrod with a gigantomachia such as is here described can be understood only in the light of the Christian legends about him, which were based on earlier Jewish legends and interpretations of Genesis X, XI. For the Jewish legends see the excellent account in Ginzberg, *Legends of the Jews* I, 177–180, cited by me in *JEGP,* XXXVII (1938), 335–336. Nimrod, who had been called γίγας in the Septuagint, was considered the first tyrant and rebel, the founder of Babylonia, and the builder of the Tower of Babel (Josephus, *Antiquities of the Jews* I, 4.2; Augustine, *De Civitate Dei* XVI, 4; Orosius II, 6; Isidore, *Etymologiae* VII, 6.22). Nimrod was called a giant by Philo, Augustine, and Orosius (Philo, *On the Giants* XV; Aug., *De Civitate Dei* XVI, 11; Oros. II, 6). Ælfric was simply following the usual Christian tradition in saying that 'Nembroð and ðā entas worhton þone wundorlīcan stȳpel æfter Nōes flōd' (A. Napier, *Wulfstan,* p. 105). In Greek writings the builders of the Tower were naturally identified with the Titans (Eusebius, *Chron.* I, 4; I, 8: *Pat. Gr.,* XIX, 116, 123; cf. *Oracula Sibyllina,* III, 97–154, ed. Geffken; a tradition that appears again in the Alfredian *Boethius,* ed. Sedgefield, pp. 98ff.; and in Dante, *Inferno* XXXI, 46–81, where Nimrod is condemned with Briareus and Ephialtes). Nimrod the giant and founder of cities also plays an important role in the Syriac *Cave of Treasures,* where he is the pupil of Jonton in astrology (C. Bezold, *Die Schatzhöhle* [Leipzig, 1883], pp. 31–36; cf. A. Goetze, *Sitzungsberichte der Heidelberger Akad., Phil.-hist. Kl.* XIII [1922], 4.59–65, on the Nimrod passages, and *Zeitschrift für Semitistik* II [1923], 51–98; III, 53–71; 153–177). In the Samaritan *Asatir,* Nimrod is involved in the wars of the nations, which began after the destruction of the Tower (ed. Moses Gaster [London, 1927], Chaps. V–VI, pp. 234–248; cf. Gaster's notes and comment on Nimrod, Introduction, esp. pp. 14–42). It is important to note further that according to Jewish legend the surviving builders of the Tower were turned into sprites, apes, and demons (Ginzberg, *Legends of the Jews,* I, 108; V, 204, note 88, citing the Midrash Haggada on Genesis XI, 8); the site of the Tower never lost its peculiar quality, whoever passed it forgetting all he knew (Ginzberg, I, 108, V, 104).

Though none of the figures in these various legends of Nimrod is easily equated with the Wolf here described, two explanations of the story here told have been suggested. M. R. James thought that the Wolf might be a reminiscence of Og the giant, because of the lost work described as 'Book of Og the giant who is said by the heretics to have fought with a dragon after the Flood' (*Lost Apocrypha of the Old Testament* [London, 1920], pp. 40–42). This *Liber de Ogia* is condemned in the so-called Gelasian decree of the sixth century (E. von Dobschütz, *Das Decretum Gelasianum, Texte und Untersuchungen zur Geschichte der altchristlichen Literatur* XXXVIII, 4 [Leipzig, 1912], p. 12). It is true that Og is connected with Nimrod in certain Jewish legends, being said to have been given to Abraham by Nimrod (Ginzberg, *Legends of the Jews*, III, 343–348, and notes VI, 118–121), but the resemblance to the extant stories of Og is only a vague one.

Another explanation was presented by me in a long article, which the reader should consult for details, called 'Nimrod and the Wolf in the Old English *Solomon and Saturn*,' *JEGP*, XXXVII (1938), 332–354. This was that the story of Wolf is a confused reminiscence of the Babylonian creation myth of Bel-Marduk as told by Greek writers. Bel destroyed the dragon of chaos, creating heaven and earth, and cut off his own head to form men and beasts. The account given by Berossus, priest of Marduk, is cited by Eusebius of Caesaraea (ca. 260–340 A.D.) in his *Chronicle* and repeated by Syncellus ca. 800 (P. Schnabel, *Berossus und die Babylonisch-Hellenistische Literatur* [Leipzig and Berlin, 1923]; for the Armenian version of Eusebius, the Greek not being preserved, see J. Karst, *Die griechischen christlichen Schriftssteller der ersten drei Jahrhunderte* XX [Leipzig, 1911]; for Syncellus, W. Dindorf, *Corpus Scriptorum Historiae Byzantinae* XIX, 52–53). Bel seems a better candidate than Og as the ancestor of the dragon-killing Wolf, first because he himself was killed, and secondly, because he is constantly connected with Nimrod as a substitute for him in the story of the Tower, or as his son, or most commonly of all as the father of Ninus, who is identified with Nimrod. In Pseudo-Eupolemos the story of the Tower is told of Bel (*Pat. Gr.*, XXI, 709), and the Armenian chronicler Moses of Chorene identifies the two: 'Nimrod, that is to say Bel' (V. Langlois, *Collections des historiens . . . de l'Arménie* I [Paris, 1867], p. 387). In Orosius II, 6, Nimrod the giant began to build Babylon and his son Ninus helped to finish it, Nimrod thus being substituted for Bel as the father of Ninus. Ninus is usually, however, the son of Bel, as in Eusebius-Jerome (*Chronici Canones*, ed. J. K. Fotheringham [London, 1923], p. 11) and many other writers, and Ninus is frequently identified with Nimrod, in the Clementine *Recognitions* and the *Chronicon Paschale*, for example (*Pat. Gr.*, I, 1327; XCII, 125). It would thus be very easy for a story told of Bel to become connected with the legend of Nimrod.

Following up a suggestion of Kemble's (p. 131) that *Weallende Wulf* might refer to *Marculf*, I pointed out (*JEGP*, XXXVII, 348–354) that since Bel is often identified with Kronos-Saturn, for example by Isidore (*Etym.*, VIII, 11; *Pat. Lat.*, XXIV, 420), and Marculf is Saturn's *alter ego*, it would be possible for Bel's story to be transferred to Marculf, which might be interpreted as 'wolf of the marches' and hence 'wandering wolf'; this conjecture would be sounder if it were certain that *weallende* meant 'wandering' (see the next note).

204a. Weallende Wulf. It seems a little safer to accept *weallende* as meaning 'raging' from *weallan*, 'boil, seethe' with Bosworth-Toller (s.v. *weallan* vii) and the *Sprachschatz*[2], in view of the gloss *weallende* 'furibundus' (Wright-Wülker, *Anglo-Saxon and Old English Vocabularies* I, 404.41), rather than assume *weallende*, 'wandering' from *weallian* (cf. line 22) as did Kemble and Vincenti (p. 69), *weallende* being then interpreted as an Anglian form for *wealliende*. *Weallende* in 212 is ambiguous since it might be either 'wandering' or 'swarming,' 'seething.' *Weallende*, 'wandering,' cannot, however, be certainly excluded. It makes an admirable variant of *mere-līðende* (203), and *Weallende Wulf* would be a good interpretation of the name *Marculf*, 'wolf of the marches' (see the end of the preceding note). It should be noted that the dragon-slayer 'was called' (*was hāten*) a sea-faring 'Weallende Wulf,' as though this were a name. On the Wolf and Woden, see 211a note.

205a. Filistīna. *Filistīna* is elsewhere in the poem *Fīlistīna*, and is always combined with another word to form half-line combinations of the E-type: *Fīlistīna flet* (183), *Fīlistīna fruma(n)* (269, 272), *Fīlistīna witan* (422); or D-type: *witan Fīlistīna* (249); or C-type: *on Fīlistīna* (246). It was therefore suggested by F. Hüttenbrenner (*Angl.*, XXVIII, 52–53) that the line is imperfect and should be read *Fīlistīna [fruma], frēond Nebrondes.* This suggestion is not unreasonable, but opens up other possibilities. If my conjecture that the creation-myth of Bel is reflected in the passage has any validity, one might, remembering that Bel is commonly represented as the father of Nimrod (cf. note on 203ff.), assume that the line read originally *Fīlistīna fruma, [fæder] Nebrondes.* With either emendation, a comma would have to be placed after *cūð* 204b. For further comment on this speculation see *JEGP*, XXXVII, 342–343, 348–351.

Nimrod is involved in wars with the Philistines in the Samaritan *Asatir* v, 11 (trans. M. Gaster, p. 240). The *Asatir*, which mentions two Nimrods, likewise remarks that the second was from the Caphtorim VI, 3 (p. 248). The Philistines are said in the Bible to be from Caphtor (Amos IX, 7, Jer. XLVII, 4; cf. Gen. X, 6, 13, 14). The Caphtorim are identified with the Philistines by the author of the Book of Jubilees XXIV, 30, and by both medieval and modern commentators (R. A. S. Macalister, *The Philistines* [London, 1914], pp. 4–14). Another connection between Nimrod and the Philistines is that in Jewish legend both were considered gigantic Anakim or Nephilim (Ginzberg, I, 151; M. Grünbaum, *Zeitschrift der deutschen morgenländischen Gesellschaft*, XXXI (1877), 229, 233–234; on the Philistines, see Jer. XLVII, 5, and Introduction, pp. 60–61).

205b. Nebrondes. The form of Nimrod's name is neither the Vulgate *Nemrod* nor the Greek Νεβρώδ. Many spellings appear in Old English, *Nembroð* in Ælfric's homily *De Falsis Deis* (ed. Napier, *Wulfstan*, p. 105), *Nebroð*, *Gen.* 1628, *Nefrod*, Alfred's *Boethius*, ed. Sedgefield, p. 99.6, 7, 8), the last two of which together with *Nebro(n)des*, M. Förster attributes to Old Irish influence, OIr. *Nebrūad* < **Nebrōd* with *d* pronounced *ð* (*Kel-*

tisches Wortgut im Altenglischen, pp. 56–57, repr. from Liebermann *Festgabe*, Halle, 1921).

207b. MS ⁊ *hine ðā of deað offeoll.* Grein suggested omitting *of* and emending to *onfēoll;* and the *Sprachschatz*[2] assumes *oferfēoll* or *onfēoll*, but the form *offeallan* seems sufficiently established in the meaning 'fall upon,' 'destroy'; cf. *B-T.* and *Suppl.*, s.v. *offeallan.*

208ff. The desert is the abode of demons in Jewish legends and in Oriental folk-lore generally (cf. Is. XIII, 21–22, XXXIV, 13–14; Jer. II, 6, IX, 11; Ps. XLIV, 19, and Oesterley, 'Demonology of the Old Testament,' *Expositor* 7, ser. III (1907), 316–332, 533). For the land that no one may visit compare such a description as that of Jer. XLIX, 33: 'And Hazor shall be a dwelling for dragons and a desolation for ever: there shall no man abide there, nor any son of man dwell in it.' To the additional detail that not even a bird may fly over this deserted land (210) a parallel may be found in the Jewish legend that Azza and Azzael are chained in a spot 'which no one, not even a bird may visit' (Ginzberg, *Legends of the Jews*, IV, 150, from the *Zohar* III, 233a–233b [Leghorn, 1866]); this is the mountain of darkness in the Book of Enoch X, 4–5. Cf. Ælfric's description in St. Bartholomew's exorcism of Ashtaroth: 'far tō wēstenne, þǣr nān fugel ne flȳhð, nē ierðling ne erað, nē mannes stemn ne swēgð' (*Cath. Hom.*, I, 464).

210b. nē ðon mā. 'Nor even more,' that is, it is even more impossible for the cattle to visit this land than for birds to fly over it.

211a. ātercynn. Kemble translated 'the poisonous race,' but the dictionaries take the word to mean 'kinds of poison,' which is perhaps more probable in view of the analogy of similar nominal compounds with *-cynn*. It has been suggested that this is parallel to Woden's slaying of the serpent in the Old English *Nine-Herbs Charm* (Grendon, pp. 191–195), and the consequent scattering of poisons (E. A. Phillippson, *Germanisches Heidentum bei den Angelsachsen*, pp. 88–89; cf. C. Singer, *Early Magic and Medicine*, pp. 13ff.). In this case the Wolf might have become identified with Woden; cf. Kemble, p. 131.

In Oriental legends poisonous exhalations are supposed to rise above the site of Sodom, as in Wisdom X, 7, where it is called a smoking waste (cf. M. Grünbaum, *Zeitschrift der deutschen morgenländischen Gesellschaft*, XXXI [1877], 236–237, 326, comparing the place of the punishment of giants). If *ātercynn* could mean 'poisonous races,' the scattering of the evil brood of the builders of the Tower might have been the starting-point of this part of the story; cf. note on 203ff., p. 122, bottom, and *JEGP*, XXXVII, 340–342. In any case, similar descriptions of the site of the Tower persisted, as in Lydgate's *Fall of Princes* 1135–48, where it is said to be the chief habitation of serpents and dragons, and so 'venomous' and horrible that no man dare approach it. This description is ultimately based on Rev. XVIII, 2, where Babylon is a 'habitation of devils,' Babel and Babylon having been regularly identified.

214. For the magic shining of the sword over the grave, one may compare *Beowulf* 1558ff., where the light in the hall seems to come from the *ealdsweord eotenisc* 1557, and the gleaming of weapons in the *Fight at Finnsburg* 3–5. The magic shining of swords and the light from the dead are reflected in such ballads as Sir Aldingar and Young Lamkin (cf. F. B. Gummere, *The Popular Ballad*, p. 303; L. C. Wimberly, *Folklore in the English and Scottish Ballad* [Chicago, 1928], pp. 82, 92).

216ff. On this and other gnomic passages, see Introduction, pp. 65f. For *dol bið*, cf. *Seafarer* 106: 'Dol biþ sē þe him his dryhten ne ondrǣdeþ'; *Exeter Gnomes* 35: 'Dol biþ sē þe his dryhten nāt.' Vincenti (p. 65) thought that this passage was an allusion to the Wolf's folly in venturing into danger and finding death.

221ff. Saturn's riddle on the dumb one who rests in a vale (that is, a cover) is obviously a book, as Solomon's answer shows: *bēc sindon brēme* (229a). It is a book by which one may be brought to see the walls of the golden Jerusalem (presumably the Heavenly Jerusalem) and its cross (226–228), and therefore a Christian book of some sort. The fact that it has seven tongues, each tongue twenty points, and each point the power to bring us to Jerusalem, is unfortunately not so helpful a description to us as it apparently was to Solomon. Vincenti suggested (p. 69) that the poet refers to the book of seven seals of Rev. v, and that each seal probably had twenty leaves. Vincenti compares (p. 69, note 1) a Solomonic book of magic for summoning demons, condemned by Pope Innocent VI (cf. Migne, *Dictionnaire des Apocryphes* II, 843); and it may be worth noting that at least one manuscript (Sloane 3885) of the *Liber sacer Salomonis* or *Liber Juratus*, mentioned by William of Auvergne in the thirteenth century, describes it as 'ex septem voluminibus artis magicae compilatus' (Lynn Thorndike, *History of Magical and Experimental Science*, II, 281, note 3, and 285–289). Seven is so common a mystic number, however, that this may be pure accident. Another possibility is that the book is the Pater Noster, whose seven petitions are expounded from Augustine to Ælfric (cf. Introduction, p. 37). The twenty points (*twēntig orda*) might possibly refer to the sort of palm-branched Pater Noster described in Poem I; cf. *tuigena ordum* 142b (143a note) and the description of the Pater Noster, which is declared to be *seofan snytro* (66), as each point is here declared to have *engles snytro*. This part of the description would simply be a fantastic way of expressing the power of the Pater Noster, as in Poem I and the prose dialogue (cf. Appendix). It is hard to see how the description could apply to the Bible as a whole; cf. *Exeter Riddles* 27, 68, both of which have sometimes been considered Bible riddles. On the riddle as characteristic of the poem, cf. Introduction, pp. 57–58, 64–65.

227b. winrōd. The half-line is metrically difficult; perhaps *and hiera* should be omitted. Because of the metre and the absence of the expected fem. acc. sg. ending in *-e*, Holthausen (*Angl.*, XXIII, 124) first proposed *wuldọr* and later (*Angl. Beibl.*, XXVII, 355) *wundọr*, suggesting a series of errors: *wundor* > *wunrod* > *winrod*. But the parallel *sōðfæstra segn* of the next half-line leads one to expect a definite rather than an abstract word for Cross; cf. *Elene* 894: *wuldres wynbēam*. On the possibility that *winrōd* is a Northumbrian fem. sg., see Introduction, p. 20, note 15.

228b. saga hwæt ic mǣne! On the formulas for beginning and ending a riddle, cf. Introduction, pp. 64f.

228ff. For similar comments on the power of books, compare *Exeter Riddle* 27 (and Tupper's excellent note on 18f.), and further Tatwine 5.6, Aldhelm 59.7–8 (ed. Ehwald).

236. Cf. *Exeter Riddle* 27.17–18.

238a. wīse, 'thing.' Mistakenly read *wīsa*, except by Pope and Dobbie.

240b. ðurh dēop gesceaft. Cf. 385, and Introduction, p. 63.

244ff. The bird Vasa Mortis here described is a demon-god of the Philistines. Solomon's remark (266ff.) that he alone discovered this creature and ordered him to be bound shows clearly that the passage is an inheritance from the Hebrew legend of Solomon's binding of the demon Ashmedai, which likewise appears in the Greek *Testament of Solomon;* cf. Introduction, pp. 59–60, and my article on this passage in [Klaeber] *Studies in Philology*, pp. 240–253. The demon seems to be a fusion of Ashmedai-Asmodeus (or some other demon of Solomonic legend), Dagon, the fish-god of the Philistines, I Sam. 5 (cf. 255b note), and the griffon. Strange griffons and bird-like demons were thought to inhabit Oriental lands. One may compare the griffon of the *Wonders of the East:* 'Ðonne is sum dūn Adamans hātte, on ðǣre dūne bið þæt fugelcynn þe Griphus hātte. Þā fugelas habbað fēower fēt and hryðeres tægl and earnes hēafod' (Fr. Knapp, *Die Wunder des Osten* [Berlin, 1906], p. 63); and the bird Hiruath of India in the Irish *Evernew Tongue* (ed. W. Stokes, *Ériu*, II, 120–121).

247a–248b. The mountain may possibly be a reminiscence of the 'mountains of darkness' where Solomon visited the chained fallen angels Azza and Azzael (Ginzberg, *Legends of the Jews*, IV, 149–150, citing *Zohar* III, 233a–233b [Leghorn, 1866]), or the mountain where Asmodeus dwelt (Ginzberg, IV, 166, from the *Tractate Gittin*). The mountain of darkness appears in the Book of Enoch XVII, 7; cf. Jer. XIII, 16.

249b. wēnað ðæs ðe nāht is. 'Expect that which is not (i.e. not true).' Vincenti suggested as an alternative (p. 70, note), 'sie glauben, dass in der Nacht ein fremdes Volk ihn rauben möchte,' which implies that MS *ðe naht* is an error for *ðā neaht* (or Angl. *næht*); cf. 252, where it is said that the guards watch Vasa Mortis 'every night.' One would, however, expect a stronger verb than *is* in this case, and it is safer to let the text stand, though the reason for the remark is unknown to us.

250–251a. 'That the whole people should snatch him (*hine*) away from them (*him . . . on*).' For the construction cf. *Gen*. 1207–09: 'þonne him God heora ǣhta . . . on genimeð'' and *Christ* 580. Vincenti's implied emendation (p. 70, note: 'ein fremdes Volk') to *elþēod* (or more probably *ælþēod*), 'a hostile people,' from *eall þēod* is very tempting. Although the manuscript is perfectly clear, Kemble, followed by Grein, omitted 248b–250 entirely, presumably because he could make no sense of the passage.

251b. 'They know a means of protection against that.'

253b. tū hund wearda. If the number has any significance it may go back ultimately to the two hundred 'watchers' (Greek ἐγρήγορες, Latin *vigiles*, in Dan. IV, 17 [Vulg. 14]), who in the Ethiopic Book of Enoch X, 4–5 are the fallen angels. The two hundred watchers could easily have been mentioned in some account of Solomon's visit to the mountains of darkness where they and their leaders are bound (cf. note on 247a–248b), and 'watchers' might have been interpreted to mean 'guardians' of one of their leaders. For details see [Klaeber] *Studies in Philology*, pp. 249–252.

254b. fēower hēafdu. Vincenti (p. 71) compares the beast in Dan. VII, 6: 'Et ecce alia quasi pardus, et alas habebat quasi avis, quattuor super se, et quattuor capita erant in bestia.' For similar many-headed monsters and demons formed from various parts of beasts and men, cf. the *Testament of Solomon, passim.*

255b. hwælen, 'like a whale,' 'made of a whale,' unrecorded elsewhere; but cf. *gǣten*, 'of goats.' This is probably a reminiscence of the tradition that Dagon, god of the Philistines, was a fish-god; Jerome defines Dagon *piscis tristitiae* (*Pat. Lat.*, XXIII, 1218). On Dagon, see *Jewish Ency.* and Macalister, *The Philistines* (London, 1911), p. 100: 'The current idea is that he was of merman form, the upper half man, the lower half fish.' A connection between Asmodeus, the demon bound by Solomon, and Dagon may have been established through the tradition recorded in the *Testament of Solomon* V, 10 that Asmodeus worshipped a fish Glanos or Glanis, and the exorcising of Asmodeus in Tobit VI, VII by means of the gall, heart, and liver of a fish. The fishy element in the Philistine demon makes Kock's emendation to *swǣ lēon* 'like a lion' unnecessary (*Jubilee Jaunts and Jottings*, p. 68).

256a. gēowes, 'of a vulture.' *Gēow* is a form of *gīw;* cf. Wright-Wülker, *Vocabularies* II, 41.3–4: 'giú, gripem; giú, griphus.' Kock's suggestion of *gēoþes*, cf. OIcel. *gjóðr*, 'sea-eagle' (*Jubilee Jaunts and Jottings*, p. 68) is unnecessary. Kemble's reading *hīwes* is one of his silent emendations, the manuscript being perfectly clear. Beginning the line with *hwælan* he read 'hwælan hiwes; hē hafað fiðeru.' This left 'and griffus fēt' an incomplete line, which Grein filled out by adding [se grimma fugol].

262b. longað. The *o* is ill formed, but resembles *o* rather than *e*, previously read. This disposes of the ghost-word *lengian*.

263–264. Frequent references appear in apocalyptic literature to demons or fallen angels that are bound until Doomsday. In Rev. XX, 2–3, the dragon, which is Satan, is bound for a thousand years, the period of the Messianic kingdom, and then 'loosed for a little season,' and in the Ethiopic Book of Enoch X, 12 the fallen angels are bound fast in the valleys of the earth 'until the day of Judgment.' Later, in both cases, the demons are to be cast forever into the lake or abyss of fire, but the fate of the fallen angels after Doomsday is not always expressly stated, in the Book of

Jubilees v, 10, for example. It is not quite clear whether the Vasa Mortis longs for Doomsday because he will be loosed a little season, or because complete destruction will then end his misery; for the second fate cf. the Old Saxon *Genesis* 147, where Antichrist is destroyed, *aldru bilōsid*. There are many mythological parallels, for example, the evil serpent Azi-Dahâka, in the Zend religion, who is fettered in the mountain for 9000 years and then released to reign for 1000 (*Zend-Avesta*, tr. L. H. Mills, *Sacred Books of the East* IV, 9 (note), 226, 245ff., V, 233–235, V, 150).

264. Cf. 317.

265ff. Solomon's explanation that he alone discovered the demon, and commanded him to be put in chains, so that the brave son of Melot bound him, seems curiously complicated, but is clarified by reference to the Hebrew legend on which it is based. According to this, Solomon, who has power over demons through his magic ring, is told by them that Asmodeus, king of the demons, is in possession of the secret of the dwelling-place of the *shamir*, a precious stone, which Solomon needs in the building of the Temple. The demons reveal to Solomon the name of the mountain where Asmodeus dwells (cf. note on 247a–248). Thereupon, 'Solomon sent his chief man, Benaiah, the son of Jehoiada, to capture Asmodeus. For this purpose he provided him with a chain. . . . Benaiah, watching him from a tree, then came and drew the chain about Asmodeus's neck.' (Ginzberg, IV, 166–167 citing the *Tractate Gittin;* cf. Introduction, pp. 22ff., 59ff.) Melot is here the intermediary who replaces Benaiah.

268b. Mēlotes. One may compare the name Mellothi, son of Heman, mentioned in I Chron. XXV, 4, 26 (Holthausen, *Angl. Beibl.*, XXVII, 355).

272b. Vāsa Mortis. The name is derived from the Vulgate Psalms VII, 14 (13): 'Et in eo paravit vasa mortis, sagittas suas ardentibus effecit.' Origen thought that this passage referred to the Devil, and interprets the *vasa mortis* or *σκεύη θανάτου* as unclean spirits or souls having death (*Pat. Gr.*, XII, 1181). The use of the phrase *vasa mortis* by Agrippa of Nettesheim (*De Occulta Philosophia* III, 18 [ed. Paris, 1567], p. 360) and other sixteenth-century demonologists to describe the third of the nine orders of devils, shows the persistence of this interpretation. Possibly the poet's curious use of the plural *vasa* as a singular arose from a traditional description of an *order* of demons by means of the term *vasa mortis*, which the poet or his predecessor mistakenly applied to the leader or chief representative of his class, Asmodeus-Dagon. Belial is leader of the third order in Agrippa, but Asmodeus is leader of the fourth. For details see [Klaeber] *Studies in Philology*, pp. 252–254.

273a. Ac hwæt is ðæt wundor. Cf. the introductory 'Hvat er þat undra,' of the riddles of Odin (*Hervarar Saga*, pp. 60–80, ed. Helgason), and Introduction, pp. 64–65. The subject of Old Age, *Yldo*, in Solomon's answer (283), was not treated as a riddle by the Anglo-Saxons either in Latin or Old English, and the riddles of the Greeks on Old Age and Time are entirely different.

288. stande[nd]ne, MS *standene*. The line continues the previous one. Old Age has destroyed the tree and broken its branches (287), and it now 'moves in its progress the standing trunk, fells it to the earth.' If one read *sīde* with Rieger for *sīðe* the line would mean 'moves the standing trunk on its side.' The line has caused much unnecessary difficulty. Kemble took *standene* to be *stāndene*, translating 'in the stony nest,' and Wyatt (*Anglo-Saxon Reader*, p. 283) translates 'it moves the upstanding prow on its journey,' in spite of Bosworth-Toller's correct citation, s.v. *stefn, stemn*. The scribe may have written *standene* for *standenne*, a possible phonetic variant of *standendne;* cf. *selerǣdenne* for *selerǣdende, Beow.* 51; Malone on *-rǣdenne, Beow.* 1142 (*JEGP*, xxv, 158); and, for the disappearance of the middle of three consonants, Bülbring, § 533; Luick, § 677.

289b–290. Grein and Assmann, following Kemble, took *wildne fugol* to be the object of *friteð*, but there is no point to *æfter ðām* unless the passage means that Old Age topples over the tree-trunk and devours it 'afterwards,' thus completing its destruction. This necessitates taking *wildne fugol* with what follows, but the word-order of the MS (*wildne fugol hēo oferwīgeð wulf*), as well as the double alliteration in the second half-line, causes difficulties. I have adopted Rieger's arrangement in the text, but there is probably a more radical error in the manuscript. Pope suggests that the division should be:

wildne fugol hēo oferwīgeð, wulf hē oferbīdeð,
stānas hē oferstīgeð, stȳle hēo abīteð.

This would put the double alliteration in the first half-line, but *oferwīgeð* seems to go more fittingly with the wolf than with the bird.

291. The metre would be improved if one adopted Pope's reading (see the previous note) or read: 'Stȳle hēo oferstīgeð, stānas (hēo) oferbīdeð,' following Rieger's reading recorded in the textual notes.

297b. oferbricgęð. Pope's reading disposes of Kemble's ghost-word *oferhrægeð*, followed by Grein and Assmann, and still in the dictionaries.

299–300. After *rēafað*, the last word of MS A, p. 18, a leaf is missing; cf. Introduction, p. 2, and note on line 389b, for the missing conjugate leaf. The omission here was not noted by Kemble, Grein, or Assmann, presumably because some kind of sense can actually be made by connecting *rēafað* with 300. The omission is certain, nevertheless, first, because *rēafað swīðor micle*, with alliteration on *sw*, is not an acceptable half-line; secondly, because the beginning of two successive speeches by the heading *Sāturnus cwæð* (before 293 and 303) and the absence of Solomon's answer to Saturn's question indicate an omission; and thirdly, because the omission of the conjugate leaf after 389, where the break in sense is more apparent, confirms the loss here. It seems likely that the enemy stronger than cunning war is death, because death is mentioned in Saturn's speech (304), which may be an answer to a question by Solomon (cf. Vincenti, p. 72).

Since the average number of normal poetic lines on a manuscript page of twenty-three lines is twenty-seven, the two missing conjugate leaves would have contained about 108 lines. If to these are added the twenty-seven lines missing because of the erasure of p. 14 (see the note on lines 193b–194), about 135 lines of Poem II must certainly be lacking. The probable disappearance of a connecting link between lines 496 and 497 (cf. Introduction, pp. 10ff.) would increase the number of missing lines further, perhaps to 150 or over.

302a. The emendation was suggested by Holthausen (*Angl.* XXIII, 124) on the basis of *Gen.* 689: '[se fēond] þe on þā frǣcnan fyrd gefaren hæfde.'

304b. slǣp bið dēaðe gelīcost. A favorite comparison in the Latin dialogues of question and answer: 'Quid est somnus? Mortis imago.' (*Altercatio Hadriani et Epicteti* no. 17, ed. L. W. Daly and W. Suchier, p. 138: *Illinois Studies in Language and Literature* XXIV [Urbana, 1939]; *Disputatio Pippini cum Albino*, ed. W. Wilmanns, *ZfdA*, XIV [1869], 533). This may come from Ovid, *Amores* II.9.41 ('somnus . . . mortis imago'); but the familiar figure of sleep and death as brothers goes back to Homer, *Il.* XIV, 231.

305ff. The familiar comparison of the passing of life and the fading of the leaf is based on such Biblical passages as Is. XL, 6–7; LXIV, 6; cf. *Guth.* 43–46. Vincenti (p. 73) compares the discourse on this theme in *Blickling Homily* V, pp. 57–59, ed. Morris, *EETS*, LVIII.

310a. hȳdað hēahgestrēon. The selfish hoarding of treasure seemed especially despicable to the Old English poets because avarice was condemned both by Christian teaching, which warned against laying up treasures on earth, and by Germanic heroic tradition, which praised the lord's liberality and expressed its scorn for niggardly behavior. For similar sentiments, cf. *Seafarer* 100–102; *Beow.* 1748–52, 2766; and for the Biblical source see especially Ps. XLIX, 6–20.

314ff. The belief that one of the portents of Doomsday would be a flood goes back ultimately to IV Ezra XV, 41; XVI, 12 (II Ezra of the Apocrypha, Authorized Version). The Exeter *Judgment Day* begins with a flood:

> Ðæt gelimpan sceal, þætte lagu flōweð,
> flōd ofer foldan; fēores bið æt ende
> ānra gehwylcum.

According to Pseudo-Bede, later than our poem, 'prima die eriget se mare in altum quadraginta cubitis super altitudines montium' (*Pat. Lat.*, XCIV, 553), and in the Old English account in Vespasian D XIV there are floods on the first and fifteenth days (R. D.-N. Warner, *Early English Homilies*, *EETS*, CLII, 89–91). The flood became one of the traditional fifteen signs of Doomsday after the eleventh century; cf. G. Grau, *Quellen und Verwandtschaften der älteren Germanischen Darstellungen des Jüngsten Gerichts*, [Morsbach's] *Studien zur englischen Philologie*, XXXI (Halle, 1908), Anhang I, pp. 261–280. On the improbability that the reference to the flood necessitates a late tenth-century date see Introduction, pp. 14f.

320b. ðæt worc. The reference is to the building of the Tower of Babel by Saturn's ancestors, the Chaldeans, as was recognized by Vincenti

(p. 73) and O. F. Emerson (*PMLA*, xxi, 909); cf. notes on 198b and 203ff. Solomon tactfully refrains from recalling too precisely the story of the pride and punishment of Saturn's ancestors, and merely urges him not to revert to the evil nature of his mighty forbears.

321b. In Solomon's use of the term *brother* for Saturn, Vogt saw a parallel to the relation of Solomon to Kitrovas, who is Solomon's brother in the Russian folk-songs, and to the similar relation of Solomon and Morolf in the German romance (*Salomon und Markolf*, p. lv). The term *brōðor* here, however, is only the natural mode of address of one prince to another, as was pointed out by Vincenti (p. 91). Saturn never addresses Solomon as brother, but only as lord or king; cf. 323, 361.

322b. in ðā. Pope's reading; previously read *on ðā*.

323b. Salomon cyning. The first half of this line may be regularized metrically if *cyning* is omitted; but cf. 325f., 328b.

325a. Gewurdene wyrda. If the text is correct this must mean 'accomplished fates,' 'fates brought to pass.' One may then compare the collocation of *wyrd* and *(ge)worden* elsewhere, *Dan.* 470, 652; cf. Vincenti (p. 73, note 2), who even considered the phrase an etymological play on words. The curious form *gewurdene* for *gewordene* is paralleled by *gewurden*, past participle, in the prose dialogue written by the same scribe (Appendix, p. 169, line 31). This makes one hesitate to adopt the tempting emendation to *gewundene* proposed by Grein and approved by Sievers. *Gewundene wyrda* could mean 'twisted' or 'woven fates,' and might be defended by the frequent connection of words for weaving and fate; cf. *Rhyming Poem* 70, *Guth.* 1322ff., *Beow.* 97; and A. Wolf, *Die Bezeichnungen für Schicksal in der ags. Dichtersprache* (Breslau, 1919), p. 27.

Solomon's explanation that the ropes of the doomed man are accomplished fates may go back ultimately to the Germanic belief that the doomed warrior is fettered on the battle-field by such goddesses as the valkyrs or *idisi*. In the Eddic *Grimnismál* (36.3), two of the valkyrs are called Hlǫkk and Herfjǫtur, Clanking Chain and Army-Fetter, and in the first of the Old High German Merseburg incantations the *idisi* (OIcel. *dísir*) are apparently summoned to bind the enemy and unbind prisoners (W. Braune, *Althochdeutsches Lesebuch* [Halle, 1911], p. 85; cf. Introduction, p. 63, on the Celtic goddesses of war). But it is plain that Solomon has given a Christian turn to the old belief, for the position of this question between two passages referring to Doomsday (314ff., 327ff.) shows that the fate of the sinful man at Doomsday is also in the poet's mind. The idea that a man may be bound by the ropes or fetters of sin is found in Old English poetry in *Elene* 1243b–44: 'Ic wæs weorcum fāh, / synnum āsǣled, sorgum gewǣled'; cf. *Christ* 736, *Jul.* 350; and is clearly expressed by Ælfric: 'Ānra gehwilc manna is gewriðen mid rāpum his synna' (*Cath. Hom.* i, 208), who is citing Proverbs v, 22: 'Iniquitates suae capiunt impium, et funibus peccatorum suorum constringitur.' Cf. Klaeber, *Anglia* xxxv, 135–136, who cites many passages from Latin writers on the *culpae* or *peccatorum vincula*. Vincenti (p. 73) tried to connect the *four* ropes with *nieht, nēd, sorg, slǣp* in lines

303–304, but this seems very unlikely. Is it possible to explain the number four by the fact that the Devil tempts man in four ways, as is mentioned in line 489? Cf. note on 489. Ælfric refers to the binding of man's soul with devil's ropes 'mid dēoflīcum rāpum' (*Cath. Hom.*, II, 34).

Line 325 seems incomplete. Kemble (printing in half-lines) divided:

Gewurdene wyrda, ðā bēoð
ðā fēowere fǣges rāpas.

Grein and Assmann made the same division of lines, but did not indicate caesural division. Sievers (*PBB*, XII, 480) divided as in the text, considering the two lines metrically irregular, the second being a long half-line of A-type with trisyllabic anacrusis. One suspects, however, that both 324a and 326a are normal A-lines (with *fēow(e)re*), or possibly unusual C-lines: cf. *Exeter Riddles* 37.3: 'hæfde fēowere fēt under wombe.'

328b. The second half of this line is too long, but I can see no solution. One might expect hypermetric lines here in view of the two following, but the words of the manuscript cannot be divided into either short or hypermetric lines. This whole passage 323–328 contains many irregularities; cf. notes on 323b, 325a.

330a. of niehtes wunde. Kemble and Schipper read *sunde*, but Assmann and Pope read *wunde*, as did Zupitza, who remarked that the letter *w* resembles an *s* because the curved down-stroke appears incomplete. Kemble translated 'from the flood of night,' and it is just possible that *sunde* is the proper reading in spite of MS *wunde*, for 'the ocean of night' might be derived from the collocation of *tenebrae* and *aquae* in Gen. I, 2. Retaining the MS reading, and remembering the constant use of the expression *synna wunde* 'the wounds of sin,' 'peccata' (*Christ* 1313, *Jul.* 710, *El.* 514), one might explain the phrase as meaning 'from the sinful state of darkness;' but the figure is too bold, and *Nergend* would hardly be used in the sense of 'the one who saved us.' Holthausen suggested *nīðes wunde* (*Angl. Beibl.*, XXVII, 355). The simplest explanation is that *wunde* is a scribal error for *wambe* or *wombe;* cf. Shakespeare, *Henry V*, Act IV, Prol. 4, and Milton, *Paradise Lost* II, 150. The genitive *niehtes* for *niehte* is not found elsewhere in the poetry, except in the adverb, but the ending in *-s* is found in Northumbrian, for example in the *Lindisfarne Gospels*, Matt. XIV, 25, Luke II, 8 (H. E. A. Carpenter, *Die Deklination in der nordhumbrischen Evangelienübersetzung*, § 455).

330b. hwæt nǣren ðē wǣron, MS *hwæt nærende wæron.* The *nærende* of the manuscript is a puzzle. Kemble translated 'saviours,' assuming that the word was the same as *nergend* in the first half of the line. This would be possible only on the assumption that *nærende* was a Mercian form with *æ* for *e* (and *-ende* for *-iende?*) and that the West Saxon scribe recognized *nergend* (Merc. *nær(i)end?*) as a familiar word in the first half-line, but not in the second. It is difficult, however, to find any connection between 'saviours' and Saturn's speech immediately following. Vincenti (p. 74) tried to bridge this gap by suggesting that the sun (338) was Saturn's indirect answer to Solomon's question 'Who were the saviours from the wound of night?' But it seems unlikely that the poet would permit Saturn to make this suggestion without refutation just after Solomon has explained that the Lord was the Saviour from the 'wound of night.' Grein in his *Sprachschatz*, s.v. ***neom***, takes the word to be a negative present participle of ***wesan***, and is followed by Clark-Hall, though the expected form would be rather ****nesende*** or possibly a Mercian ****næsende***. Some desperate suggestions of Holthausen are recorded in the textual notes.

It is probable that Grein and Clark-Hall were on the right track in connecting ***nærende*** with the verb ***wesan***, even though the participial form is impossible. A solution must satisfy three requirements: (1) that the question in the second half of the line should have some connection with the statement in the first half; (2) that Saturn's following question should show indirectly that he understood the answer to Solomon's question, since it is plain that he makes no direct and obvious answer (cf. Introduction, p. 52 and lines 229ff., 335ff., 342ff., 353ff., 427ff.); and (3) that the question or riddle itself should have a parallel. I suggest that we have hidden in the question the 'shadow' or 'light' riddle, which is itself one of a larger group of 'Quid est, quod est et non est?' puzzles. Alcuin's answer to what is and is not is the echo (*Disputatio Pippini cum Albino*, ed. W. Wilmanns, *ZfdA*, XIV [1869], 542, cf. 555). But in the *Strassburger Rätselbuch*, the answer is the shadow of the sun or a light: 'Etwas ist nichts, und nichts ist etwas. So nun nichts etwas ist, so muss etwas nichts sein. Antwort: der schette von der sonnen oder ein liechts ist ein schein eins dings und doch an ym selbs nichts' (Wilmanns, p. 555). This riddle satisfies the condition that the question should be suggested by what precedes (***niehtes***) and answered indirectly by what follows, for Saturn's mention of the sun, its bright shining and its shadowing (***sunne . . . scīre geondscīnan . . . besceadeð***, 331–332) shows that he is aware of the correct answers: 'shadow of the sun' or 'light.' This would be much more characteristic of the style of the dialogue than an awkward repetition of ***nergend***. The original may have read ***hwæt nǣren ðe wǣron*** (or ***wǣren***), 'what (sort of things) might not exist that (yet) would exist?' Other possibilities would be ***hwæt nesende wǣre(n)***, 'what not being, might be (for ***nǣre*** and ***wǣre*** in the same line, cf. *Metres of Boethius* XX, 103) or, more improbably, ***hwæt næron*** [***nearon***] ***ðe earon***, 'what things are not that are?' For ***næron*** one may compare *Seafarer* 82–83 (Krapp-Dobbie): 'næron nū cyningas nē cāseras / nē goldgiefan swylce iū wǣron,' where ***næron*** apparently stands for ***nearon***.

338b. ēadgum. This is Pope's reading, Kemble, Schipper, and Assmann having read *endgum*, though Grein had suggested *ēadgum* as an emendation, a reading approved by Holthausen in the corrections of the *Sprachschatz*[2]. The construction remains difficult. 'One has too little, though desirous of good; him God places, because of his merits, at rest with (?) the blessed.' For a similar construction cf. *Guth.* 1005: 'Ond þā in ēode ēadgum tō sprǣce.' Solomon's justification of the unequal distribution of sunshine (Saturn's question, 339ff.) and riches (335f.) in the world is that God rewards the righteous but poor man hereafter; *ēadig* which has come to mean 'blessed' still retains something of its original meaning of 'rich.'

342–343. Solomon hardly attempts to answer Saturn's unanswerable question, but condemns excessive and desperate mourning. Cf. Cassian's distinction between a proper and improper *tristitia*, the latter proceeding 'de irrationabili mentis anxietate seu desperatione' (*Collationes* v, 11, *Pat. Lat.*, XLIX, 627).

346ff. Solomon's answer implies that evil and good, like other opposites, dwell together. Cf. the Alfredian *Boethius:* 'Hū ne wāst þū þæt hit nis nāuht gecynde ne nāuht gewunelīc þæt ǣnig wiðerweard þing bīon gemenged wið ōðrum wiðerweardum, oððe ǣnige gefērrǣdenne wið habban? Ac sēo gecynd hit onscunað þæt hī ne magon weorðan tōgædere gemenged, [þe] mā ðe þæt good and ðæt yfel magon ætgædere bīon' (XVI, iii, p. 37, ed. Sedgefield); and further, the *Cotton Gnomes* 50ff.

350ff. Saturn wonders why the more wicked man who does not enjoy greater respect among his kinsmen [than the better man] should live longer [thus apparently finding more favor with God]. Solomon hints that the longer life of the wicked man is unimportant since he must eventually meet death. Cf. Job XXI, 7 (esp. the Septuagint and Old Latin versions); Ps. XXXVII (XXXVI), 35, 36; and further, the note on 338b. The *Elucidarium* of Honorius of Autun contains the same question and a similar answer (*Pat. Lat.*, CLXXII, 1136): 'Cur mali hic divitiis affluunt, potentia florent, sanitate vigent, et contra boni inopia tabescunt, a malis injuste opprimuntur, debilitate marcescunt.' . . . 'Omnia enim quae faciunt, pro terrenis agunt, unde et mercedem suam recipiunt.'

353a. forild*a*[n], MS *for ildo.* Kemble emended silently to *foryldan.*

357a. twēgen getwinnas. The problem of the different fate of twins was discussed in ancient times by Cicero, *De Divinatione* II, 43, among others, and became a favorite one in the Middle Ages, when the case of Jacob and Esau was frequently cited (cf. Augustine, *De Civ. Dei* V, 2–4). Augustine repudiated astrology because the different fate of twins seemed to him to prove the folly of astrological prediction (*De Civ. Dei* V, 6). Cf. T. O. Wedel, *The Mediaeval Attitude towards Astrology, Yale Studies in English* LX, pp. 11–12.

358–359. These are two hypermetric lines, as Pope suggests to me, rather than three regular lines, as has been assumed hitherto. Kemble's division *ōðer . . . ēadig, swīðe . . . duguðum, ōðer leofað . . . hwīle,* was followed by Grein and Assmann. Holthausen, recognizing the irregularity, lifted *on eorðan* out of the first line (likewise transposing to *ēadig bið ōðer*), and placed it after *leofað* in the third line. In all these arrangements, the third *ōðer* must be taken to refer once more to the twin who is *unlǣde* (358). One would expect a correlative.

361a. hlāford. Emendation to *frēa* is unnecessary, since the alliteration is probably *f h h f;* cf. the crossed alliteration of the type abab in 303, 320.

362ff. Solomon seems to declare that fate determines a man's earthly destiny, but that the mother has no control over it (and cannot predict it?). Perhaps the poet intends Solomon's answer to be a denial of the belief that man's good or evil destiny is in any way affected by the stars, a belief implied in Saturn's question about the twins. Solomon's speech develops the theme of the exile in the typical manner of the Old English elegy. Cf. J. H. W. Rosteutscher, *Engl. Stud.* LXXIII (1938), 7–8.

365–366. Kemble translates 'to her own sorrow, after she must bear his griefs, his fatal hour.' If the mother is the subject and *siððan* a conjunction, one might better render 'to her own sorrow, when she endures,' etc. In view of the use of the phrase *orleg drēogeð* (Exeter *Judgment Day* 29) and OIcel. *ǫrlǫg drýgja* in the meaning 'endure one's fate,' 'dree one's weird,' one would expect the subject of *drēogeð . . . orlegstunde* to be the son rather than the mother. Though the change of subject is abrupt, this interpretation is perhaps preferable, unless one takes *orlegstunde* as a dative.

373–374. 'From the wretched man his only lord's looks are often turned.' Kemble following the MS *locað geneahhe fram ðam unlædan ængan hlaford* translated 'shutteth himself enough from his ungentle own lord'! Holthausen (*Angl. Beibl.*, XXVII, 355) proposed *frēgan* for *hlāford*, since a suggested *hlāford*[*e*], dative after *fram*, would be a metrically irregular D-type in the second half-line. Bosworth-Toller's translation (*Suppl.*, s.v. *ǣnga*) is 'from the wretched solitary often are his lord's looks turned.' This is certainly the correct interpretation of *unlǣdan*, which must refer, not to the lord, but to his follower, as is obvious from the use of *unlǣde* in the passage preceding and following (358, 383). On the other hand *ǣnga*, *ānga* never seems to mean 'solitary,' 'lonely' but 'only,' 'unique,' translating Latin *unīcus*, and it is preferable to emend MS *ængan* to *ǣnga* both for this reason and because of the rhythm. Solomon's words, which seem to refer only to the characteristic plight of the exile deprived of his lord's favor, here probably have a double meaning, since he is thinking of a follower of Christ; *ǣnga hlāford* is thus parallel to *ānne æðeling* (383), where the Christian application is more obvious. Cf. note on 381ff.

376b. gebyrd. The word here means neither 'birth,' the usual sense, nor 'succession' (Kemble, *B-T. Suppl.* vii), but 'fate,' 'what is determined by nature for a person'; cf. *Beow.* 1074; Wright-Wülker I, 213: 'conditio, i. status, indicio, procreatio, natura, sors, regula, lex, rectitudo, *gescæp*, *gewyrd*, *gescæft*, *gebyrd*'; OHG. *giburt*, 'sors'; and Wolf's discussion, *Die Bezeichnungen für Schicksal*, pp. 119–120.

379. dǣdfruma. Kemble emended silently to *dǣd fremman*, which is still accepted by the *Sprachschatz*[2] (perhaps an oversight). The preceding passage and the following (Solomon's answer) both refer to the relation of the lord and his follower (373–374; 381–383), showing clearly that the MS reading is right. Saturn inquires why a man will not in his youth win for himself illustrious renown for courage and an heroic prince (as his lord). B-T., s.v. *dryhtscipe*, translates *dēores dryhtscipes* 'bold rulership', but I take *dēores* to be genitive of *dēore*, 'precious,' 'desirable,' 'noble,' not *dēor;* cf. the frequent combination of *dēore* and *dryhten*, *Sprachschatz*, s.v. *dȳre*. Is it possible that the phrase means 'desirable lordship' (to serve under) and is exactly parallel to *dǣdfruman?*

381ff. Solomon's answer is, I think, intentionally ambiguous, referring superficially to worldly advancement, but with the deeper meaning that the *mildne hlāford, ānne æðeling* whom the young man should choose is Christ. *Ēadig* means both 'fortunate' and 'blessed' and *unlǣde* both 'unfortunate' and 'morally wretched,' 'wicked.'

385a. drēogeð dēop gesceaft, 'undergoes the mysterious course destined for it by nature.' Cf. 240, 377, and Introduction, pp. 62f. Wolf, *Die Bezeichnungen für Schicksal*, p. 68: 'durchdringt die tiefe Schöpfung.'

386a. neahtes nēðeð (MS *neahtes neðyð*), 'at night it fares boldly.' Similarly Kock, *Jubilee Jaunts and Jottings*, p. 69, who keeps the MS form *nēðyð*.

386b. [nearo]craefte tȳð. It is hard to choose between this emendation of Holthausen, suggested by *Beow.* 2243 (*Angl. Beibl.*, XXVII, 356), which means 'proceeds with oppressive power' (or 'with power when confined') and Kock's *nēodcræfte*, 'with eager might' (*Jubilee Jaunts and Jottings*, p. 69). It should be noted that *tȳð*, pres. 3 sg. of *tēon*, may be for *tīð*, the regular Anglian form, to which corresponds WS *tīehð* or *tȳhð* (Sievers-Cook, § 374, note 2; Luick, § 244).

389b. neahtes. The last word of MS A, p. 22, and probably the last word of Saturn's speech, since half a line is left blank after the word and the usual three dots (·.·) delimiting the speeches are to be found at the end of the line. Although there is no indication of the fact in the manuscript, a leaf is undoubtedly missing between pp. 22 and 23. This is clearly shown both by the fact that two speeches of Saturn (384ff., 416ff.) occur in succession in the manuscript as it is, and by the lack of continuity between 389 and 390ff., the subject being changed from water to light and fire. The loss of a leaf is corroborated, moreover, by the manuscript indication of the conclusion of Saturn's speech mentioned above. Kemble rightly noted an omission, but was not followed by the editors; cf. Vincenti, pp. 75–76; Introduction, p. 2, and note on line 299, where the conjugate leaf is missing. On the possible import of Solomon's missing speech on water see Introduction, p. 69; Vincenti, p. 77.

391. Since the second part of this line is hypermetric, the first half is probably incomplete, and the whole may have been the last of a series of hypermetric lines.

393. ðonne . . . snǣd. The punctuation of the manuscript with a space and three dots after *gesamnod*, together with capital Đ, favors Kemble's punctuation with a semi-colon (or a period) after *gesamnod* rather than that of the text, which follows Grein and Assmann; but the sense seems to indicate a subordinate clause: the Devil's power is humbled, when a morsel of food slips to the floor, which the wise man perceives by means of light, and blesses. The reference here is to the superstition that a bit of food when dropped becomes the Devil's property, and consequently, when recovered, must be blessed before being eaten. This explanation, proposed by Holthausen (*Angl. Beibl.*, XXVII, 356), is confirmed by the superstition that fallen fruit belongs to the Devil (*Handwörterbuch des deutschen Aberglaubens*, s.v. *Fallen*, p. 116.6). Cf. the next note.

396–399. These lines are parenthetical in Solomon's speech on light and fire. The reference seems, at first sight, to be simply to the blessed morsel just mentioned, and the clause *gif hē hit geðencan cann* seems to confirm the view that the poet is merely saying that a blessing on food has great value 'if a man can remember it.' I suspect that there is also a deeper implication and that *sēo ān snǣd* may refer to the consecrated host, which is better than 'seven days feasting.' Vincenti, p. 77, suggested that the whole passage (393–399) might refer to the host (or the *corsnǣd* of the ordeal), but the reference in line 393 can hardly be to the sacramental bread when the man finds it, blesses it himself, and *flavors* it (*gesyfleð*, 395).

400. The allusion is to the descent of the Holy Ghost at Pentecost in the 'linguae tamquam ignis,' Acts II, 2 (3). Light and fire are considered aspects of the same element throughout this passage.

409–410. 'It is wholly visible to the hero who can share in the Lord's light,' i.e. in the light of the Christian faith.

411ff. The primacy of fire among the elements is a familiar conception from the philosophy of Heraclitus to Schiller's *Lied von der Glocke.* The description in this passage of the all-pervasive nature of fire may depend on Boethius; cf. the Old English *Metres of Boethius* XX, 125–129 (ed. Sedgefield):

þonne is þæs fȳres frumstōl on riht
eard ofer eallum ōðrum gesceaftum
gesewenlīcum geond þisne sīdan grund;
þēah hit wið ealle sīe eft gemenged
weoruldgesceafta.

417a. swerian. Perhaps 'make solemn declarations,' a meaning not paralleled elsewhere. Grein suggested 'loqui,' 'dissere,' and compared *andswerian*, an explanation retained in the revised *Sprachschatz. Spyrian* (cf. *āspyrian*, 426) might satisfy the conditions, but it is unlikely that the poet would alliterate *sp* and *s*; cf. Introduction, p. 16.

419a. wyrd ðe warnung. The antithesis is not between Boethian fate and providence, nor between Augustinian predestination and free-will, but between Germanic destiny and foresight; cf. the note on Solomon's answer, 427ff.

427ff. Solomon's explanation, that Wyrd is turned aside with difficulty, but that man's wisdom, with the help of friends and the divine spirit, may moderate every blow of fate, is a Christian modification of the Germanic belief in inexorable destiny, reminding us of the compromises of the poet of *Beowulf*, e.g. *Beow.* 1056f.: 'nefne him wītig God wyrd forstōde / ond ðæs mannes mōd.' Cf. note on lines 434ff.

429a. scyð[eð]. MS *scyð* is LWS for *scyðeð* (Angl. *sceðeð*) from *scieððan* 'harm,' rather than for *scȳ[e]ð* from *scȳan* 'tempt' as Sievers thought (*PBB*, x, 475); cf. *And.* 1561b: 'ūs sēo wyrd scyðeð.' It is hard to say whether Kemble's *scȳt* 'shooteth' is a silent emendation or a misreading, since he provides no comments whatever on the text of Poem II; his corresponding emendation of the second half-line to *gār* from *gēr* 'years' is equally unnecessary.

434ff. Saturn, extending the view of Wyrd as a bearer of woe in Solomon's previous speech (428–429), depicts mighty Wyrd as the source of all human evils. Saturn's declaration that Wyrd is the father and mother of every original sin, and the daughter of death, seems, at first sight, rather out of character, being obviously a Christian interpretation foreshadowing Solomon's explanation that the evil in the world is a result of Satan's revolt against God. But the poet himself probably had no clear conception of the original heathen belief in Wyrd and intends Saturn's speech to be merely a pagan's inquiry concerning the reason for the existence of the evil in the world brought to men by fate. One may compare the inquiry of Boethius about the exaltation of the wicked by Fortune, a passage in which Alfred translates *fortuna* by *wyrd* (*Consolatio* I, 5; Alfredian version IV, ed. Sedgefield, pp. 10, 156).

Solomon's answer differs markedly from most Christian explanations of Wyrd. It is not the common explanation that Wyrd is simply a false belief (Ælfric, *Cath. Hom.* I, 114), nor the philosophical explanation that the only destiny was the execution of God's foreknowledge (Boethius, ed. Sedgefield, p. 131), nor the explanation that Wyrd was subordinate in some degree to God, who could temper it, the typical poetic interpretation which still accorded some respect to the traditionally powerful figure (*Beow.* 1056f.; Introduction, pp. 62f.; Brandl, *Forschungen*, p. 83; Kauffmann, p. 368). Solomon recounts the story of Lucifer's fall, and declares that the fallen angels are the enemies who fight against us and bring us *wōpes ēaca*. Bouterwek thought that the poet intended to identify Wyrd and the fallen angel who becomes Satan (*Cædmon's biblische Dichtungen*, p. lxiv); but the poet does not actually say this, and the implication is rather that the evils men endure are the result of Lucifer's rebellion. Solomon, in spite of his partial acceptance of the power of Wyrd in lines 427ff., seems to substitute Satan for Wyrd as the originator of evil. It is curious that there is no mention of the temptation and fall of man, through which death and all our woe came more directly. It should be noted that Saturn's characterization of Wyrd attributes all evil to her much more definitely than any other passage in Old English. Wyrd is elsewhere often represented as an evil fate, and the frequent mention of Wyrd as the bringer of death and an evil end made the transformation of the figure into the source of evil an easy one, a process that was further facilitated by the depiction of God and Wyrd as ethical opposites (cf. Ehrismann, *PBB*, xxxv, 237).

434b. wyrd sēo swīðe. Cf. *Ruin* 25.

439–440. 'Lo, as long as she lives, she will be slow to tire of engendering enmity by means of sinful disputes (*literally* the conflicts of crimes).' *Late* is equivalent to 'never' by litotes; cf. the Middle English *Purity* 1804. For *āðrēotan* with an irrational negative in the subordinate clause see *B-T. Suppl.* I, 3.

443b. dier[n]e (MS *diere*) **cræftas.** Cf. *Beow.* 2168, and the *Cotton Gnomes* 43. The secret arts by which the rebellious angels make standards and corselets go back to the legend in the Book of Enoch VIII, 1ff. about the discovery by the evil angels under Azazel of metals and magic arts; cf. further Ginzberg, *Legends of the Jews*, I, 125; V, 153–156. For various unnecessary emendations resulting from the failure to recognize a long line here, see the textual variants. The second half of the long line is somewhat overweighted, but Holthausen's proposed shift of *ongan wyrcan* to the beginning of a new line of which the remainder has been lost raises more problems than it solves.

446. Pope's careful study of this line, very obscure in the manuscript, has made the text much more intelligible. 'Propogate for himself with the tenth part until he should know no end of his spite (?) through internal generation,' i.e. Lucifer will continue his rebellious race by producing heirs within his own order. *(t)ȳ(d)ran*, Pope's reading, must be correct as opposed to Kemble's [*cyrran*], which is followed by Grein and Assmann. Pope reports the cross of *t* missing but the shape more like *t* than *c*, the third letter either *d* or *ð*, though obscured by a crack in the vellum. Zupitza read *ran* certainly, *cy* less certainly, and considered the first *r* doubtful. The alliteration requires initial *t*. For *(to)r(nes) (ne) cūðe* (the letters in parenthesis very faint) Kemble printed [*āgenne cūðe*], but, as usual, it is impossible to tell how much he actually read and what is guesswork. Zupitza read only *cūðe*. For *tornes* I have been tempted to read *tēames*, especially in view of the alliteration in the poetry of *tȳdran* and *tīeman*, *tuddor* and *tēam* (e.g. *Gen.* 1512, 1535, 1613; and the *Cotton Gnomes* 48), but though 'no end of his generation' would be more obvious, it is perhaps not so poetically effective as *tornes*, and Pope's reading can hardly be set aside without further study of the manuscript. We may safely disregard guesses and emendations, recorded in the textual variants, of editors and commentators who have not concerned themselves with the appearance of the line in the manuscript. Bouterwek has an elaborate rewriting of the whole passage based on Kemble and Grein.—**tēoðan dǣle.** In other Old English versions of the fall of the angels, the rebellious angels are actually considered to form a tenth order (*Gen.* B 246–248; Ælfric, *Cath. Hom.* I, 10), a conception which may go back to the *Book of the Secrets of Enoch* XXIX, 3. Cf. Bouterwek, *Cædmon's biblische Dichtungen*, pp. cxli–cxlviii; M. D. Clubb, *Christ and Satan*, line 366 note.

447a. insceafte. This *hapax legomenon* probably means 'internal generation,' that is, the creation or propogation within Lucifer's own order of rebellious angels; one may compare the function of *in* in such compounds as *inbyrde* 'born on the estate,' *inādl*, *incoðu* 'internal disease,' *inlende* 'native.'

447b. se æðel(a) (ð)ēoden, Pope's reading. Kemble read *sēo æðele gedryht* without comment or brackets. Assmann could not make anything of the last word.

449. Grein and Assmann made a rather curious short line beginning with *āfielde* and ending with *scēatas,* considering *heht* to *feohtað on* another long line. Since it is very unlikely that the poet would write six long lines, one short line, and then another long line, I have followed Holthausen's division and emendation (*Angl. Beibl.*, XXI, 175).

451b. wōpes ēaca. Cf. *wōpes hēafod* 436b, and 428.

454a. āweorp hine. Vincenti (p. 79) suggested emendation to *hīe*. Either reading involves difficulties. Retaining the manuscript reading, as in the text, one may translate 454ff.: 'cast him (Lucifer) down then from glory and drove (him) far away and entrusted to him the sons of heaven-dwellers so that they, also, must ever dwell in surging flame while they lived.' The objections to this are that *hine* must refer to Satan who has not been mentioned since 449, and that the poet has already described Satan's fall (448–449), and would hardly repeat himself thus. On the other hand the change to *hīe*, though it makes the repetition less obvious by having the description here concerned solely with Satan's followers, involves the difficulty of interpreting *bearn heofonwara* 'son of heaven-dwellers' as a kenning for God (cf. Hertha Marquardt, *Die altenglischen Kenningar, Schriften der Königsberger Gelehrten Gesellschaft, Geisteswissenschaftliche Kl.*, XIV.3 (1938), 150. One would then translate: 'cast them down then from glory and scattered them afar, and the Son of heaven-dwellers commanded them that they must also ever dwell,' etc. Kemble's translation, 'commanded them children of the dwellers in heaven,' equates *him* and *bearn,* but this syntax seems out of the question. *Bearn* might be more easily referred to God if it stood for *beorn,* 'hero,' but *beorn* is not used with the genitive plural in this way.

459a. wælcealde wīc. Cf. *Christ* 1546 (and Cook's note); *Gen. B* 313ff.; *Christ and Satan* 132 (and Clubb's note), 335, 627. For general discussions of the descriptions of hell in Old English literature see R. W. Deering, *The Anglo-Saxon Poets on the Judgment Day* (Halle, 1890); E. J. Becker, *A Contribution to the Comparative Study of the Medieval Visions of Heaven and Hell* (Baltimore, 1899); G. Grau, *Quellen und Verwandtschaften der älteren germanischen Darstellungen des jüngsten Gerichts,* [Morsbach's] *Studien zur englischen Philologie* XXXI (Halle, 1908); and A. B. Van Os, *Religious Visions* (Amsterdam, 1932).

464a. ēgna egesan. Kemble printed *ēacne*, probably a silent emendation. 'Dread of eyes' probably refers to the 'horribilis visio dæmonum et draconum' listed as an infernal punishment by Honorius of Autun, *Pat. Lat.*, CLXXII, 1160.

468b. ā manige, MS *man man āge*. I propose this emendation as the best parallel to *ābǣde* that can be reconciled with the scribe's error. 'Is there any man of earthly race in this world who may ever claim death, compel it, before that day shall come when the calendar of his life has entirely run out and he be suddenly summoned forth?' For *manian*, 'claim,' 'demand,' see *B-T.*, and cf. *āmanian*, 'exact'; *manige* would then be an exact parallel to *ābǣde*, 'compel,' 'constrain,' 'exact,' and *dēað* would be construed with both. For parallels to the noun at the beginning of a line which is the object of a preceding and following verb, see Kock, *Jubilee Jaunts and Jottings*, pp. 29–30, who punctuates *Phoenix* 188f.: 'timbran onginneð / nest, gearwian,' and H. Meritt, who would consider such a case the construction ἀπὸ κοινοῦ (*The Construction* ἀπὸ κοινοῦ *in the Germanic Languages* [Stanford, 1938], cf. 158 note). For the metre cf. *Resignation* 85: 'yrmþu ofer eorþan, þæt ic ā þolade.' Other attempts to emend this line have changed *man man* to an alliterating noun beginning with a vowel, such as *ǣðm* (Bouterwek), or *oroð*, with *ðe* added before *dēað* (Holthausen), or *endemān* 'final pain' (Kock); see the textual notes for references.

470b. [clǣne]. Holthausen ingeniously supplied *clāne* (*clǣne* is a somewhat commoner form). For the meaning 'entirely,' 'to the full,' cf. *Phoenix* 226, *B-T.* and *Suppl.*, s.v. *clǣne*, adv., and the modern 'clean gone.'

472ff. Solomon's speech on the guardian angel contains no direct answer to Saturn's question, but the missing portion, 497ff., may have made the connection obvious. The implication may be that the guardian angel cannot prevent man's bringing about his own destruction if he succumbs too easily to the counsel of the wicked angel. On the guardian angel see Ælfric, *Cath. Hom.* I, 516f., and on the origin of the belief the article *Angélologie*, section viii, in Vacant and Mangenot, *Dictionnaire de Théologie Catholique.* For the two angels, good and evil, see the note on 477b.

This passage, much of which is very obscure in the manuscript, has caused the editors much trouble. Kemble, printing by half-lines, divided:

> .... onsendeð
> dryhten hē ... .
> se sceal behealdan hū his hyge . . .
> . .. dig grōwan in Godes sibbe.

Grein, depending on Kemble's text, placed *dryhten* after *onsendeð*, and supplied [*mōte*] after *hyge*, and [*gōdspē*]*dig* in the next line. Assmann, depending partly on the collations of Zupitza and Skeat, the latter reported by Schipper, read:

> Æghwylc[um men e]ngel onsendeð dryhten
> he ......eð se sceal behealdan, hu his hyge
> g ....dig growan in godes sibbe.

Pope's readings, on which I depend, show clearly that Kemble, though he left many gaps, perceived the correct division of the lines; cf. likewise Holthausen, *Angl.* XXIII, 125. Pope thinks the word after *hyge* might be *wille*, but the MS is almost entirely illegible.

473. heo(fona ðonne dæg styr)eð. Pope's reading, the letters in parenthesis being almost illegible and somewhat doubtful; *ðonne* is abbreviated, as usual, as *ðoñ*. Previous editors and collators read only *he* and ...*eð*, Schipper supposing that twelve letters were missing after *he*.

475a. (grǣ)dig grōwan. Pope's reading. For the favorable sense of *grǣdig*, i.e. 'desirous,' 'eager,' cf. 337. 'Grow eager in the will of God' (cf. *Christ* 1580–81, *Guth*. 348), is paralleled by 476a.

477b. gāstas twēgen. The belief that two spirits, one good and one evil, accompany a man, is an extension of the belief in the guardian angel. The two spirits are sometimes both emissaries of God, one reporting on a man's virtuous deeds, the other accusing him of crimes, but sometimes the second is an emissary of Satan, representing man's evil inclinations (see Ginzberg, *Legends of the Jews*, v, 76–77, on Jewish and early Christian views of the two angels, and Hoops, *Reallexikon* s.v. *fylgjen*, on the development in Scandinavian literature, under Christian influence, of two guardian spirits, white and black, from the original heathen figure of the *fylgja*, 'follower'). The two angels of wickedness and righteousness appear as early as the *Shepherd of Hermas* (Mandate vi). In Old English one may compare the *Vercelli Homilies* (ed. M. Förster) iv, p. 106, and *Guth*. 114–116 (85–87):

hine twēgen ymb
weardas wacedon, þā gewin drugon,
engel dryhtnes ond se atela gǣst.

479–480. It seems probable that in these two lines one clause beginning with *ōðer* has been omitted, since the correlatives *ōðer . . . ōðer* refer to the good and evil angels in 478 and 481, 483. Grein assumed a missing line after 478, and supplied it, printing:

[ōðer cymeð of hēahþrymme heofona rīces]
ōðer cymeð [of stēame] þǣre stȳlenan helle.

But 478 is a hypermetric line, and since *ofer ðǣre stȳlenan helle* is also a good hypermetric half-line, one may guess that after writing the first *ōðer cymeð*, beginning the clause descriptive of the good angel, the scribe omitted the rest of the clause, and the beginning of the clause on the evil angel. Possibly both clauses began with *ōðer cymeð;* in that case perhaps 480b should read: 'ōðer cymeð of (MS ofer) ðǣre stȳlenan helle.' There is a curious parallel to the phrase *stȳlenan helle* in the passage on the two angels in the *Vercelli Homilies* (ed. M. Förster) iv, p. 106: 'Ōðer cymð ufan of heofonum, þe ūs sceall gōde bysena on-stellan and ūs gōde þēawas tǣcan, and hæfð him on handa þā scyldas, þe ic ǣr nemde, and þæt sweord, and wyle ūs forstandan æt þām āwyrgdan dīofle, þe of þǣre stȳlenan helle cymð mid his scearpum strǣlum ūs mid tō scotianne.' The similarity of the phraseology suggests that there is a relation between the poem and the homily, both perhaps going back to the same source. One might even conjecture that the first *ōðer*-clause in the poem originally read as in the homily 'ōðer cymeð ufan of heofonum,' in which case, as Pope suggests to me, this might be the first half of a hypermetric line, and possibly 'ōðer of ðǣre stȳlenan helle' the second.

489b. on fēower gecynd. The Devil fights, that is, tempts man, in four ways. For four kinds of sin one may compare the *Blickling Homilies*, p. 35; Honorius of Autun, *Pat. Lat.*, CLXXII, 1143.

493a. wēpende. The reporting angel who weeps at man's succumbing to the Devil's temptations goes back to the *Visio Pauli:* 'ecce angeli alii venerunt adorare . . . qui flebant' (ed. M. R. James, *Texts and Studies*, II, 3 [Cambridge, 1893], p. 14).

497a. swīce. This is the first word on p. 13 of MS A; *tōmiddes* (496b) is the last word on p. 26 of MS A. On the conclusion of the poem and the misplacement of the final lines (497–505), see Introduction, pp. 8–12.

503a. forcumen and forcȳðed. Cf. 198a.

504a. was. The manuscript plainly has *was* (so Schipper), not *wæs* as given by Kemble and Assmann. Cf. *was*, 173, 203, the latter unnoted by editors and collators.

505. On the joy of the disputant conquered by the truth, cf. Introduction, p. 54.

GLOSSARY

The order of words is strictly alphabetical; *æ* is considered a separate letter and comes after *a*, and *ð* (and *þ*) after *t*. Nouns in *ge-* are under *g*, but verbs follow the simplex. Roman numerals indicate the classes of ablaut verbs; w.1, etc., those of the weak verbs, prp. the preterite-presents; mi., mu., mja., mc., etc., denote masc. i-, u-, ja-, consonant-stems; m. or n. alone denotes a masculine or neuter a-stem (or occasionally a noun of indeterminable declension).

To save space the forms of nouns, adjectives, and verbs are not cited, unless they differ from those normally expected, or unless more than one form appears in the text. All occurrences of every word are, however, indicated by numbers, except in the case of a few common words, when "etc." is added after selected references. Unless otherwise noted, the mood of verbs is indicative, and the case of nouns and adjectives nominative singular.

The dagger, †, designates words found in poetry only; (†) is used when the word is found rarely outside the poetry. The double dagger, ‡, designates words not found elsewhere.

Small capitals indicate modern descendants of the Old English words, but the modern words are not necessarily derived directly from the exact form of the head-word. If the word is recorded in the *NED.*, but is obsolete or has developed a different meaning, it is put in brackets.

Textual changes are indicated by italicizing the line-number. After a line-number n. calls attention to a note. The letter A or B after a number, e.g. 76A, indicates that a form occurs only in MS A or MS B (in lines 30–94 of MS A and 1–94 of MS B). When the form is the same in both MSS (in lines 30–94) no letter follows. From line 95 on, no letter is added, all the references being to MS A.

Ā, the letter and the *āc*-rune, 93A; the letter only, 93B.

ā, adv., *ever, always*, 91A, 96, 342, 456, 466, *468*.

ābannan, VII w. ūt, *summon, call forth;* pres. opt. 3 sg. 471. [ABANNE].

ābǣdan, w.1, *compel, constrain;* pres. opt. 3 sg. 469.

ābelgan, III, *make angry, offend*, 321. [ABELGEN].

ābītan, I, *bite, consume;* pres. 3 sg. 292.

ābrēdan, III, w. ūt, *draw quickly, unsheath*, 164. [ABRAID].

ābrēotan, II, *destroy;* pres. 3 sg. 287.

ac, conj., *but*, 166, 278, 330, 348, 354, 376; w. interr. 36, 53, 221, 273, 293, 327, 331, 335, 339, 350, 355, 378, 384, 434, 438.

ācennan, w.1, *bring forth, bear;* pp. ācende 356. [AKENNE].

ādrēogan, II, *suffer, endure*, 354. [ADREE].

ādwǣscan, w.1, *quench, put out;* pres. 3 sg. 42.

āfēdan, w.1, *feed, nourish, bring up;* pres. 3 sg. 364. [AFEDE].

āfiellan, w.1, *fell, bring down;* pres. 3 sg. āfilleð 289; pret. 3 sg. āfielde 449. [AFELLE].

afora†, wk.m., *son;* gs. afran 367.

āgan, prp., *possess, have;* neg. pres. 3 sg. nāh 375. [OWE].

āhīeðan, w.1, *destroy;* pres. 3 sg. 73A.

āhliehhan†, VI, *laugh, rejoice;* pret. 3 sg. āhlōg 505.

aldor(†), n., *life;* as. 348.

āmyrgan‡, w.1, *cheer, delight;* 3 pl. 232.

ān, num. adj. and subst. (1) ONE; nsm. ān æfter ānum, *one after another*, 377; dsm. 377; asm. ānne, *unique*(?), *peer-*

less(?), 383n.; nsf. 396 (emph.); asf. 356; gp. in ānra (ge)hwylc, *each one*, 225, 348; (2) *a certain* 238, 246; *alone*, wk. nsm. āna 35, 266.

and, conj., AND (always abbrev. 7), 3B, 15B, 18B, 31, 34, etc.

ānnunga, adv., *certainly, necessarily*, 471.

ansacan, VI, w. gen., *deny, contradict*; pres. 3 sg. ansæceð 173.

ār, f., *honor*; as. 352.

Arabia, prop. n., *Arabia*; gs. 186.

ārinnan, III, *run out*; pp. 470.

ārunnen, see **ārinnan**.

āscēadan, VII, *separate, keep apart*, 56.

āspyrian, w.1, *trace out, discover*, 426.

āstǣnan, w.1, *adorn with precious stones*; pp. adj. 63.

āstyrian, w.1, *move from its place, remove*; pres. 3 sg. 288.

ātercynn‡, nja., *kind of poison*; np. 211n.

atol, adj., *terrible, horrible*; asf. atole 129; asn. 461. [ATEL].

attor, n., *poison*; gs. attres, 213. [ATTER].

āðrēotan, II, impers. w. acc. and ðæt-clause, *weary, tire*, 439; w. acc., pres. 3 sg. 420.

āðringan, III, *press out*, 495.

āwa, adv., *ever*, 315.

āweaxan, VI, *grow*; pp. 28B.

āweccan, w.1, *arouse, call forth*; pres. 3 sg. āweceð, 275. [AWECCHE].

āweorpan, III, *cast down, depose*; pret. 3 sg. āweorp 454. [AWARP].

āwrītan, I, *inscribe*; pres. 3 sg. 161. [AWRITE].

ǣdre, wk.f., *vein*; np. 144. [EDDRE].

geæfnan, w.1, *carry out, endure*, 348.

ǣfre, EVER, 33, 261.

æfter, (1) prep. w. dat., (local) AFTER, *about, through, along*, 61, 116, 150, 377, 380, 394; (temporal), 289. (2) adv., *behind*, 135.

æfðanca, wk.m., *offence, vexation*; dp. 487.

ǣghwæt, n. pron., *everything*; gs. 283.

ǣghwæðer, pron., *each* (*of two*), 108. [EITHER].

ǣghwylc, pron., *each* (*one*), *every* (*one*), 64, 115, 465; dsm. (adj.) 396, 472.

ǣht, fi., *possession*; gs. 11B. [AUGHT].

ǣled†, m., *fire*; as. 129.

ælmihtig, adj., ALMIGHTY, 313; dsm. 34A, 34B.

ǣnga, wk.adj., *only, sole, 374*n.

ǣnig, pron., ANY, 208, 265, 467; adj., asf. 353, 402.

æppel, m., APPLE, i.e. *ball*; dp. aplum, 28Bn.

ǣr, (1) adv., ERE, *before, earlier*, 308, 420, 505; comp. ǣror, 408; superl. ǣrest, *first*, 88, 211; (2) conj., *before*, w. neg. *until*, 264, 469, 497.

ǣren, adj., *brazen*; wk. nsf. -e, 46.

ǣrðon, conj., *before, until*, 242, 266.

æt, prep., AT, 104, 133, 159.

ætgædre, adv., *together*, 339.

æðele, adj. ja., *noble*; wk. nsm. 447. [ATHEL].

æðeling, m., *chief, prince*; as. 383. [ATHELING].

bald, adj., BOLD, 175, 234.

baldlīce, adv., BOLDLY, 298.

bān, n., BONE; np. 144.

bana, wk.m., *slayer, destroyer*, i.e., *devil*; np. 131n. [BANE].

bāncofa†, wk.m., *bodily frame, body*; ds. 150.

bærnan, w.1, BURN; pres. 3 sg. 404.

bæð, n., BATH; as.(?), 157.

be, prep., BY, *by means of*, 100, 113, 394.

bealu(†), nwa., BALE, *harm, ruin*; ds. bealwe, 364.

bealu(†), adj.wa., *harmful, baleful*; ap. bealwe 162.

bēam, m., *tree*; as. 287. [BEAM].

bearm, m., *lap*; as. 423. [BARM].

bearn, n., *child, son*, 268, 455n.; gs. 376; as. 364; ap. 197. [BAIRN].

bēatan, VII, BEAT *upon, strike*; pres. 3 sg. 274.

bebēodan, II, *command, decree*; pret. 3 sg. 455. [BIBEDE].

bebrecan‡, V, *break in pieces*; pres. 3 sg. bebriceð, 287.

bēc, see **bōc**.

beclemman‡, w.1, *bind, enclose*; pres. opt. 3 sg. 71.

bedǣlan, w.1, *deprive*, pp. 371.

begongan, VII, *cultivate, honor;* ger. -ne, 54A, begangenne, 54B.
begyrdan, w.1, BEGIRD, *encompass;* pres. 3 pl. 124.
behealdan, VII, BEHOLD, *watch,* 474.
behelman‡, w.1, *cover;* pp. 104.
behȳdan, w.1, *hide, cover;* pres. 3 sg. 293. [BEHIDE].
belūcan, II, *lock up, enclose,* 270. [BELOUKE].
bemurnan, III, *be anxious about, care for;* pres. 3 sg. 110. [BEMOURN].
gebendan, w.1, *put in bonds,* 267 (see 265n.).
bēon, anom.v., BE; 2 sg. eart, 321; 3 sg. biȣ, 21B, 30B, 34, 66, 102, 104, 116, 136, 216, 234, 235, 303², 304², 314, 318, 342, 343, 357, 358², 361, 390, 396, 397, 409, 427, 431, 478², 487; bēoȣ, 283; is, 53, 63, 75, 77, 78A, 89, 221, 238, 244, 247, 249, 255, 273, 377, 451, 467; his, 78B; 3 pl. bēoȣ, 28B, 295, 305, 324, 326, 339, 356; sindon, 229, 450; pres. opt. 1 sg. sī, 16B; 3 sg. sīe, 263, 399, 415, 470; pret. 3 sg. was, 173, 203, 504; pret. 3 sg. wǣron, 198; opt. 3 sg. wǣre, 10B; wǣron, 330n.; neg. pres. 3 sg. nis, 411; pret. 3 pl. nǣron, 335; opt. 3 sg. nǣre, 425; 3 pl. nǣren(?), 330n.
beorht, adj., BRIGHT, *beautiful, excellent;* dsn. wk., 43.
beran, IV, BEAR; pres. 3 sg. byreȣ, 429.
besceadian, w.2(?), *overshadow;* pres. 3 sg. besceadeȣ, 332. [BESHADE].
besceāwian, w.2, *look to, consider;* pres. 3 sg. 101.
beswīcan, I, *deceive, circumvent, evade,* 277. [BESWIKE].
betra, see **gōd,** adj.
betȳnan, w.1, *enclose,* 500.
beȣeccean, w.1, *cover;* pp. adj. apn. beȣeahte, 459.
bewrēon, I, *cover, veil;* pres. 3 sg. bewrīhȣ, 294. [BEWRY].
beyrnan, III, *run into, incur;* imp. sg. 322.
bīdan, V, BIDE, *wait;* pres. 3 sg. 137.
biddan, V, BID, *pray;* 168.
bīgan, w.1, *subdue;* pres. 3 pl. 125. [BEY].
bill, mja., BILL, *sword;* as. 162.
gebindan, III, *bind,* 269, 449. [IBINDE].
gebisigian, w.2, *vex, overcome;* pp. 116.
bismorlīce, adv., *shamefully, contemptuously,* 27B.
biter, adj., BITTER, *cruel;* gsn. bittres, 321; asm. 125, 131.
Bitȣinia, prop.n., *Bithynia;* as. *188.*
blæc, adj., BLACK; dsf. blacere, 27B; apf. 462.
blǣd, mi., *prosperity, life;* gs. 376.
blēdan, w.1, BLEED; pres. 3 pl. 144.
blēo, nja., *color, appearance, form;* dp. blēoum, 150. [BLEE].
blīcan, I, *shine, gleam,* 227; pres. 3 pl. 144, 215. [BLIK].
bliss, fjō., BLISS, *joy;* ds. 168.
geblissian, w.2, *gladden;* pres. 3 sg. 40.
blōd, n., BLOOD, 156; as. 43.
blōdig, adj., BLOODY; apm. 462.
bōc, f(n)c., BOOK; ds. 6Bn. (here neut.); np. 229; gp. 2B, 175, 234; dp. 61, 423; ap. 49.
bōcstæf, m., *letter, character;* gp. 99; ap. 162. [BOCSTAFF].
bodian, w.2, *proclaim, declare;* 3 pl. 229. [BODE].
boldgetimbre‡, nja., *building;* ap. 404.
brād, adj., BROAD; asn. 267.
brecan, V, BREAK, *shatter,* 71; *disturb, vex,* 239; *fail to keep*(?), *break into*(?), 132n.; inf. 100; pres. 3 sg. briceȣ, 71; brieceȣ, 95; bryceȣ, 404; pres. 3 pl. 132n.; pret. 3 sg. 239.
gebrecan, V, *break down;* pres. 3 sg. gebryceȣ, 298.
bregdan, III, *shake,* 99; *change, shift,* 150; pres. 3 sg. 99; 3 p. 150. [BRAID].
brego†, mu., *chief, prince,* 99.
brēme, adj. ja., *famous;* np. 229; comp. nsm. 173. [BREME].
gebrengan, see **gebringan.**
brengeȣ, see **bringan.**
brēosttoga, wk.m., *chieftain,* 175.
bri(e)ceȣ, see **brecan.**
bringan, w.1, BRING, 225; pres. 3 sg. brengeȣ, 108.

gebringan, w.1, *bring, lead,* 16B; w. acc. and pres. part. 87, 147; inf. gebringan, 87B, gebrengan, 87A, 147; pres. 2 sg. gebringest, 16B.
brōga, wk.m., *terror;* as. 125, 131.
brōðor, mc., BROTHER, 321.
brūcan, II, w. gen., *enjoy, possess,* 433. [BROOK].
bryceð, see **brecan.**
gebryddan‡, w.1, *frighten, overawe*(?); pp. 16Bn.
bryne, mi., *burning, fervor,* 61. [BRUNE].
bū, num., n. of bēgen, *both,* 168.
burg, fc., *town;* gp. 298. [BOROUGH].
būtan, prep., *without,* 23B, 86, 403, 418, 466. [BOUT].
Buðanasan, prop.n., error for Baðanǣan(?); as. 188n.
byreð, see **beran.**
byrgen, fjō., *burial-place, grave;* ap. -na, 215. [BURIAN].
byrne, wk.f., *corslet;* ap. 444. [BURNE].
byrðen, fjō., BURDEN, 304.
bysig, adj., BUSY, *diligent;* nsm. 61A; bisi, 61B.

C, n., the letter and the *cēn*-rune, 123.
Caldēas, prop.n., *Chaldeans;* np. 198; gp. 185, 503; ap. 20B.
cālendcwide‡, mi., *number of months, tale of days,* 470.
cantic, m., *canticle, song* (*of Pater Noster*), 49; gs. -es, 17B; as. 24B.
Cappadocia, prop.n., *Cappadocia;* as. 191.
cǣg, fjō., KEY; gp. *175.*
ceald, n. (sb. from adj.), COLD; ds. 296.
ceaster, f., *city;* as. 179. [CHESTER].
cempa, wk.m., *warrior;* as. 139.
cennan, w.1, *bear, bring forth;* pres. 3 sg. 362, 375. [KEN].
gecēosan, II, *choose,* 381. [ICHEOSE].
cile, mi., CHILL, 346.
cirice, wk.f., CHURCH; gs. cirican, 107.
cīð, m., *seed, shoot;* as. 294. [CHITHE].
clausum, see **clūse.**
clǣne, adv., CLEAN, *entirely, 470*n.
clǣnsian, w.2, CLEANSE, *purify;* pres. 3 sg. 387.
geclingan, III, *shrivel, wither;* pp. adj., np. geclungne, 296.
clūd, m., *rock;* ap. *185*n. [CLOUD].
clūse, wk.f., *bolt, bar;* dp. 71A; clausum, 71Bn.
clymman‡, wk. 1 (?), CLIMB; pres. 3 sg. 406.
Cōferflōd, prop.n., *the river Chebar;* as. 20Bn.; Cōfor- 196.
Coref, prop.n., (*Mount*) *Horeb;* gs. Coreffes, 185n.
gecostian, w.2, *try, afflict;* pres. 3 sg. 296.
cræft, m., CRAFT, *power,* 71, 234; *science, skill, art,* 186, 443; gs. 234; as. 71; ap. 186, 443.
cræftig, adj., *powerful,* 283. [CRAFTY].
Crēcas, prop.n., *Greeks,* gp. 183n., 186; Grēca, 3Bn.
Crīst, prop.n., *Christ;* gs. 17B, 49, 139, 191, 401; ds. 327; as. 24B.
crīstnian, w.2 CHRISTEN *baptize;* pres. 3 sg. 387.
cuiclifigende† part. adj. *living,* 411.
cuman, IV COME; pres. 3 sg. cymeð, 111, 316, 479; opt. 3 sg. cyme 169, 469; pret. 3 sg. cwōm, 504; cuōm, 408.
cunnan, prp., *know,* 33, 251, 388, 446; *know how to, be able,* CAN, 24B, 398, 410; pres. 1 sg. cann, 388; 3 sg. cann, 398; can, 24B, 410; 3 pl. cunnon, 251; pret. opt. 3 sg. cūðe, 33, 446.
cunnian, w.2, *try,* 406; *tempt,* 219; pres. 3 sg. 219, 406. [CUN].
cūð, adj., *well known;* nsm. 204. [COUTH].
cūðe, see **cunnan.**
cwealm, m., *torment;* ds. 118. [QUALM].
cwēman, w.1, *please;* pres. opt. 3 sg. 165. [QUEME].
cweðan, V, *say, speak;* only in pret. 3 sg., cwæð. 444; in extrametrical lines before 1B, 21B, 36, 39, 53, 63A, 216, 234, 238, 273, 303, 305, 314, 323, 327, 329, 331, 339, 350, 355, 378, 381, 384, 416, 441, 467; with capitals CVÆÐ (= cuæð), before 203, 221, 229, 236, 283, 325, 335, 342, 362; abbrev. C̄, 63B, 293, 318, 344, 346, 353, 427, 434, 472; C̄ð, 244. [QUETHE].

cwic, adj., *living;* dpf. 139; gp. (as noun), 387. [QUICK].
cwide, mi., *saying, words,* 17B; Godes cwide (*Pater Noster*), 63, 84, 146; as. 84; cwyde, 17B. [QUIDE].
cyme(ð), see **cuman.**
cyning, m., KING, 323n.
cynn, n. ja., *race, tribe,* 186, etc.; *quality,* 415; gs. 266, 321, 415, 468; ap. 186. [KIN].
gecȳðan, w.1, *show, prove;* pret. 3 sg. 401; pret. 3 pl. 319.
cȳðð, f., *native land;* as. 196. [KITH].

D, n., the letter and the *dæg*-rune, 135.
Dāuid, prop.n., *David, King of Israel;* gs. 13B, 323, 502.
dǣd, fi., DEED, *action;* dp. 491.
dǣdfruma†, wk.m., *doer of deeds, mighty lord;* gs. 379n.
dæg, m., DAY, *daylight,* 469, *473,* 476; gs. 317; as adv., *by day,* 240; ds. 328; as. 385; gp. 399.
dæglong‡, adj., *lasting all day;* asm. 491.
dægrēd, n., DAYRED, *dawn, break of day;* as. 207.
dǣl, mi., *part;* is. 446. [DEAL].
gedǣlan, w.1, *divide, 335; share in, take part in,* 410; inf. 410; pp. *335.*
dēad, adj., DEAD; gp. as noun 78B.
dēaf, adj., DEAF; gp. as noun 78A.
dear, see **durran.**
dēað, mu., DEATH, 207; gs. 438; ds. 304; as. 469.
gedēgan, w.1, *carry through, complete;* pret. 3 pl. 320.
dēman, w.1, DEEM, *judge,* 329; pres. 3 sg. 327, 328.
denu, f., *vale;* ds. 221. [DEAN].
dēofol, m(n.), DEVIL, 25B, 122; gs. 42, 44, 391, 448, 491; ds. 145.
dēop, adj., DEEP; asn. 216; *mysterious, profound;* asn. 240, 385.
dēor, n., *beast;* as. 461. [DEER].
dēor, adj., *grievous, severe,* gp. 122; wk. asm. 354. [DEAR: *NED*'s adj. 2].
dēore, adj. ja., DEAR, *noble, illustrious;* gsm. 379n.
dierne, adj. ja., *secret, hidden;* apm. *443.* [DERNE].
dohtor, fc., DAUGHTER, 438.
dol, adj., *foolish, presumptuous,* 216.
dōm, m., DOOM, *judgment;* gs. 317, 328.
dōmdæg, m., DOOMSDAY; gs. 264; ds. 26B.
dōn, anom.v., DO, 172; repres. preceding verb, 241, etc.; inf. 383; pres. 3 sg. dēð, 172, 241, 292.
draca, wk.m., *dragon,* 26B; gp. dracena, 207. [DRAKE].
gedrēfan, w.1, *disturb, vex;* pp. 448.
drēogan, II, *perform, fulfill,* 385; *endure,* 365; *be employed,* 60B; pres. 3 sg. 60B, 365, 385. [DREE].
drēor†, m., blood; as. *44A*n. (MS drēam).
drēosan, III, *fail, sink;* pres. 3 sg. 60A.
drohtian, w.2, *lead life, live;* pres. 3 sg. 438.
dropa, wk.m., DROP; np. 44.
drȳ, mi., *magician;* as. 44Bn.
Dryhten, m., *Lord* (*God*), 242, 452, 473; gs. Dryhtnes, 220, 320, 410; ds. Dryhtne, 329, 443; w. Crīste, 327. [DRIGHTIN].
dryhtscipe†, mi., *lordship, renoun;* gs. 379n.
dugoð, f., *host, multitude,* 359; *power,* 391; as. 391; dp. duguðum, 359. [DOUTH].
dumb, adj., DUMB; gp. as noun 78A; wk. nsm. 221.
dūn, f., DOWN, *height;* of dūne, *down-(wards),* 448.
durran, prp., DARE; pres. 3 sg. dear, 329.
duru, fu., DOOR; ap. duru, 37.
dūst, n., DUST; ds. 307, 329.
dynn, mja., DIN, *tumult;* as. 264; dyn, 317.
dynt, mi., DINT, *blow, stroke;* gp. 122.
dyslīce, adv., *foolishly,* 220. [DIZZILY].

Ē, n., the letter and the *eoh*-rune, 96.
ēac, adv., EKE, *likewise, also,* 4B, 93, 296, 391; ēc, 333, 456.
ēaca, wk.m., *increase, access,* 451. [EKE].
ēadig, adj., *prosperous, fortunate,* 358, 381; *blessed,* 338n., 442, 452; gs. ēadiges, 442; dp. ēadgum, 338n. [EADI].
eald, adj., OLD, *ancient;* nsf. 377.
eall, adj., ALL; nsf. 30, 250; asn. 286, 315, 445, 494; npm. 28B, 335, 344; gpm.

76A, 97, 147; gpf. ealra, 36A; eallra, 36B, 435; gpn. eallra, 1B; dpf. 328; dpn. 7B; apm. 72, 76B; apf. 49; apn. 176.
ealle, adv., *in all,* 13B.
eallenga, adv., *altogether, entirely,* 409. [ALLINGE].
eard, mu., *native land;* ds. 494; as. 180. [ERD].
eardian, w.2, *dwell, live,* 347. [ERDE].
earfoð, n., *labor, suffering,* 366n.; *torment,* 465; gp. eorfeða, 465; ap. earfoðu, 366n.
earhfaru†, f., *flight of arrows;* as. 129.
earm, adj., *poor, wretched;* gpm. 81, 484, 488. [ARM].
earn, m., *eagle;* ap. 462. [ERNE].
Ēast-Corsias, prop.n., *East Cosseans;* ap. *177*n.
ēaðe, adv., *easily,* 381; superl. ēaðost, 36A; ēaðusð, 36B. [EATH].
eccg, f., EDGE (*of weapon*); as. eccge, 165; dp. ecggum, 251.
ēce, adj., *eternal,* 242, 313. [ECHE].
ēce, adv., *eternally,* 465.
ēc, see **ēac.**
edwend†, f., *change;* ds. 466.
edwitt, n., *shame, scorn;* gs. -es, 29Bn. [EDWIT].
eft, adv., *afterwards, back, again,* 306, 360, 408. [EFT].
ēge, wk.n., EYE, 487; gp. ēgna, 464n.
egesa, wk.m., *fear, dread;* as. 464.
egesfullīc, adj., *terrible;* comp. npm. -ran, 46A; -ra, 46B.
egeslīce, adv., *terribly, dreadfully,* 26B.
Ēgiptas, prop.n., *Egyptians;* gp. 184.
ellen, n., *strength, power;* gs. elnes, 11B. [ELNE].
ende, mja., END; as. 447.
enge, adj.ja., *narrow, confined;* superl. gsn. engestan, 106.
engel, m., ANGEL, 138, 494; gs. 224, 442; as. 472; gp. 111, 452; dp. 35.
eorl, m., EARL, *nobleman, warrior, chief,* 381, 503; ds. *409.*
eorlscipe†, mi., *lordly power, nobility;* gs. 11B.
eormenstrȳnd‡, f., *mighty race;* gs. 322.
eorre, see **ierre.**
eorðe, wk.f., EARTH; gs. 266, 468; ds. in phrase on eorðan, 21B, 283, 358; as. 306.
eorðwela, wk.m., *earth's wealth, riches;* np. *335.*
ēðel, m., *native land, home;* ds. 408; as. *191*n. [ETHEL].
ēðelrīce†, nja., *native realm;* gs. 106.

F, the letter and the *feoh*-rune, 127.
fāmig, adj., FOAMY; asn. 157.
faran, VI, FARE, *go, proceed,* 376, 493; pres. 1 sg. fare, *18B;* pres. 3 sg. færeð, 135, 273; *fare forth,* 368; 3 pl. 119.
fæder, mc., FATHER, 437; gs. faeder, 407.
fǣge, adj.ja., *doomed to death;* gsm. 158; as noun, 326; fǣgæs, 324. [FEY].
fǣhðo, f., *feud, hostility, enmity;* gs. fǣhðo, 435; as. fǣhðo, 440.
fæst, adj., FAST, *fastened,* 257.
fæste, adv., FAST, *firmly,* 97, 269, 449.
fæsten, nja., *stronghold, fortress;* as. 183; ds. -ne, 311. [FAESTEN].
gefæstnian, w.2, *fasten;* pres. 3 sg. 70.
fæðm, m., *embrace*(?), *power*(?); ds. 390. [FATHOM].
feallan, VII, FALL; pres. 3 sg. 293; 3 pl. 306.
gefeallan, VII, *fall;* pres. 3 pl. 308.
fealewian, w.2, *fade, wither;* pres. 3 pl. 306. [FALLOW].
feax, n., *hair;* ds. 100; as. 130. [FAX].
gefeccan, w.3, *fetch, bring forth,* 69A; gefetian, 69B. [YFET].
feld, mu., FIELD, *plain;* ds. -a, 206; as. feld, 201.
feldgongende†, part. adj., *field-roaming,* 23B, 154.
feng, mi., *grip, grasp,* 346.
feoh, n., *cattle,* 23B; as. 154. [FEE].
feohgestrēon, n., *treasure;* gp. 32A.
feohtan, III, FIGHT; pres. 3 sg. 489; 3 pl. w. on, 450; pres. part. as adj. asm. feohtende, 87A; feohtenne, *87B.*
fēond, mc., *enemy,* 302; FIEND, *devil;* ns. 69, 169, 489; gs. 130; ds. 302; as. 87, 91, 100, 113; np. *450;* gp. 97, 147; dp. 311; ap. 501.
feor, adj., FAR, 373.

feorbūende, part. adj., *far-dwelling;* npm. 271.
feorh, mu., *life;* as. 110, 169.
feorran, adv., *from afar*, 505. [FERREN].
fēower, num., FOUR; an. 254 (iiii); an. 489; nm. -e, 324, 326.
fēran, w.1, *fare, proceed;* pres. 3 sg. 298. [FERE].
ferhð†, m., *soul, spirit*, 505.
geferian, w.1, *carry, bring;* pp. 505.
ferigend‡, mc., *bearer*, 80A; feriend, 80B.
feter, f., FETTER; dp. 70.
feterian†, w.2, FETTER, *bind;* pres. 3 sg. 158.
gefetian, see **gefeccan.**
feðerhoma, wk.m., *plumage;* ds. 151. [FEATHERHAM].
feðersceātas‡, m.pl., *four quarters;* dp. 32A. See **feðerscētte.**
feðerscētte, adj.ja., *in four quarters, in every part;* nsf. 32B. See **feðersceātas.**
fīf, num., in fīf and twēntig (MS xxv), *twenty-five*, 206.
fīfmægn‡, n.pl., *quintuple powers;* dp. 136n.
fīftig, num., FIFTY; as. (L) 239; dpf. 70.
Filistīnas, prop.n., *Philistines;* gp. 183, 205n., *246*, 249, 269, 272, 422.
findan, III, FIND, 8B.
fīras†, mja.pl., *men, human beings;* gp. 208, 265, 467; fȳra, 47, 202.
fisc, m., FISH, 412; gp. 81A; fixa, 81B.
fiðere, nja., *wing;* ap. 256.
flān, m., *arrow;* gp. 130n. [FLANE].
flǣschoma(†), wk.m., *body;* as. 110.
geflēogan, II, *fly to*, 210.
flēon, II, FLEE; pres.p., asm. in flēondne gebrengan, *put to flight*, 147; flēonde geb. 87.
flet, nja., *hall, dwelling;* as. 183. [FLET].
flint, m., FLINT; as. 100.
flītan, I, *dispute, contend*, 170. [FLITE].
flōd, mu., FLOOD, *water;* gs. 80, 157.
flota, m., *sailor;* as. 151. [FLOTE].
flōwan, VII, FLOW, 314.
flyht, mi., FLIGHT, *power of flying;* as. 218.
folc, n., FOLK, *people;* gs. 80.
folctoga†, wk.m., *leader, commander;* np. 119.
folde, wk.f. *earth, ground, land;* gs. 210, 412, 449; ds. 265, 289, 467; as. 69, 157, 208, 293. [FOLD].
folgoð, mu., *condition, destiny*, 361.
folm(†), f., *hand;* as. 169.
fōn, VII, *take up*, w. gen.; pret. 1 pl. 424. [FANG].
for, prep., FOR, 47.
forcinnan‡, III (?), *destroy* (?); pres. 3 pl. 107n.
forcuman, IV, *overcome;* pp. 198, 503.
forcȳðan, w.1, *reprove, rebuke;* pp. 503; -cȳððed, 198.
foreweard, adv., FORWARD, 113.
forhwon, conj., *for what reason, why*, 293, 331, 344, 350; forhwan, 339, 378, 389; forhwām, 332, 335, 384.
forildan, w.1, *delay, put off*, *353*n.
forlǣtan, VII, *let, cause* (*to*); pret. 3 sg. 448. [FORLET].
forscrīfan, I, *bewitch by writing†;* pres. 3 sg. 162.
forst, m., FROST; gs. 335.
forð, adv., FORTH; *further, still*, 415.
forðon, conj., *for that reason, therefore*, 49A, 163, 320, 411, 451; forðan, 49B, 208, 375.
forweornian, w.2, *wither, decay;* pres. 3 pl. 307.
fōt, mc., FOOT; dp. 113, 202, 218; ap. 256.
fracoð, adj., *vile, abominable*, 34; superl. -ast, 343. [FRAKED].
fram, prep., FROM, 31, 374; from, *about*, 201.
frǣcne, adj.ja., *terrible, bold;* wk. as. (?) 302n.
frēa†, wk.m., *lord;* ds. 34.
fremede, adj. ja., *estranged from*, 34A; fremde, 34B; *unfriendly, hostile;* asm. fremdne, 110.
frēond, mc., FRIEND, 205; dp. 135, 432.
fretan, V, *eat, devour;* pres. 3 sg. friteð, 289, 395. [FRET].
fricgan(†), V, *ask;* pres. 1 sg. 361.
gefrignan, III, *learn by inquiry†, hear;* pret. 1 sg. 170.
frīnan, III, *ask, inquire;* pres. 3 sg. 58. [FRAYNE].
frōd(†), adj., *wise, old;* apm. 416.
from, adj., *active, bold;* npm. 119.

from, prep., see **fram.**
fruma, wk.m., *origin, cause,* 435; *prince, ruler,* 269; np. *272.* [FRUME].
frumsceaft, fi., *origin;* as. 407. [FRUMSCHAFT].
frumscyld‡, fi., *chief sin;* gp. 437.
fugol, m., FOWL, *bird,* 210; fugel, 246, 254, 412; gs. fugles, 218; as. 290; fugel, 271.
full, adj., FULL, 25B, 136; nsf. 32; nsn. 487; asf. 501.
full, adv., FULL, *very,* 220; f. oft, 57, 296, 340, 391, 401, 416.
fultum, m., *aid, help, support;* as. 135, 432. [FULTUM].
fūs, adj., *eager;* nsn. 58. [FOUS].
fylgean, w.3, *follow, pursue;* pres. 3 sg. fylgeð, 92A; filgið, 92B.
gefyllan, w.1, *strike down;* pres. 3 sg. *41A;* gefilleð, 41B. [YFELL].
fȳr, n., FIRE, 136n., 407; gs. 346, 501; as. 42.
fyrd, fi., *army;* as. *302*n.
fȳren, adj., *fiery;* gsn. 415. [FIREN].
fyren, f., *sin, crime;* gp. 435, 440; ap. 308.
fyrn, adv., *of old,* 416. [FERN].
fyrndagas, m.pl., *days of old;* dp. 170.
fyrngestrēon‡, n., *ancient treasure;* gp. 32B.
fyrngewryt†, n., *ancient writing,* dp. 8B.
fyrst, m., *time, space of time;* as. 491.
fyrwit, nja., *curiosity,* 58A; fyrwet, 58B, 239.

G, n., the letter and the *gēar*-rune, 134n.
gād, f., GOAD, *point;* as. 91.
Galilēa, prop.n., *Galilee,* 192.
gān, anom.v., GO, *proceed;* pres. 3 sg. gǣð, 126, 216, 274, 278.
gangan, VII, *go,* 345. [GANG].
gegangan, VII, *go,* 280; *happen,* 355; pres. 3 sg. 355.
gārtorn‡, m., *spear-anger, wrath shown by spear-throwing;* as. 145.
gāst, m., GHOST, *spirit, soul,* 54, etc.; hālig g., *Holy Ghost,* 400; *(evil) spirit,* 86A; *(guardian) spirit,* 477; ns. 54A, 241; gǣst, 54B; gs. gāstes, 65A, 400; gǣstes, 433; gǣstæs, 65B; as. gāst, 429; gǣst, 86A; np. gāstas, 477.
gæd‡, n., *society, fellowship,* 441.
geador(†), adv., *together,* 441.
Geador, prop.n., *Gadara* (?), 182n.
Geallbōe, prop.n., *Gilboa,* 182n.
gēap, adj., *vaulted,* 248; *broad,* 405; *curved, crooked,* 124n., 134; nsn. 405; wk. nsm. 134. [YEPE].
gēar, n., YEAR; gp. 280; ap. gēr, 429.
geāra, adv., *of* YORE, *formerly,* 421.
geard, m., YARD, *court,* 83; ap. 407.
geat, n., GATE, as. (?) 298.
gebed, n., *prayer;* ds. 43. [IBED].
gebregdstæf‡, m., literally *skill-letter;* ap. *cunning skill in letters,* 2B.
gebyrd, fi., *fate,* as. 376n.
gecynd, fni., *nature, kind, manner,* 411; ap. 489.
gecyndo, f. (see Sievers-Cook, § 267, n. 4), *nature,* 401; *natural home, native place,* 406; as. -o, 401, 406.
geearnung, f., *merit;* ap. -a, 338.
geflit, n., *dispute, debate;* dp. 422; *contention, strife;* ap. 440.
gehwā, pron., *each one, every one;* gsn. 437; dsm. 236, 451; asm. gehwane, 97, 147.
gegnum†, adv., *forwards,* 345.
gehwylc, pron., *each, every (one),* 223, 224, 348 (w. ānra); gsm. 232; dsm. 146, isn.-hwelce, 280; a(d?)sf.-hwylce, 252, 430.
gehygd, ni., *thought, counsel;* ap. -o, 448.
gelīc, adj., ALIKE, 357; *like,* superl. -ost, 304.
gelīce, adv., ALIKE, *equally,* 336.
gelōme, adv., *often, frequently,* 367.
gemǣre, nja., *boundary, border;* as. (p.?) 189.
gēna, adv., *yet,* 241.
geneahhe, adv., *abundantly,* 229; *often, frequently,* 370, 373, 427.
geōmorlīce, adv., *mournfully,* 259.
geōmrian, w.2, *be sad, mourn,* 343; pres. part. as adj. geōmrende, *troubled,* 241. [YOMER].
geond, prep., *throughout, through,* 115, 273, 363, 384, 486. [YOND].
geondhweorfan†, III, *wander through, traverse;* pret. 3 sg. 176.

geondmengan‡, w.1, *disturb;* pres. 3 sg. 59B.
geondscīnan, I, *shine upon*, 332.
geong, adj., YOUNG, 368; *new*, gsn. 140.
georne, adv., *eagerly, zealously, carefully*, 248, 310, 378. [YERNE].
geornlīce, adv., *zealously, diligently*, 84.
gēotan, II, *pour;* pres. 3 sg. 145. [YET].
gegēotan, II, *found, cast;* pp. 31.
gēow, m., *vulture;* gs. 256n.
gepalmtwigod‡, pp. adj., PALM-TWIGGED, *adorned with palm-branches;* wk. nsm. -twigoda, 12B; nsn. -twigede, 39A; -twigude, 39B.
gēr, see **gēar.**
gerǣswa†, wk.m., *leader, prince*, 111.
gesǣlig, adj., *happy, blessed;* superl. gesǣlgost, 67B. [ISELI].
gesceaft, f(n)i., *created thing, creature*, 36, 328; *creation*, 30, 319, 360; *destiny*, 240, *377*, 385; ns. 30, *377*; ds. 319, 360; as. 240, 385; -e, 331; gp. 36; dp. 328.
gesegled, pp.adj., *equipped with a sail;* asn. 217.
gesīene, adj. ja., *seen;* nsn. 314.
gesihð, fi., *sight, vision;* ds. 409.
gesīð, m., *companion;* as. 86B (prob. error); np. 339; dp. 444.
gesund, adj., *safe and sound*, 18B.
getæl, n., *number, series;* gs. getales, 38B. See **getælrīm.** [ITEL].
getælrīm‡, n., *number, order;* ds. 38A.
getrum†, n., *legion, host;* dp. 142.
getwinnas, m., *twins;* np. 357; -tuinnas, 107.
geðōht, m., *thought, purpose;* as. 231.
geweald, n., *power, control;* as. 235, 375.
gewin, n., *labor, toil;* as. 463. [I-WIN].
gewitt, nja., *understanding;* ds. 23B. [I-WIT].
gewrit, n., *writing*, in pl. *scriptures;* ap. 50. [I-WRIT].
gewurdene, see **geweorðan.**
gielpen, adj., *boastful;* npm. gielpne, 199.
gierd, fjō., YARD, *rod, staff;* as. -e, 90A; gyrde, 90B.
gif, conj., IF, 16B, 33, 88A, 195, 397, 398, 402, 431; gyf, 88B.
gifan, V, GIVE, opt. 3 sg. 168; pret. 3 sg. geaf, 56.
gīfre, adj., *greedy, rapacious;* dsm. 145. [YEVER].
gīfre, adv., *greedily, ravenously;* comp. gīfrust, 48A; gīfrost, 48B.
gifu, f., *gift, grace;* as. 65.
gihðu†, f., *anxiety, grief;* ds. 343.
gillan, III, YELL; pres. 3 sg. 259.
gilp, m., *boasting;* as. 132.
gilpan, III, *boast*, 197.
gimm, m., GEM; dp. 63A; gymmum, 63B.
giogoð, f., YOUTH; ds. 378.
gīt, adv., YET, *still*, 214; þā gīt, *further*, 9B.
glæd, adj., GLAD, *bright;* comp. nsm. 478.
glēaw, adj., *keen, prudent*, 431. [GLEW].
glēd, fi., *glowing coal, flame;* gp. 48. [GLEED].
God, m., GOD, 134, 313, 337; gs. 63, 84, 140, 146, 219, 345, 441, 475; ds. 343.
gōd, adj., GOOD, 102; wk. nsn. 355; comp. betra, BETTER; nsm. 361; nsf. sēlre, 397.
gōd, n., GOOD; gs. 337.
godcund, adj., *divine;* gsm. 433.
godspel, n., GOSPEL; as. 65A.
godspellian, w.2, *declare the gospel*, 65B.
gold, n., GOLD, gs. 15B, 31; ds. 478.
goldwlonc†, adj., *proud with gold;* npm. 199.
grǣdig, adj., GREEDY, *eager, zealous*, *475*n.; w. gen., *eager for*, 337.
Grēca, see **Crēcas.**
grēne, adj. ja., GREEN; npn. 305.
grēotan, II, *weep, lament*, 368. [GREET].
griffus, m., *griffon;* gs. griffus, 256.
grimm, adj., GRIM, *fierce, cruel;* wk. asm. *91A;* grymman, 91B.
grimme, adv., *cruelly*, 132; *bitterly*, 368.
grīpan, I, *seize, attack;* pres. 3 pl. 151. [GRIPE].
gegrīpan, I, *seize;* pres. 3 sg. 112.
gripe, mi., GRIP, *grasp;* ds. 48, 76.
gripu‡, f., *kettle, cauldron*, 46A; -o, 46B.
grōwan, VII, GROW, 475.
grund, m., GROUND, *bottom*, 31, 219; *abyss (of hell)*, 478; ds. 31; as. 219; dp. 478.
grundbūend†, mc., *earth-dweller;* gp. -ra, 280.

guma†, wk.m., *man;* gp. 146, *197.* [GOME].
gūð†, f., *battle, war;* ds. 124, 199.
gūðmāga‡, wk.m., *warrior,* 90B.
gūðmæcga‡, wk.m., *warrior,* 90A.
gylden, adj., *golden,* 63, 248; asf. 91; wk. gsf. -nan, 226. [GILDEN].
gyrd, see **gierd.**
gyrn†, mi., *sorrow, misfortune;* as. 259.

H, n., the letter, 138.
habban, w.3, (1) HAVE, pres. 3 sg. hafað, 49, 64, 90, 222, 223, 224, 235, 254, 256, 336, 349, 369, 400; 3 pl. habbað, 120, 128; w. neg. pres. 3 sg. nafað, 217; pret. opt. 3 sg. hæfde, 174. (2) as auxiliary, pres. 1 sg. hæbbe, 1B; pret. 3 sg. hæfde, 502; pres. opt. 2 sg. hæbbe, 197.
hād, mu., *nature, form;* as. 400.
hālig, adj., HOLY; gsm. 400; ap. -e, 40A; hālie, 40B; wk.apf. 37B; hālgan, 37A.
hand, fu., HAND; as. 278, 490; ap. 159.
hangiende, pres. part., HANGING, 105n.
hātan, VII, *command, order,* 267, 268, 449, 500; *call, name,* 203, 271; pres. 3 sg. 500; 3 pl. 271; pret. 1 sg. hēt, 267; 3 sg. heht, 268, 449; pp. 203. [HIGHT].
hædre†, adv., *anxiously, oppressively,* 62A.
hæft, m., *bond, fetter;* dp. 403.
hæftling, m., *captive, prisoner;* as. *126.*
hæleð†, mc., *man, hero;* gp. 60. [HELETH].
hǣlo, f(īn.), *salvation, safety;* gs. hǣlo, 237.
hē, pers. pron., HE, (*she*), (IT); hē, 33, 34, 50, 66, etc. (44 times); nsf. hēo, 286, 287, 290, 291, etc. (20 times); hīo, 291, 292; nsn. hit, 390, 391, 401, 402, etc. (7 times); gsm. (poss.) his, 54, 102, 161, 166, etc. (20 times); gsf. (poss.) hiera, 227; gsn. (poss.) his, 407; dsm. him, 30B, 44, 56, 88, etc. (21 times); refl. 378, 381, 443; dsf. hire, 316; asm. hine, 25B, 85, 93, 94, etc. (32 times); refl. 115, 260, 301 (?); hiene, 96, 98, 103 (refl.), 118, 127, 250; asf. hīe, 69A, 70A, 439; hī, 69B, 70B; asn. hit, 276, 398, 402; np. hīe, 132, 149, 152, 251, etc. (17 times); gp. hira, 235, 348, 361; poss. 172, 357, 420; dp. him, 122, 250, 458, 496; refl. 309, 446; ap. hīe, 231, 237, 295, 312.
hēaf, m., *lamentation;* as. 458.
hēafod, n., HEAD, 29B, 254; *source,* 436; dp. 29B; ap. 254.
Hēahcining(†), n., *high king* (*God*), 500.
hēahgestrēon†, n., *rich treasure;* as. 310.
healdan, VII, HOLD, *keep;* pres. 3 sg. 51; 3 pl. 248, *252,* 310, 403; opt. 3 sg. 481.
healf, adj., HALF; dsn. 445.
healf, f., HALF, *side;* ap. 253.
heall, f., HALL, *dwelling;* as. 372.
hēap, m., HEAP, *host, throng;* as. 115, 148, 161.
heard, adj., HARD; gsn. (as noun), 278; dsn. 7B; asm. 495; superl. -ost, 303.
hearde, adv., HARD, *with difficulty,* 427; *exceedingly, greatly,* 62B, 262.
heardlīce, adv., *harshly, severely,* 131. [HARDLY].
gehēawan, VII, *hew;* pres. 3 sg. 156.
gehefegian, w.2, *make heavy, weigh down;* pres. 3 sg. 159.
hell, fjō., HELL; gs. 105, 115, 126; ds. 480, 499; as. 73, 458, 500.
hēo, see **hē.**
heofon, m., HEAVEN; gp. heofona, 37A, 52A, 445, 473; heofna, 37B; dp. heofnum, 60B; hefenum, 60A; hefonum, 458; ap. heofonas, 40A; heofnas, 40B.
heofonrīce, nja., *kingdom of heaven;* gs. 52B. [HEAVENRIC].
heofonware, mi., pl., *inhabitants of heaven;* gp. 455. [HEAVENWARE].
heolstor, m., *darkness;* ds. 104.
heorte, wk.f., HEART; gs. 156; ds. 62, 495; heartan, 104; as. 369.
hēow, nja., HUE, *appearance, form;* as. 400.
hēr, adv., HERE, 318.
heregeatewa, fwō., pl., *war-gear;* ap. 52A, -owe, 52B. [HERIOT].
geherian, w.1, *praise,* 24B.
hettend†, mc., *enemy;* dp. 499.
gehīdan, w.1, *hide;* pres. 3 sg. 73B (error). See **āhīeðan.**
hider, adv., HITHER, 275.

hielt, mi., HILT; np. (with sg. meaning), 215.
hīeran, w.1, HEAR, *obey;* pret. 3 sg. 443.
gehīeran, w.1, *hear, heed;* inf. -hīran, 313; pres. opt. 3 sg. 317; -hȳre, 264; pret. 1 sg. -hȳrde, 416. [YHERE].
Hiērusālem, prop.n., *Jerusalem;* gs. 226; as. *192*n.
Hierycho, prop.n.; as. *Jericho,* 192.
hige, see **hyge.**
higegeōmor†, adj., *sad in mind,* 372.
hild†, fjō., *war, combat;* ds. 159.
hildewrǣsen‡, f., *chain for war-captive;* ds. -wrǣsne, 284.
hinder, adv., *behind, back;* on h. *backward,* 126.
hīo, see **hē.**
hīðan, w.1, *plunder, ravage,* 445; pres. p., dsf., 284.
hladan, VI, *heap up;* pres. 3 sg. 429. [LADE].
hlāford, m., LORD, 361, 374n.; as. 382.
hleahtor, m., LAUGHTER, 340.
hlēor, n., *cheek;* as. 113. [LEER].
gehnǣgan, w.1, *humble, vanquish,* 118, 391; *bring down,* 155; pres. 3 sg. 155, 391; 3 pl. 118.
hnesce, adj. (ja.), *soft;* gsn. (as noun) 278. [NESH].
holt, n., HOLT, *forest, wood,* 82.
horn, m., HORN; dp. 156, 461.
hrægl, n., *garment;* gs. 140. [RAIL].
gehrēosan, II, *fall,* 448.
hricg, mja., RIDGE, *height, 19B.*
hringan, III, RING; pres. 3 sg. 258.
hrōf, m., ROOF; as. 403.
hū, adv., conj., HOW; in direct question, 334, 341, 355; in indirect question, 60, 363, 474.
hūlīc, interr. pron., *of what sort,* 53.
hund, n.num., *hundred,* 253.
hungor, n., HUNGER; as. 73, 463.
hunig, n., HONEY, 66.
hūru, adv., *truly,* 56, 104, 219. [HURE].
hwā, interr. pron., WHO, (WHAT); ns. 36, 327, 329; nsn. hwæt, 221, 273, 324, 330; asn. 228, 434; isn. tō hwon, *to what purpose, why,* 438.
hwælen‡, adj., *like a whale,* 255n.
hwænne, adv., conj., *when,* 406.
hwæt, interj., *lo, truly,* 1B, 170, 381, 439.
hwæðer, interr. pron., *which of two,* 418; gsm. 361; asm. 420. [WHETHER].
hwæðre, adv., *yet, nevertheless,* 321, 430, 504. See **ðēhhwæðre.** [WHETHER].
hwearfian, w.2, *turn, wander;* pres. 3 sg. 35A; hwarfað, 35B. [WHARVE].
hwettan, w.1, WHET, *incite;* pres. 3 sg. hweteð, 485.
hwīl, f., WHILE, *time, space of time;* as. 109, 305, 353, 359; ǣnige h. 402; dp., adv., *sometimes, at times,* 61A, 372; hwȳlum, 61B; correl. 151, 152, 155, 158.
hwylc, pron., WHICH, *of what sort,* 10B; w. ānra, *each one,* 225.
hycgan, w.3, *think, consider;* pres. 1 sg. hycgge, 194; 3 sg. hygeð, 230.
hȳdan, w.1, HIDE; pres. 3 sg. 115; 3 pl. 310.
hyge†, mi., *mind, spirit,* 474; hige, 60, 62. [HIGH].
hȳrsum, adj., *obedient;* nsn. 390. [HEARSUM].
hȳð, fjō., *harbor, refuge;* as. 237.

I, n., the letter, 123.
ic, pers. pron., *I,* 1B, 7B, 9B, 13B, 16B, 18B, 193, etc. (20 times); ds. mē, 5B, 61, 201, 242, etc. (7 times); mec (?), 18Bn.; as. mē, 239, 243; mec, 16B, 18B, 19B, 57; np. wē, 344, 422; dp. ūs, 434, 438; ap. ūs, 329; ūsic, 292, 450.
idese, fi., *woman*†; as. 356.
iēo, adv., *once, formerly, of old,* 319.
ieorrenga, adv., *angrily, fiercely,* 98n.
ierre, adj.ja., *perverse, depraved,* 322, 488; *angry, fierce,* 88, nsn. yrre, 488; asm. ierne, 88A; yorn (error), 88B; gsf. eorre, 322; wk. nsm. yrra, 123.
īgland, n., ISLAND, *land bordering the sea;* gp. 1B.
in, adv., IN, 460.
in, prep., IN, *into;* w. dat. 309, 351, 441, 457, 475; w. acc. 152, 322, 345.
Indēas, prop.n., *Indians;* gp. 4B, 177.
ingang, m., *entrance;* as. 213. [INGANG].
ingemynd†, fi., *memory, mind;* dp. 53.
insceaft, fi., *internal propagation;* as. 447n.

intinga, wk.m., *cause* (?); dp. -um, 45An.; ds. (?) -an, 45B.
inwitgecyndo‡, f. (see **gecyndo**), *evil nature;* as. -o, 322.
īren, adj., IRON; dp. 28B, 461.
īren, n., IRON; as. 292.
Israēlas, prop.n., *Israelites;* gp. *14B.*
istoria, n., *history;* as. -m, 4Bn.
īð, see **ȳð.**

L, n., the letter and the *lagu*-rune, 123.
laguswemmende‡, part. adj., *swimming in the sea;* gp. as noun 281.
lama, wk.m., LAME *person, cripple;* gp. -ena, 77A; -ana, 77B.
land, n., LAND; ds. 201; as. 486; lond, 187; ap. land, 176; lond, 315.
lang, adj., LONG; dsf. 286; asf. 90; apm. 120.
lange, adv., LONG, 309; comp. leng, 350, 453; superl. lengest, 318.
lār, f., LORE, *learning;* as. 187; *counsel;* as. 453.
lārcræft, m., *knowledge, science;* ap. 3B.
lārēow, mwa., *teacher, master;* dp. 390.
late, adv., LATE, 439n.
lāð, adj., LOATH, *hated, hostile;* nsn. 122; asn. 160; wk. asm. lāðan, 86A; lāþan, 86B; apn. 301.
læccean (**lǣcean**?), w.1, *seize, take;* pres. 3 sg. lǣceð, 486. [LATCH].
lǣce, mja., LEECH, *physician*, 77, 102.
lǣdan, w.1, LEAD; pres. 3 sg. 486.
gelǣdan, w.1, *lead;* pres. 3 sg. 301.
lǣne, adj., *transitory;* wk. dsf. 319.
lǣran, wk.1, *teach;* pres. 3 sg. 50, 481 (*urge*), 483. [LERE].
lǣsse, see **lȳtel.**
lǣstan, w.1, *continue to do;* pres. 3 pl. 309. [LAST].
lǣtan, VII, LET, *cause, make;* pres. 3 sg. 100, 113; 3 pl. 129.
lēaf, n., LEAF; np. 305; ap. 64.
leahtor, m., *sin, offense;* dp. 86.
lēas, adj., *without, bereft of;* nsm. 371. [LEASE].
lecgan, w.1, LAY; pret. 1 pl. 423.
leng, see **lange.**
lengu, f(īn.), *length, height;* as. 405.
lēode, mi. pl., *people, men;* np. 319; gp. 359; dp. 336, 373.
lēodgryre‡, mi., *terror of the people;* ds. 270.
lēof, adj., LIEF, *dear;* comp. nsn. 30.
leofað, see **lifian.**
lēoftǣle, adj.ja., *friendly, agreeable, well liked*, 359.
lēogan, II, LIE, *deceive;* pres. 3 sg. līehð, 172n.
lēoht, n., LIGHT, 77, 400; ds. 394.
lēoht, adj., LIGHT, *bright, fair;* apn. 120; wk. nsf. 30.
leorneng, f., LEARNING; gs. -a, 176.
Libias, prop.n., *Libyans;* gp. 3B, 187.
līc, n., *body;* as. 152.
licgan, V, LIE, 181, 257; *lie still*, 262; pres. 3 sg. ligeð, 181, 257; 3 pl. licggað, 262.
līehð, see **lēogan.**
līf, n., LIFE; gs. 21B, 160, 233, 390.
līfgetwinnan‡, wk.m.pl., *twins*, 141.
lifian, w.3, LIVE; pres. 3 sg. leofað, 350, 359, 373; 3 pl. lifiað, 309, 319; lifigað, 466; pret. 3 pl. lifdon, 456; pres. part. lifigende, 439.
lim, n., LIMB; np. leoma, 262; gp. leomona, 102.
gelimpan, III, *happen, befall;* pret. 3 sg. gelomp, 200. [ILIMP].
līne, wk.f., LINE, *rope*, 286; *rule* (?), 17B; ds. 286; as. (p. ?), 17B.
lissan‡, w.1, *subdue;* pres. 3 sg. 286.
lið, n., *joint;* ap. 102n.
liðere, wk.f., *sling;* ds. liðran, 27B. [LITHER].
līxan, w.1, *shine, gleam*, 227.
loca, m., LOCK; ap. 176.
lōcian, w.2, LOOK, 257; *turn one's gaze?*, 273; pres. 3 sg. 257, 373.
lond, see **land.**
longian, w.2, impers. w. acc., LONG; pres. 3 sg. 262.
lonn†, f., *chain, fetter;* dp. 257, 270.
lufian, w.2, LOVE, *cherish*, 86; pres. 3 sg. 237.
lufu (lufe), (wk.) f., LOVE; ds. lufan, 481.
lūtan, II, *bend, stoop;* pres. 3 sg. 394. [LOUT].
lyft, fi., *air;* ds. 141. [LIFT].

lyftflēogende‡, part. adj., *flying in the air;* gp. as noun, 281.
lȳt, indecl.n., *little*, 336. [LITE].
lȳtel, adj., LITTLE; asf. lȳtle, 305, 359; comp. asn. lǣsse, 349.

M, n., the letter and the *man*-rune, 127.
mā, see **micle.**
Macedonia, prop.n., *Macedonia*, 190.
māga†, wk.m., *son;* ap. 362, 375.
magan, prp., MAY, *be able, can;* pres. 2 sg. miht, 43; 3 sg. mæg, 36, 64, 68, 86, 146, 202, 208, 218, 276, 346, 353, 381, 383, 430; pret. 1 sg. mihte, 8B; meahte, 495; 3 sg. 426.
man, mc., MAN, 163; monn, 243, 378; mon, 209, 353, 471 (indef.); gs. 148, 158; ds. men, 393, 396, *472*; gp. 232, 255, 425, 484; monna, 59B; dp. monnum, 318; ap. menn, 416; men, 171.
mān, n., *crime, sin;* ds. 309, 318.
mānful, adj., *evil, wicked;* gp. as n. -ra, 148.
manian, w.2, *exact, claim;* opt. pres. 3 sg. manige, *468*n.
manigo, f(īn.), *multitude;* as. 387.
māra, see **micel.**
Marculf, prop.n., *Marcolf;* gs. 180n.
Māthean, prop.n., *Midian;* gs. (?), *184*n.
maððumsele‡, mi., *hall of treasures;* ap. 180.
mǣg, m., *kinsman;* gp. 482. [MAY].
mǣgwine†, mi., *friendly kinsman;* dp. 352.
mægn, n., MAIN, *power, strength;* as. *349.*
mægenðrymm, mja., *power, greatness, virtue;* gs. 10B.
mǣnan, w.1, MEAN; pres. 1 sg. 228.
mǣre, adj.ja., *famous;* wk. nsm. 203.
mǣrðo, f., *glory*, 163; *glorious deed*, 67B, 200; as. mærðo, 163; gp. -a, 67B, 200.
mǣte, adj.ja., *moderate, small;* gsn. (as noun), 279.
M.ces, see note on 7a.
meahta, see **mieht.**
mēce, mja., *sword;* gs. 163.
Mēdas, prop.n., MEDES; gp. 180.
medume, adj., (orig. superl.) *middling, average;* gpm. 255.
Mēlot, prop.n., *Melot* (?); gs. 268n.
meltan, see **miltan.**
mengan, w.1, *mingle in, join in;* pret. 1 p. 424. [MENG].
gemengan, w.1, *disturb, confuse;* pres. 3 sg. 59A. [IMENG].
meolc, fc., MILK, 67B.
mercstede‡, mi., *borderland, desolate region;* as. 209.
mere, mi., *sea†, ocean;* as. 177. [MERE].
merelīðende, part. adj., *sea-faring*, nsm. *203.*
mergan, w.1, *cleanse, purify*, 55A; merian, 55B. [MERE].
Mesopotamie, prop.n., *Mesopotamia;* as. 190.
gemetigian, w.2, *moderate, control*, 431.
Metod†, m., *God;* gs. 476, 482; as. 41.
meðelcwide†, mi., *discourse;* ap. 424.
micel, adj., *great;* gsn. (as noun), 279; wk. dsn. -an, 6B; comp. asf. māran, 352. [MICKLE].
micle, adv., MUCH, *by far*, 300, 397; comp. mā, in phrase ðon mā, *the more*, 210n.
mid, adv., *likewise*, 501.
mid, prep., *with, together with;* w. dat. and instr., 18B, 43, 70, 168, 218, 284, 292, 318, 344, 359, 360, 420, 438, 444, 446, 499; w. acc. 302, 453. [MID.] See also **mid ðȳ ðe.**
middangeard, m., *world, earth*, 414; gs. 75B, 171, 425; ds. 75A. [MIDDENERD].
midde, wk.f., *middle*, in phrase on middan, 255.
middelgemǣre‡, mja., *central region;* dp. 247.
mid ðȳ ðe, conj., *while*, 476.
mieht, fi., MIGHT, *power;* gp. meahta, 220; dp. 320.
milde, adj.ja., MILD, *generous;* asn. 382.
miltan, w.1, MELT, *refine by melting*, 55B; meltan, 55A.
milts, f., *mercy;* as. 482. [MILCE].
gemiltsian, w.2, *make merciful;* pres. 3 sg. 41.
mīn, pron. adj., MINE, MY, 60; apm. 15B.
misgemynd‡, fi., *evil thought;* ap. -a, 485.
mōd, n., MOOD, *spirit, heart, mind*, 59; gs. 10B, 67B, 431; as. 369, 485.
mōdig, adj., *high-souled, brave*, 75, 268; *proud*, 200, 318; npm. 200; wk. nsm.

mōdega, 268; dp. mōdgum, 318; comp. nsm. mōdigra, 75. [MOODY].
mōdglēaw‡, adj., *wise;* apm. 171.
mōdor, fc., MOTHER, 362, 375, 435, 437.
mōdsefa†, wk.m., *mind, heart;* ds. 382; as. 232.
monig, adj., MANY; asn. 461; gsn. (as noun), 424; apf. 333.
moning, f., *warning, admonition,* 200.
mon(n), see **man.**
mōr, n., MOOR, *mountain,* 414; ap. 333.
morðor, n., *crime, mortal sin;* ds. 55; as. 41. [MURDER].
mōs, n., *food;* ds. 279.
mōtan, prp., *may, be permitted to, must;* pres. 3 sg. 314, 331, 385, 389; 1 pl. 344; opt. 3 sg. 406. [MOTE].
munt, m., MOUNT, *mountain,* 247, 414; ap. 333.
murnan, III, MOURN; *care about, long for,* 476.
mūð, m., MOUTH; as. 148.

N, n., the letter, 108.
nafað, see **habban.**
nāh, see **āgan.**
nāht, n.pron., NAUGHT, *nothing,* 249n.
nama, wk.m., NAME, 89.
nāmon, see **niman.**
nǣdre, wk.f., ADDER, *serpent;* ap. 462.
nǣfre, adv., NEVER, 7B, 505; næfre . . . ðæs, *never so,* 69n., 149.
genǣman, w.1, *take away by force, seize,* w. on (*from*), 250n.
nǣnig, pron., *none, no one, not any,* 59, 202; adj., 163, 425; nsf. nǣnegu, 411.
ne, adv., *not,* 8B, 24B, 101, 110, etc. (28 times).
nē, conj., *nor,* prec. clause, 102, 210; correl. (ne) . . . nē . . . nē, 217, 218²; 276², 277; 346, 347; 412³, 413³, 414³.
nēah, adj., NIGH, *near,* 62, 137; superl. dsn., in phrase æt nīehstan, *next, shortly,* 133.
neahtes, see **nieht.**
nearocræft†, m., *oppressive power* (?); ds. *386*n.
nearwe, adv., NARROW*ly, strictly, forcibly,* 133.
nēat, n., NEAT, *cattle, 210.*

Nebrond, prop.n., *Nimrod;* gs. 205n.
nēd, fi., NEED, *necessity,* 303.
nele, see **willan.**
nerigend, mc., *saviour,* 80A; *Saviour, God,* 330; neriend, 80B; Nergend, 330.
nēðan, w.1, *venture, fare boldly;* pres. 3 sg. nēðeð, *386*n.
nieht, f(m)c., NIGHT, 303; gs. -es, 330; as adv. 240; neahtes, 386, 389; gp. 252.
nīeten, n., *animal, cattle,* 22B; as. 153.
niman, IV, *take;* pret. 3 pl. nāmon, 453. [NIM].
Niniue, prop.n., NINEVEH; gs. -n, 179.
nīð, m., *hostility, war,* 300. [NITH].
niðer, adv., NETHER, *down,* 69.
nō, adv., *not at all,* 101, 194.
norð, adv., NORTH, *to the north,* 182.
norðan, adv., *from the north,* 252.
Norð-Predan, prop.n., *North Parthians* (?); ap. 179n.
Noster, see **Pāter Noster.**
nū, adv., NOW, 12, 212, 318; nū gēna, *still, even, yet, 241.*
nyste, see **witan.**
nytt, adj. ja., *useful, profitable;* gsn. (as noun), 194.

Ō, n., the letter, *108*n.
of, prep. w. dat., OF, *from,* 27B, 29B, 55, 56, etc. (13 times).
ofer, prep., OVER, *above, beyond;* w. dat. 48, 480; w. acc. 20B, 49, 196, 215, 267, 315.
oferbīdan, I, *outlast;* pres. 3 sg. 291. [OVERBIDE].
oferbricgan, w.1, *bridge over;* pres. 3 sg. 297n.
ofermægen†, n., *overpowering might;* ds. 93.
ofermōd, adj., *too proud, insolent;* wk. gsm. 442.
oferstīgan, I, *surpass, overcome;* pres. 3 sg. 291. [OVERSTY].
oferwīgan‡, I, *overcome, vanquish;* pres. 3 sg. 290.
offeallan, VII, *fall upon;* pret. 3 sg. 207n. [OFFALL].
ofslēan, VI, *strike down, destroy;* pres. 3 sg. -slihð, 93A; -slehð, 93B; pret. 3 sg. -slōg, 206. [OFSLAY].

oft, adv., OFT, *often, frequently,* 57, 132, 164, 275, 296, 340, 364, 367, 391, 401, 416, 419.

ōm, m., *rust;* ds. 292.

on, prep., ON, *in, among;* w. dat., 6B, 7B, 21B, 38, etc. (37 times); postpos. 250, w. acc., *into, to, against, toward, with, on,* 19B, 94, 114, 195 (19 times); postpos. 450; in adv. phrases, on hinder, 126; on weg, 493; on willan, 19B.

onǣlan, w.1, *set fire to, kindle;* pres. 3 sg. 42. [ANNEAL].

onbyrgan, w.1, *taste;* pres. 3 sg. onbyregeð, 234; pp. 2B.

ōnettan, w.1, *hasten;* pres. 3 sg. 138.

onfindan, III, *discover;* pret. 1 sg. 266; 3 sg. 452.

onfōn, VII, *take on, put on;* pres. 3 pl. 151. [ONFANG].

ongieldan, III, *atone for, pay for* (w. gen.); pres. 3 pl. 132n.

onginnan, III, *begin;* pret. 3 sg. 443. [ONGIN].

onhǣtan, w.1, *heat,* 43.

onlīðigan‡, w.2, *weaken, yield,* 349.

onlūcan, II, *unlock;* pp. 3B. [UNLOUK].

onlūtan, II, *bow, submit,* 349.

onmēdla, wk.m., *courage;* ds. 344.

onsendan, w.1, *send forth;* pres. 3 sg. 472; 3 pl. 236.

ontȳnan, w.1, *open, reveal,* 38; pres. 3 sg. 40. [UNTINE].

onwæcnan, VI, (wk.1), *spring, be born;* pp. onwæcned, 212.

ord, m., *point;* gp. 224; dp. 142. [ORD].

organ, m., *canticle, song* (*of Pater Noster*), 53A; organan (prob. error), 53Bn.; gs. 33.

orlegstund‡, f., *hour of destiny;* as. 366n.

ormōd, adj., *despairing, spiritless,* 342. [ORMOD].

oroð, n., *breath;* as. 213.

orðanc, m., *skilful device;* ap. 72A;-þ-72B.

orðances‡, adv., *thoughtlessly, heedlessly,* 164.

ōðer, pron., OTHER; ōðer . . . ōðer, *one . . . an* (*the*) *other,* 358², 359; 443²; 478², 479, 481, 483.

oððæt, conj., *until,* 144, 156, 446, 487, 490.

oððe, conj., *or,* 10B, 11B², 173, 193, 355.

oðglīdan‡, I, *glide away, slip away, escape;* pres. 3 sg. 393.

ōwiht, n., AUGHT; as. 33.

P, n., the letter and the *peorð*-rune, 89A; the letter only, 89B.

Palestinion, prop.n., *Palestine;* as. 178n.

Palmtrēow, n., *palm-tree;* as. 167.

Pamphilia, prop.n., *Pamphilia, 189.*

Pāter Noster, m., n., *Pater Noster;* ns(m). 12Bn.; ns(n). 39; as. 167.

Persēas, prop.n., *Persians;* gp. 178.

Pōrus, prop.n., *Porus, King of India;* gs. Pōres, 189n.

prīma, adj., PRIME, *first;* asm. 89A; prīm, 89B.

prologa, m., *prologue;* as. 89An.; -o, 89B.

pund, n., POUND; gp. 14B.

Q, n., the letter and the *cweorð*-rune, 118.

R, n., the letter and the *rād*-rune, 98.

racentēag, f., *chain;* ds. 285.

rāp, m., ROPE; np. 324, 326.

rǣcan, w.1, REACH; pres. 3 sg. rǣceð, 285.

gerǣcan, w.1, *reach,* 219.

rǣd, m., REDE, *advice, counsel;* as. 482.

rǣdan, VII, *have control over;* pres. 3 sg. 362. [REDE].

ræst, fjō., REST; ds. 338.

rǣswa†, wk.m., *leader, counsellor, chief;* ap. *171*n.

rēafian, w.2, *plunder, ravage;* pres. 3 sg. 299. [REAVE].

recene, adv., *instantly, quickly,* 244.

restan, w.1, REST, 385; pres. 3 sg. 221.

rīce, nja., *realm, kingdom;* gs. 4B, 37, 52A; as. 178, 181, 185, 345, 441, 445.

rīm, n., *reckoning, count;* ds. 38B. [RIME].

rūm, adj., *wide, long;* dsf. 285.

rȳman, w.1, *open up;* pres. 3 pl. 213.

S, n., the letter and the *sigel*-rune, 111.

Salomon, prop.n., *Solomon, King of Is-*

rael, 323, 361; Saloman, 173; in headings preceding lines 39A, 63A, *193*, 216, 229, 236, 244, 283, 305, 318, 325, 329, 335, 342, 346, 353, 362, 381, *390*, 427, 441, 472; abbrev. Salom̄ (see textual notes), 21B, 39B, 63B.

samnian, w.2, *gather, collect;* pp. 392; apf. as adj. samnode, *9B*.

samod, adv., *simultaneously, together*, *108*; somod, 347; w. ætgædere, 339.

Sanere, prop.n., *Shinar, site of the Tower of Babel* (Gen. x, 10); gs.(?) 201.

sārgian, w.2, *wound, afflict;* pres. 3 sg. *109*.

Sātan, prop.n., *Satan;* gs. 117.

Sāturnus, prop.n., *Saturn, prince of Chaldea, 174;* in headings preceding lines 1Bn., 36, 53, 203, 221, 234, 238, 273, 293, 303, 314, 323, 327, 331, 339, 344, 350, 354, 378, 384, 416, 434, 467.

Saulus, prop.n., *Saul;* gs. Saulus, 181.

sāwol, f., SOUL, *spirit;* gs. sāwle, 66B; sāule, 66A; as. sāwle, 68B; sāule, 68A; np. sāula, 498.

sǣl, mi., *time*, 316; *happiness*, in phrase on sǣlum, *happy*, 504. [SELE].

gesǣlan, w.1, *happen;* pres. 3 sg. 341.

sǣlð, f., *fortune, happiness, blessing;* ap. 341.

gescǣnan, w.1, *make shine, render brilliant;* pp. 214.

scead, n., *shade, shadow;* gs. 116. [SHED].

sceaft, m., SHAFT, *spear;* ap. 120.

sceapen, see **scieppan.**

scearp, adj., SHARP; apn. 128.

scēat, m., *region, quarter;* ap. 449.

sceaða, wk.m., *enemy, fiend, devil,* 116; as. 128.

Sceppend, see **Scippend.**

sceððan, VI, *injure, harm;* pres. 3 sg. scyðeð, *429*n.

scieppan, VI, SHAPE, *destine;* pp. sceapen, 363.

gescieppan, VI, *create;* pret. 3 sg. 458. [ISHAPE].

scierpan, w.1, *clothe;* pres. 3 sg. 138. [SHARP].

scild, m., SHIELD, 79B; scyld, 79A.

scima, wk.m., *twilight, gloom;* ds. 116.

scīnan, I, SHINE; pres. 3 sg. *214*.

scinn, n., *spectre, evil spirit;* gs. *101*.

scip, n., SHIP; as. 217.

Scippend, mc., *Creator;* Scippend, 56A; Sceppend, 56B; gs. Scippendes, 79B; Scyppendes, 79A. [SHEPPEND].

scīre, adv., *brightly*, 332. [SHIRE].

sconca, wk.m., SHANK, *leg;* ap. 101.

gescōp, see **gescieppan.**

sculan, prp., SHALL, *must;* pres. 1 sg. sceall, 321; 3 sg. sceall, 159, 279, 354, 367, 376, 474; sceal, 166, 348; opt. 3 sg. scyle, 250; scile, 163; pret. opt. (?) 3 pl. scoldon, 456.

scyld, fi., *guilt, crime;* as. 488; dp. 56B.

scyld, m., see **scild.**

scyldig, adj., *guilty, criminal;* asm. 128; gp. 79A; scildigra, 79B; dpm. 56An. [SHILDY].

Scyppendes, see **Scippend.**

scyðeð, see **sceððan.**

sē, se, sēo, ðæt, dem. pron., dem. adj., and def. article, THE, THAT, *he, she, that, that one;* nsm. sē, *he, that one*, 219, 343; as rel. sē, 301, 474; *he who*, 24B; sē ðe, 84, 172, 216, 217, 221, 234, 342, 504; se, art., 12B, 49, 53, 63, etc. (25 times); nsf. sēo, 46, 331, 375, 396, 434; nsn. ðæt, 39, 122, 167, 273, 334, 355, 377, 450; rel. (= sē) 415, 426, gsm. ðæs, 33A, 130, 315, 367, 391, 442; 448, 492 (*of him*); þæs, 17B, 33B, 44B; gsf. ðǣre, 226; gsn. ðæs, 57A; rel. 132; þæs, 57B; rel. w. ðe, 249; ðæs, used as adv., *so*, 69, 149, 199², 200; dsm. ðām, 31, 201, 206, 374; rel. ðām, 89A; þām, 89B; rel. with ðe, 54A, 230, 237; þām þe, 54B; dsf. ðǣre, 265, 480, 495; dsn. ðām, 100, 260, 289, 454; þām, 6B; asm. ðone, 24B, 71A, 86A, 91A, 204, 271, 354; þone, 86B, 91B; þane, 71B; rel. ðone, 134; asf. ðā, 68A, 94, 208, 245, 322; rel. 239, 394; þā, 68B; asn. ðæt, 95, 319, 320, 401, 452, 485, 494; rel. 244, 286; after nouns of time (dæg, sǣl), 317, 470; ism. ðȳ, 446; isn. ðȳ, 43A; ðē, w. comp., *so much the*, 235; ðon, in phrase ðon mā, *the more, either*, 210; npf.m.n. ðā, 107, 215, 324, 339, *450*, 498; þā, 5B; rel. 450; w. ðe, 212, 308; gpm. ðāra, 426; rel. w. ðe, 225,

468; dpm. ðām, 113, 200; rel. w. ðe, 318; dpn. þām, 8B; apm.f.n. ðā, 37, 72A; 215, 301, 302, 501; þā, 72B.

searo, nwa., *armor*, *trappings;* as. 258.

sēcan, w.1, SEEK, *inquire*, 9B; *seek out*, *visit*, 20B, 103, 196, 432; inf. 20B, 432; seccan, 196n.; pres. 3 sg. 103; pret. 1 sg. sōhte, 9B.

gesēcan, w.1, *seek out*, *visit*, 209; *go to*, *reach*, 157; *attack*, 98; inf. 209; pres. 3 sg. 98, 157. [ISECHE].

secgan, w.3, SAY, *tell*, 65A; secggan, 417; pres. 2 sg. sagast, 244; 3 sg. sagað, 494; opt. 1 sg. secgge, 245; pret. 3 pl. sægdon, 421; imper. sg. saga, 228, 323; sæge, 201, 330.

sefa, wk.m., *mind*, *spirit*, *heart;* gs. 66B, 45Bn.; seofan, 66A, 45An.; as. 370.

sefian, w.2, *sigh forth*, *lament;* pres. 3 sg. 259.

segn, m,. *sign*, *standard;* as. 228; as. 444. [SENYE].

gesegnian, w.2, *bless by making the sign of the cross;* pres. 3 sg. 395; pp. 397.

seld†, n., *hall*, *palace*, 79n. [SELD].

seldum, adv., SELDOM, 261.

sēlre, see **gōd**, adj.

sēman, w.1, *put (a person) right*, *satisfy;* pres. 1 sg. 244.

gesēman, w.1, *put (a person) right*, *satisfy;* pres. 2 sg. -sēmesð, 18B; opt. 3 sg. 243.

sendan, w.1, SEND; pres. 3 sg. 134; pret. 3 sg. 460.

sēo, see **sē**.

seofan, see **sefa**.

seofon, num., SEVEN, 222, 399.

seolf, pron., SELF, *own;* dsf. 365; nsm. sylf, after him, 395.

seolfor, n., SILVER; gs. seolfres, 31A; silofres, 31B.

seolfryn, adj., SILVERN, *made of silver;* apn. seolofren, 64B; sylfren, 64A; dp. seolfrynum, 143.

seomian†, w.2 *remain suspended*, *hang;* pres. 3 sg. 405.

gesēon, V, *see*, *catch sight of;* pres. 2 sg. -siehst, 226; 3 sg. -sihð, 394. [ISEE].

settan, w.1, SET, *place*, pres. 3 sg. 337.

sīd, adj., *spacious*, *wide;* asf. 331; apf. 444; wk. dsf. 360.

sienful, adj., SINFUL, *guilty*, wk.apf. 498.

siennihte, see **synnihte**.

sige, fi., *victory*, *success;* as. 236.

sillan, w.1, *give;* pres. 1 sg. *13B*. [SELL].

silofres, see **seolfor**.

simle, adv., *ever*, *always*, 146, 390; symle, 85B, 166, 235; siemle, 85A.

singan, III, SING, *chant*, 85, 166; pres. 3 sg. singgeð, 261.

sittan, V, SIT, 445; pres. 3 sg. 246; pret. 1 pl. 422.

sīð, m., *journey*, *going*, *course;* gs. 316; ds. 109, 288, 504; as. 354 (of death). [SITHE].

siððan, conj., *when*, *after*, 314, 365; sioððan, 316. [SITHEN].

slǣp, m., SLEEP, 304.

slīdan, I, SLIDE, *err*, *lapse;* pres. 3 sg. 370.

smǣte, adj., *pure*, *refined;* gsn. 15B.

smēalīce, adv., *accurately*, *carefully*, 85B.

snāw, mwa., SNOW, 293, 347.

snǣd, fi., *morsel*, *piece of food*, 393, 396. [SNEDE].

snotor, adj., *wise*, *clever*, *prudent;* dsm. snottrum, 393; wk. nsm. snotra, 502; comp. nsm. snoterra, 243. [SNOTER].

snytro, f(īn.), *wisdom*, *sagacity*, 66A; snytero, 66B; ds. snytro, 380; as. 224.

snyttrian, w.2, *be clever*, *wise;* pres. 3 sg. 222.

somod, see **samod**.

sōna, adv., SOON, *presently*, *at once*, 99, 125, 314.

sorg, f., SORROW, *grief*, 304; ds. 55, 365; dp. 360.

sorgfull, adj., SORROWFUL; asm. 370.

sōð, adj., SOOTH, *true;* nsn. 244; isn. in phrase tō sōðon, *truly*, 421.

sōð, n., SOOTH, *truth;* gs. 173; ds. 9B, 18B; as. 497.

sōðfæst, adj., *righteous*, *just;* gp. 228, 236. [SOOTHFAST].

sōðlīce, adv., *truly*, 85A.

spanan, VII, *entice*, *mislead*, *seduce;* pres. 3 sg. 486, 492.

spere, ni., SPEAR; ap. 120, 128.

sprecan, V, SPEAK; opt. 1 sg. *194*.

spyrigan, w.1, *request*, w. gen.; pres. part. as adj. spyrigende, *140*n.
stān, m., STONE, *rock*, 276, 412; as. 114, 496; gp. 76; ap. 291.
standan, VI, STAND; pres. 3 sg. stondeð, 465; pres. part. asm. standendne, *288*n.
gestaðelian, w.2, *establish, confirm;* pres. 3 pl. 231.
staðol, m., *base, foundation;* ds. 76; ap. 274. [STADDLE].
staðolfæst, adj., *steadfast;* asm. 231. [STATHELFAST].
stæf, m., STAFF, *letter*, 112, 124, 137.
gestæppan, VI, *tread, step upon*, 202.
stēap, adj., STEEP, *high;* nsn. 405; *bright, brilliant;* wk.nsm. 276.
stede, mi., STEAD, *place;* as. 51.
stefn, m., STEM, *trunk*, 288; *race, people*, 51; as. 288; dp. 51.
stēoran, w.1, STEER, *guide, direct*, w. dat.; pres. 3 sg. 51A; stēreð, 51B.
steorra, wk.m., STAR, 276.
stician, w.2, STICK, *stab*, 94; *remain fixed, cling*, 496, 498; pres. 3 sg. 94, 496; opt. 3 pl. 498.
sticol, adj., *biting;* gsm. 153.
stīgan, I, *mount, rise, ascend;* pres. 3 sg. 61, 405; 3 pl. 44. [STY].
stillan, w.1, STILL, *quiet, silence*, 133; *be still*, 389; pres. 3 sg. 133.
gestillan, w.1, *quiet, silence;* pp. 117.
stille, adv., STILL, *quietly*, 137.
stingan, III, STING, *bite;* pres. 3 sg. 153.
standan, see **standan.**
gestondan, VI, *stand up against*, 97.
stōw, fwō., *place, spot;* ap. 334. [STOW].
strang, adj., STRONG, *powerful, firm;* gsm. stronges, 153; asm. 114; comp. nsm. strengra, 76, *418*.
gestrangian, w.2, *strengthen;* pres. 3 pl. -strangað, 231.
strǣt, f., STREET; ds. 137.
strēam, m., STREAM, 389.
stregdan, III, *strew, scatter*, 130; *be scattered;* pres. 3 pl. (?), 114n.
gestrūdan, II, *despoil, plunder, carry off;* pres. 3 sg. 73, 154.
stȳle, nja., STEEL; as. 291.
stȳlen, adj., *of steel*, 480; *hard as steel*, 496; asm. 496; wk. dsf. 480. [STEELEN].
styrian, w.1, STIR; pres. 3 sg. 473.
styrnenga‡, adv., *inexorably*, 274.
sum, adj., SOME, *one, a certain;* dsf. 221; asf. 417; gpf. 174 (*many*, by litotes); nsm. as noun, 336.
sund, n., *power of swimming;* as. 217. [SOUND].
sundor, adv., *severally, separately*, 64.
sunne, wk.f., SUN, 331, 347.
sunu, mu., SON, 13B, 323, 502; ap. 15B.
sūð, adv., SOUTH, 181, 201.
sūðan, adv., *from the south*, 252.
swā, adv., SO, *thus, likewise*, 241, 292, 308, 383, 489; conj., *as*, 22B; introducing clause, 96, 181.
swāpan, VII, *sweep, drive;* pres. 3 sg. 92B. [SWOPE].
swār, adj., *heavy, grievous;* superl. nsf. swārost, 304. [SWEER].
swāt, m., *sweat, blood;* ds. 45n. [SWOTE].
swaðu, f., *track;* ds. 92.
sweart, adj., SWART, *black;* asm. 149; comp. nsm. 478.
geswencan, w.1, *vex, torment*, 149.
sweng, mi., *stroke, blow;* gp. 121. [SWENG].
sweopan, see **swipe.**
sweopian†, w 2, *whip, scourge;* pres. 3 sg. 92A.
sweord, n., SWORD, 214; as. 166.
swerian, VI, SWEAR, *declare* (?), 417n.
swīcan, I, *fail, weaken*, 360; *yield* (?), *depart* (?), 497; pres. 3 sg. 360; opt. 3 sg. (?), 497. [SWIKE].
geswīcan, I, *cease* (*from*), w. gen., 316. [ISWIKE].
swīgian, w.2, *be silent;* pres. 1 sg. 193. [SWIE].
swilc, adj., SUCH; nsf. 396.
swilce, adv., *likewise, also*, 43B, 78, 118; swylce, 4B, 43A. [SUCH].
swingan, III, SWING, *beat, flap with wings;* pres. 3 sg. 258.
swipe, wk.f., *whip, scourge;* as. sweopan, 109; dp. sweopum, 143; ap. sweopan, 121. [SWEPE].
swipor, adj., *cunning;* wk. nsm. swipra, 300.

swīð, adj., *strong, mighty;* wk. nsf. 434.
swīðe, adv., *very (much), exceedingly*, 117, 143, 214, 258, 321, 358, 427; swȳðe, 222; comp. swīðor, 300. [SWITH].
geswīðan, w.1, *strengthen* (?), *forced out* (?); pp. 45n.
swīðmōd†, adj., *stout-hearted*, 92; ap. (?) 121.
swylce, pron., *such as*, 7Bn.
gesyflan, w.1, *flavor;* pres. 3 sg. 395.
sylf, see **seolf.**
sylfren, see **seolfryn.**
syllīce, adv., *strangely, wondrously*, 149, 261. [SELLY].
symbelgereord‡, n., *feasting, banquet;* np. -u, 399.
symle, see **simle.**
synnihte†, nja., *continual night, perpetual darkness;* ds. 68B; sien-, 68A.
Syria, prop.n., *Syria;* gs. 187.

T, n., the letter and the *tīr*-rune, 94A; the letter only, 94B.
talu, f., TALE, *story;* ap. 5B.
tæso, f., *ruin, wrong;* as.tæso, 483.
telga, wk.m., *branch;* dp. 287.
tēon, II, *proceed* (?); pres. 3 sg. tȳð, 386n. [TEE].
getēon, II, *draw;* pres. opt. 3 sg. 166.
tēoða, num., *tenth;* wk. ism. 446.
teswian‡, w.2, *injure;* pres. 3 sg. 94.
getīgan, w.1, *tie, bind;* pres. 3 sg. 294.
tiligan, w.2, *strive for, contend for*, 160. [TILL].
getimbran, w.1, *build;* pres. 3 sg. -timbreð, 74A; -tymbreð, 74B.
tīr(†), m., *fame, glory, honor*, 357.
tō, prep., TO, *toward*, w. dat., 200, 302, 307, 408, 421; w. ger., 54, 398; *for*, 279; w. gen., tō ðæs, *to such a point, so*, 69.
tō, adv., TOO, 336.
tōbrǣdan, w.1, *spread out, open*, w. dat.; pret. 1 pl. 423. [TOBREDE].
tōdrīfan, I, *drive away, scatter;* pret. 3 sg. 454. [TODRIVE].
tōgegnes, prep., *against*, 119. [TOGAINS].
tōmiddes, prep., *in the midst of*, 496, 499.
torhte, adv., *brightly, clearly*, 38.
torn, n., *anger, wrath;* gs. *446*n.
tōslītan, I, *tear apart*, 72; *divide, destroy*, 341; pres. 3 sg. 72; 3 pl. 341.
tōð, mc., TOOTH; n.(a.?)p. tōðas, 114.
tōweorpan, III, *turn aside, avert, scatter;* pres. 3 sg. 74A; -worpeð, 74B. [TOWARP].
treahtere, mja., *interpreter, expounder;* np. 5B.
tuig, n., TWIG, *branch;* gp. tuigena, 142.
tuīon, see **twēo.**
tunge, wk.f., TONGUE, 78; as. 94; gp. 223; ap. 222.
tungol, n., *star;* gp. 142.
twēgen, num., TWAIN, TWO; nm. 357, 477; g. twēgra, 419; twēga, 426; af. twā, 253; nn. tū, 253.
twelf, num., TWELVE; d. 47; am. postpos. -e, 15B.
twēntig, num., TWENTY, 206 223.
twēo, wk.n., *doubt*, 418; *difference*, 426; ds. twēon, 418; as. tuīon, 426.
tȳdernes, fjō., *branch, generation;* dp. 47.
tȳdran, w.1, *bring forth, beget, propagate*, *446*n.; pres. opt. 3 sg. 440n.
tyhtan, w.1, *lead astray, seduce;* pres. 3 sg. 483.
tȳð, see **tēon.**

ðā, adv., *then*, 207, 267, 448, 454, 502; þā gīt, *still*, 9B. [THO].
ðā, conj., *when*, 452.
ðā, pron., see **sē.**
þane, see **þonne.**
ðanon, adv., *thence*, 211; *whence*, 408. [THENNE].
ðǣr, adv., THERE, 449; conj., *where*, 200, 202, 392.
ðæt, pron., see **sē.**
ðæt, conj., THAT, introd. subst. clause, 168, 197[2], 198, 243, 245, 250, 263, 312, 440, 444, 453, 456, 481, 498; þæt, 16B; *so that*, 126, 226, 268, 295, 425.
ðē, rel. pron., *that, who, which*, 235, 273, 329, *330*n., 349, 492. See also **sē, ðēah.**
ðe, conj., *or*, 419.
ðē, pers. pron., see **ðū.**
ðē, art., see **sē.**
ðēah, conj., THOUGH, *although*, 70A, 194; þēah, 70B; ðēah ðe, 165, 174.

ðearle, adj., *heavy, severe;* wk. asn. 463.
ðecele, wk.f., *torch, light;* as. 410.
ðegn, m., THANE, *follower, retainer,* 117.
ðēhhwæðre, adv., *yet, moreover,* 433. [THOUGHWHETHER].
geðencan, w.1, *be mindful, remember,* 398 (see 396n.). [ITHENCHE].
ðenden, conj., *while,* 456, 466.
ðēod, f., *people, nation,* 250n.
ðēoden, m., *chief, ruler,* 14B; *Lord, 447*n.; as. þēoden, 14B.
ðes, dem.pron., THIS; nsm. 414; nsf. ðēos, 30A; þēos, 30B; nsn. ðis, 384; gsn. ðisses, 233; dsf. ðisse, 319, 360, 467; asf. ðās, 273; gpn. ðissa, 465; dp. ðissum, 318.
ðīestre, adj.ja., *dark;* superl. -ost, 303. [THESTER].
ðīn, pron.adj., THINE, *thy;* npm. 319.
ðon, see **sē.**
ðonne, (1) adv., THEN, 34A, 98, 103, 107, 111, 123, 127, 133, 141, 195, 306, 308, 318, 327, 329, 344, 350, 360, 445, 467, 477, 489, 493, 500; þonne, 30B, 34B; (2) conj., *when,* 47A, 105, 159, 166, 328, 356, 362, 368, 375, 393n., 419, 422, *473;* þonne, 47B; THAN, 30, 46A, 76A, 300, 399; þone, 76B; þane, 46B.
ðrāg, f., *time, period, season;* as. 295. [THROW].
ðrēanīedla†, wk.m., *compulsion, compelling force, 420; inevitable misfortune, 233;* ds. *233, 420.*
geðrēatian, w.2, *restrain, check;* pres. 3 sg. 295.
ðrēotēne, num., THIRTEEN; an. ðrēotēno, 282.
ðria, num., THRICE, 263, 282. [THRIE].
ðridda, num., THIRD; nsm. 136.
ðrītig (XXX), num., THIRTY, 14B, 263.
ðrōwian, w.2, *endure, suffer,* 457. [THROW].
ðrym, mja., *glory;* as. 476. [THRUM].
ðū, pron., THOU, 43, 88A, 195, 197², 226, 244, 321, 322, 323; þū, 16B, 88B; ds. þē, 13B; as. ðē, 225, 244, 321; ðec, 361.
ðurh, prep., THROUGH, *by means of, by;* w. acc., 17B, 65A, 148, 213, 240, 338, 356, 403, 440, 443, 447, 448, 485, 488; þurh, 2B, 24B, 65B.
ðurst, m., THIRST; as. 463.
ðūsend, num., THOUSAND, 263.
ðūsendgerīm‡, n., *thousand-count, reckoning by thousands;* gs. 282.
ðȳ, see **sē.**
ðycggan, V, *partake of, eat;* ger. 398. [THIG].
geðȳn, w.1, *crush;* pres. 3 sg. -ðȳð, 295.
ðyncean, w.1, impers., *seem;* pres. 3 sg. 263. [THINK].

Ū (MS V), n., the letter and the *ūr*-rune, 118.
ufan, adv., *from above,* 88B; on u., *above, over,* 88A.
under, prep., UNDER; w. dat. 60, 103, 142, 458; w. acc. 69, 449.
ungelīc, adj., *unlike,* 35A. [UNILICHE].
ungesibb, adj., *not related,* 35B. See **ungelīc.**
unhīere, adv., *horribly, fiercely,* 257.
unlǣde adj. ja, *miserable, wretched, unfortunate,* 21B, 342, 358, 383n.; wk. dsm. 375.
unlust, mu., *joylessness;* dp. (semi-adv.), 260.
geunnan, prp., *grant, allow;* opt. 3 sg. 242.
unnit, adj., *useless, 21B.*
unrōtnes, fjō., *sadness, sorrow;* as. 464.
unðanc, m., *displeasure;* as. 98. [UNTHANK].
unwita, wk.m., *ignorant person, foolish man;* np. 402.
uppe, adv., UP, 225.
ūt, adv., OUT, *forth,* 164, 471.
ūtan, adv., *without,* 127. [OUTEN].

Vāsa Mortis, prop.n., *Vasa Mortis, idol of the Philistines,* 272n.

wā, adv., WOE, 104, *318.*
wadan, VI, WADE, *advance, stride,* 380; pres. 3 sg. wædeð, 403.
wanhoga, wk.m., *thoughtless man, fool;* np. 312.
warian, w.2, *remain* (?); pres. 3 sg. warað (probably error for wōrað, *wanders,* A), 25Bn.
warnung, f., WARNING, *foresight,* 419.
wāt, see **witan.**

wǣd, fi., WEED, *garment;* dp. 139.
wǣlan, w.1, *torment, scourge;* pres. 3 sg. *143*n.
wælceald‡, adj., *deadly cold;* apn. -e, 459.
wællnōt‡, m., *fatal letter;* gp. 161.
wǣpen, n., WEAPON; gs. 165; ds. 161; gp. 251.
wǣr, f., *protection, guardianship;* as. 251n.
wæstm, m., *growing thing, plant;* ap. 294. [WASTUM].
wǣta, wk.m., *wetness, moisture;* dp. 297.
wæter, n., WATER, *sea, ocean*, 277, 384; gs. 19B, 413; ds. 155; as. 184, 216, 267, 460.
wēa, wk.m., WOE, *misfortune;* gp. 436; ap. 428.
weall, m., WALL, 248; ap. 227.
weallan, VII, *seethe, boil*, 48; *burn, surge*, 62, 427; *swarm*, 212; *rage* (?), 204n.; pres. 3 sg. 48A, 62, 427; -aδ, 48B; pres. part. 204n., 212.
weallian, w.2, *wander, roam;* pres. 3 sg. 22B.
weard, m., WARD, *guardian*, 83; gp. 253.
weardian, w.2, WARD, *guard;* pres. 3 sg. 372.
weccan, w.1, *arouse, call forth;* pres. 3 sg. 428. [WECCHE].
weder, n., WEATHER; gp. 303.
weg, m., WAY; as. in phrase on weg, *away*, 493.
wegan, V, *carry, bear;* pres. 3 sg. wigeδ, 52A, 124; wegeδ, 52B. [WEIGH].
welm, see **wylm.**
wēnan, w.1, WEEN, *believe, expect;* pres. 3 pl. 249, 312.
wendan, w.1, WEND *one's way, turn*, 19B, 103; *turn aside, change*, 427; pres. 1 sg. 19B; 3 sg. 103; pp. 427.
Wendelsǣ, prop.n., *the Mediterranean sea;* ds. 195.
gewendan, w.1, *turn, change;* pres. 3 sg. 490; 3 pl. 152.
weorδan, III, *become*, 488; *turn*, 307; as auxil. 363, 447; pres. 3 pl. 307; opt. 3 sg. 363; pret. 3 sg. 447; pp. 488. [WORTH].
geweorδan, III, *happen*, 334; *become;* as auxil. 211; pres. 3 sg. 334; pret. 3 pl. 211; pp. as adj. gewurdene, 325n. [IWORTH].
weorδgeorn, adj., *desirous of honor;* gp. as noun, 340.
weorδmynd, fi., *honor;* gp. -a, 83A; -mynta, 83B.
weotod, part.adj., *appointed, ordained, certain;* asm. 230.
wēpan, VII, WEEP; pres. part. 493.
wērig, adj., WEARY, *wretched*, 371; asf. 369.
werδēod(†), f., *people, nation;* dp. 204.
werud, n., *troop;* as. 160. [WERED].
gewesan‡, anom.v., *be busy (about), debate*, 172n.
wēste, adj. ja., *waste, desolate*, 334; *barren*, 22; nsm. 22A; wēsδe, 22Bn.; apf. 334. [WESTE].
wēsten, nja., *waste place, desert;* gs. -es, 83B; ds. wēstenne, 83A.
wīc, n., *dwelling-place, habitation;* ap. 301, 459. [WICK].
wicg, n., *horse;* as. 155. [WIDGE].
wīde, adv., WIDE, *afar, far and wide*, 212, 285, 454.
wīdmǣre, adj.ja., *celebrated;* superl. apn. -ost, 50.
wīdsīδ†, m., *long journey*, 363.
wīgsteall, n., *defense, entrenchment;* as. 103.
wiht, fi., WIGHT, *creature*, 245; *anything*, 230; as. 230, 245; ds. as adv., *at all*, 277, 388.
wilde, adj.ja., WILD, 290; *uncontrolled*, 369; asm. 290; asn. 369.
wildēor, n., *wild beast*, 277; gp. 82. [WILD-DEER].
willa, wk.m., WILL, *purpose, desire*, 230, 475, 492; *pleasure, joy*, 302, 311, 371; ds. 302, 311, 475; in phrase on w. *gladly*, 19B; as. 230, 492; gp. wilna, 371.
willan, anom.v., WILL; pres. 2 sg. wilt, 245; 3 sg. wile, 54, 84, 85A, 86B, 96, 225, 286, 315, 342, 432, 439; opt. 2 sg. wille, 197; 3 sg. 312, *474;* pret. 3 sg. wolde, 444; neg. pres. 3 sg. nele, 378; pret. 3 sg. nolde, 441.
wincende, part.adj., WINK*ing, blinking;* as noun, gp. 77A; winciendra, 77B.

wind, m., WIND; gs. 25B.
winnan, III, *strive, contend*, 320, 380, 419; *toil, struggle, make one's way*, 275, 384; inf. 380; pres. 3 sg. 275, 384; 3 pl. 419; pret. 3 pl. 320. [WIN].
winrōd‡, f., *joy-giving cross;* as. -rōd, 227n.
winter, mu., WINTER; ds. wintre, 459; gp. 239, 263.
wīs, adj., WISE; comp. nsm. wīsra, 235.
wīscan, w.1, WISH, *long for;* pres. 3 sg. 105.
wīsdōm, m., WISDOM; gs. 22B; as. 172, 380.
wīse, wk.f., *thing, matter*, 238; as. 417. [WISE].
wīsian, w.2, *point out, show;* pret. 3 pl. wīsedon, 5B.
wīssefa‡, wk.m., *wise-minded man*, 430.
wita, wk.m., *wise man, sage, counsellor;* np. 249, 422; gp. witena, 451; weotena, 392. [WITE].
witan, prp., *know;* 1 sg. wāt, 195, 198, 421; 3 sg. 59, 351; opt. 3 sg. wite, 497; neg. pret. 3 sg. nyste, 265. [WIT].
wītan, I, *lay to one's charge;* pres. 3 sg. 434. [WITE].
gewītan, I, *go, depart, proceed;* pres. 2 sg. 195; 3 sg. 58, 360, 493.
wīte, nja., *punishment, torment;* ds. 260.
wið, prep., WITH, *against;* w. dat., 55, 270, 320; w. acc. 160.
wlenco, f., *pride, glory, wealth*, 82B (probably error).
wlite, mi., *fair form, beauty*, 165; as. 57. [WLITE].
gewlitigan, w.2, *beautify, make fair;* pres. 3 sg. 388.
woddor‡, n., *throat, gullet;* as. 95.
wōh, n., *error, wrong;* as. 492. [WOUGH].
wolcen, n., *cloud;* dp. 103. [WELKIN].
wonge, wk.n., *jaw, cheek;* ap. 95. [WANG].
wōp, m., *weeping, lamentation*, 340; gs. 436, 451; as. 428, 457.
wōpdropa‡, wk.m., *tear;* ap. 275.
worc, n., WORK, *structure;* as. 320.
word, n., WORD; ap. 50.
worn, m., *troop, company, multitude*, 392; as. 297.
worold, f., WORLD; ds. -e, 57A; worulde, 57B; as. worold, 273, 363.
woroldrīce, nja., *earthly kingdom, world;* ds. woruld-, 238, 351; as. 384.
worpian, w.2, *strike by throwing, pelt;* pres. 3 sg. 25B.
wrāð, adj., WROTH, *angry, hostile;* asm. 112.
wrǣstan, w.1, WREST, *twist;* pres. 3 sg. 95.
wrǣtlīc, adj., *curious, wondrous;* wk. asf. 245.
wudu, mu., WOOD, *forest;* as. 184.
wudutelga‡, wk.m., *branch of a tree*, 413.
wuldor, n., *glory, honor;* gs. 112; wuldres, 371; ds. wuldre, 388, 454; as. 74.
Wuldorcining(†), m., *glorious king* (*God*), 312.
wuldorlīc†, adj., *glorious;* asm. 57A.
wulf, m., WOLF (as prop. n.) 204n.; as. 290.
wund, f., WOUND; ds. 330n.
wundor, n., WONDER, *strange thing*, 273.
wundorlīc, adj., *wondrous;* asm. 57B.
wunian, w.2, *dwell, remain*, 457; pres. 3 sg. 260. [WONE].
wyllan, w.1, *roll, wallow, twist;* pres. 3 sg. 260.
wylm, mi., *surging current, stream*, 82A, 413; *surging flame, conflagration*, 74, 457; ns. 413; welm, 82A; ds. 457; as. 74. [WALM].
wyrcan, w.1, WORK, *make, do*, 443; pres. 3 sg. wyrcð, 492.
gewyrcean, w.1, *make*, 329; *strive after, win*, 378; inf. 378; pret. 3 sg. 329.
wyrd, fi., *fate, destiny, destined event*, 419, 427, 434; np. -a, 325; gp. 303, 430. [WEIRD].
wyrm, mi., WORM, *serpent;* gs. 152; gp. 82.
wyrmgeard‡, m., *enclosure full of snakes;* ap. 460.
wyrnan, w.1, *refuse, withhold;* pres. 3 pl. 121.
wyrs, adv., comp. (of yfele), WORSE, 172.
wyrsa, adj., comp. (of yfel), WORSE; asf. 490; nsm. as noun, 350, 351.
wyrt, fi., WORT, *herb, plant;* gp. 294.
wyrtwela, wk.m., *root*, 436.

yfel, adj., EVIL; wk. nsn., as noun, 355.

yflian, w.2, *injure;* pres. 3 sg. 96. [EVIL].

yldo, f(īn.), ELD, *old age,* 283.

ymb, prep., w. acc., *around,* 182, 201; *about, concerning,* 172, 239, 245, 417; ymbe, 172, 182 (first instance), 201. [UMB].

ymbegangan, VII, *go around (with), accompany;* pres. 3 pl. 477.

ymbðringan, III, *press about;* pres. 3 pl. 127.

ymbūtan, prep., w. acc. *round about,* 247.

yorn, see **ierre.**

yppan, w.1, *disclose, reveal;* pres. 3 sg. 484. [UPPE].

yrfeweard, m., *hereditary lord and guardian,* 81.

yrre, see **ierre.**

ȳð, fjō., *wave, sea, flood,* 315; gp. 81; īða, 29B. [YTHE].

ȳwan, w.1, *show, reveal;* pres. 3 sg. 484.

APPENDIX

The Prose Dialogue of MS A[1]

Sāturnus cwæð, 'Ac hū moniges blēos bið ðæt dēofol and se Pāter Noster ðonne hīe betwīh him gewinnað.' Saloman cwæð, 'Þrītiges blēos.' Sāturnus cwæð, 'Hwæt sindon ðā ǣrestan?' Saloman cwæð, 'Þæt dēofol bið ǣrest on geogoðhāde on cildes onlīcnisse; ðonne bið se Pāter Noster on hāliges gāstes onlīcnisse. Þriddan sīðe bið ðæt dēofol on dracan onlīcnisse. Fēorðan sīðe bið se Pāter Noster on strǣles onlīcnisse ðe *brahhia dei* hātte. Fīftan sīðe bið ðæt dēofol on ðȳstres onlīcnisse. Sixtan sīðe bið se Pāter Noster on lēohtes onlīcnisse. Seofoðan sīðe bið ðonne ðæt dēofol (p. 7) on wildēores onlīcnisse. Eahtēoðan[2] sīðe bið se Pāter Noster on ðæs hwales onlīcnisse ðe *leuiathan* hātte. Nygoðan sīðe bið ðæt dēofol on atoles swefnes onlīcnisse. Tēoðan sīðe bið ðonne ðæt Pāter Noster on heofonlīcre gesihðe onlīcnesse. Enleftan sīðe bið ðæt dēofol on yfles wīfes onlīcnesse. Twelftan sīðe bið se Pāter Noster on heofonlīcre byrnan onlīcnisse. Þrēotēoðan sīðe bið ðæt dēoful on sweordes onlīcnesse. Fēowertēoðan sīðe bið se Pāter Noster on gyldenre byrnan onlīcnisse. Fīftēoðan sīðe bið ðæt dēofol on brēmles onlīcnisse. Sixtēoðan sīðe bið se Pāter Noster on seolfrenes earnes onlīcnesse. Seofontēoðan sīðe bið ðonne ðæt dēofol on sleges onlīcnisse. Eahtēoðan sīðe bið se Pāter Noster on seolfrenes earnes onlīcnesse. Niogontēoðan sīðe bið ðæt dēofol on fylles onlīcnisse. XX sīðe bið Pāter Noster on Crīstes onlīcnesse. On xxi sīðe bið ðæt dēofol on ǣtrenes fugeles onlīcnisse. On xxii sīða bið ðæt Pāter Noster on gyldenes earnes onlīcnisse. On xxiii sīða bið ðæt dēofol on wulfes onlīcnisse. On xxiiii sīða bið se Pāter Noster on gyldenre racentēage onlīcnisse. On xxv sīða bið ðæt dēofol on wrōhte onlīcnisse. On xxvi sīða bið se Pāter Noster on (p. 8) sybbe onlīcnisse. On xxvii sīða bið ðæt dēofol on yfeles geðōhtes onlīcnes. On xxviii sīða bið se Pāter Noster on ārfæstes gāstes onlīcnesse. On xxviii sīða bið dēoplicor gehwyrfed ðæt dēofol on dēaðes onlīcnesse.' Saloman cwæð, 'Dōmlīcor bið ðonne se Pāter Noster gehwyrfed on Dryhtnes onlīcnesse.'

[1] See Introduction, pp. 8–10, 55–56.

[2] MS Eeahteoðan.

Sāturnus cwæð, 'Ac hwā āspyreð ðæt dēofol of hefones [1] holte and hine gebringeð on ðāra Crīstes cempena fæðmum ðe ðus hātton: Cherubin and Seraphin?' [Saloman cwæð,] 'Uriel and Rumiel.' Sāturnus cwæð, 'Ac hwā scotað ðæt dēofol mid weallendum strǣlum?' Salomon cwæð, 'Se Pāter Noster scotað ðæt dēofol mid weallendum strǣlum, and sēo līget [2] hēo bærneð and tācnað and se regn hit ufan wyrdeð and ðā genipu hit dweliað and se ðunor hit ðrysceð mid ðǣre fȳrenan æcxe and hit drīfeð tō ðǣre īrenan ræccentēage ðe his fæder on eardað, Satan and Sathiel. And ðonne ðæt dēofol swīðe wērgað, hit sēceð scyldiges mannes nīeten oððe unclǣne trēow; oððe gif hit mēteð ungesēnodes mannes mūð and līchoman and hit ðonne on forgietenan mannes innelfe gewīteð, and ðurh his fell and ðurh his flǣsc on ðā eorðan gewīteð, and ðanon helle wēsten gespyrreð.'

Sāturnus cwæð, 'Ac hūlīc hēafod hafað se Pāter Noster?' (p. 9) Salomon cwæð, 'Pāter Noster hafað gylden hēafod and sylfren feax, and ðēah ðe ealle eorðan wæter sīen gemenged wið ðām heofonlīcum wætrum uppe on āne ǣdran and hit samlīce rīnan onginne eall middangerd mid eallum his gesceaftum, hē mæg under ðæs Pāter Nosters feaxe ānum locce drīge gestandan. And his ēagan sindon xii ðūsendum sīða beorhtran ðonne ealles middangeardes eorðe, ðēah ðe hīo sīe mid ðǣre beorhtestan lilian blōstmum ofbrǣded, and ǣghwylc blōstman lēaf hæbbe xii sunnan, and ǣghwylc blōstma hæbbe xii mōnan, and ǣghwylc mōna sīe sinderlīce xii ðūsendum sīða beorhtra ðonne hē iēo wæs ǣr Ābeles slege.'

Sāturnus cwæð, 'Ac hūlīc is ðæs Pāter Nosters sēo wlitige heorte?' Saloman cwæð, 'His heorte is xii ðūsendum sīða beorhtre ðonne ealle ðās seofon heofonas ðe ūs syndon ofergesette, ðēah ðe hīe sīen ealle mid ðī dōmescan fȳre onǣled, and ðēah ðe eall ðēos eorðe him neoðan tōgegnes byrne, and hēo hæbbe fȳrene tungan and gyldene hracan and lēohtne mūð inneweardne, and ðēah ðe eall middangeard sīe fram Ādames frymðe ednīowe gewurden and ānra gehwelc hæbbe ðā xii snyttro Habrahames and Isaces and Iacobes, and ānra gehwylc mōte lifigan ðrēo hund wintra, ne magon (p. 10) hīe ðǣre tungan gerecnesse ne hire mægnes swīðmōdnisse āspyrian. Ond [3] his earmas siendon xii ðūsendum sīða lengran ðonne ealles middangeardes eorðe oððe bēamas, ðēah ðe hīe sīen mid ðȳ beorhtestan wyrhtan folmum tōsomne gefēged and ānra gehwylc ende sīe fram ōðrum tō ðām midle mid ðȳ gulliscan

[1] K. emends to *geofones* without comment.

[2] An obscure letter after the *t* of *liget*.

[3] When spelled out the word is always *ond;* 7 I have, perhaps inconsistently, expanded *and*.

seolfre oferworht and mid ðām neorxnawonges compgimmum āstǣned; and his handa twā hīe sint brādran ðonne xii middangeardas ðēah hīe sīen ealle tōsomne gesette. Ond se hālga cantic hē hafað gyldene fingras and ðāra is ānra gehwylc synderlīce xxxtigum ðūsendum dǣla lengran ðonne eall middangeard oððe eorðe. And on ðæs Pāter Nosters ðǣre swīðran handa is gyldennes sweordes onlīcnis ðæt is eallum ōðrum wǣpnum ungelīc; his lēoma hē is hlūtra and beorhtra ðonne ealra heofona tungol oððe on ealre eorðan sīen goldes and seolfres frætwednessa and fægernessa; and ðæs dryhtenlīcan wǣpnes sēo swīðre ecglāst hē is mildra and gemetfæstra ðonne ealles middangeardes swētnissa oððe his stencas. Ond sēo wynstre ecglāst ðæs ilcan wǣpnes hē is rēðra and scearpra ðonne eall middangeard ðēah hē sīe binnan his fēower hwommum full gedrifen wildēora, and ānra gehwylc dēor hæbbe synderlīce xii hornas īerene and ānra gehwylc (p. 11) horn hæbbe xii tindas īerene and ānra gehwylc tind hæbbe synderlice xii ordas and ānra gehwilc sīe xii ðūsendum sīða scearpra ðonne sēo ān flān ðe sīe fram hundtwelftigum hyrdenna geondhyrded. Ond ðēah ðe seofon middangeardas sīen ealle on efen ābrǣdde on ðēoses ānes onlīcnisse, and ðǣr sīe eall gesomnod ðætte heofon oððe hell oððe eorðe ǣfre ācende, ne magon hīe ðā līfes līnan on middan ymbfæðman. Ond se Pāter Noster hē mæg āna ealla gesceafta on his ðǣre swīðran hand on ānes weaxæples onlīcnisse geðȳn and gewringan. Ond his geðōht hē is spryngdra and swyftra ðonne xii ðūsendu hāligra gǣsta, ðēah ðe ānra gehwylc gǣst hæbbe synderlīce xii feðerhoman and ānra gehwylc feðerhoma hæbbe xii windas and ānra gehwylc wind twelf sigefæstnissa synderlīce. Ond his stefen hēo is hlūdre ðonne eall manna cynn oððe eall wildēora cynn, ðēah ðe hīe sīen ealle on ðone munt gesomnod ðe sīe in ðǣre lengo ðe [1] sēo līne ðe wile xxxiiitigum sīða ealle eorðan ymbehwyrft ūtan ymblicggan. Ond ðēh ðe ðǣron gesomnod sīe eall ðætte heofon oððe hell oððe eorðe ǣfre ācende, and ānra gehwylc ge ðāra cweðendra ge ðāra uncweðendra (p. 12) hæbbe gyldene bȳman on mūðe, and eallra bȳmena gehwylc hæbbe xii hlēoðor, and hlēoðra gehwylc sīe heofone hēarre and helle dēopre, ðonne gēna ðæs hālgan cantices se gyldena organ hē hīe ealle oferhlēoðrað and ealle ðā ōðra hē ādȳfeð.'

Sāturnus cwæð, 'Ac hūlīc is ðæs Pāter Noster' . . . [Saloman cwæð,] . . . 'hafað gyldene fonan, and sēo fane is mid xii godwebbum ūtan ymbhangen, and ānra gehwylc godweb hangað on hundtwelftigum hringa gyldenra. Ond ðæt ǣreste godweb is hāten *aurum celæstium*, ðām ðīostro ne magon cxxtigum mīla nēah gehleonian.

[1] So MS, perh. for *lengðe;* K. *lengoðe.*

Ðonne nemnað englas ðæt æftere godweb *spiritum paraclitum;* in ðām godwebcynne bið Sanctus Mihhael gescyrped on dōmes dæg. Ðonne nemnað englas ðæt ðridde godwebb *pastoralices;* ðæt godwebb wæs on ðæs godwebbes onlīcnisse ðe iēo ymb mīnes fæder Dāuides columban hangode on ðeosum ilcan temple. Ðonne is ðæt fēorðe godwebb hāten *solacitum;* ðæt godweb wæs on ðæs godwebbes onlīcnisse ðe gēo Abimelech, se gōda cining, brōhte Crīste tō lācum and tō ansǣgdnesse. Ðonne is ðæt fīfte godwebb hāten *uita perpetua;* ðæt godwebb is ðonne ðǣre hālgan ðrinisse. Ðonne is ðæt syxte godwebb hāten *sacrificium dei;* ðæt is ðonne on eallra dēora onlīcnisse. Ðonne is ðæt seofoðe' . . .

INDEX

The index covers the Introduction and Notes, and includes most proper names and the chief subjects of discussion. Authors merely cited in the Notes are not usually listed. The references to the Introduction are to pages and occasionally also to notes at the bottom of the page; the references to the Notes are to pages and the numbers of the lines annotated. Thus, 56 n.16 means note 16 at the bottom of p. 56, while 109 n.30 means note on line 30 on p. 109. In the latter case only the number of the line is given: thus 109 n.44 (not 109 n.44a), unless there are notes on both half-lines (44a and 44b). The glossary should be consulted for proper names in the text. Since the names Solomon and Saturn occur on almost every page, unimportant references to these names, especially in the analysis of the poems, are omitted. Italics indicate the main discussion of a subject.

Abdemon, 22, 28, 29
Ælfric, 14, 36 n.4, 38, 39, 40, 42, 106 n.12, 122 n.203, 133 n.325
Æsop, 34
Aethicus Cosmographicus, 30, 31, 32, 34
Alcuin, 38, 44 and n.46, 46, 55, 56 n.16, 64, 134 n.330
Aldhelm, 44 n.46, 64, 109 n.28
Alfred, King, and his works, 1, 12 and n.3, 13, 15, 16, 38, 56
Alfredian *Metres of Boethius*, see Boethius
alliteration, 15, 16, 37, 105 n.7a, 120 n.186, n.192b, 130 n.289, 135 n.361
alphabetic magic, 42, 45, 46, 47, 112 n.89, 115–116 n.136
Altercatio Hadriani et Epicteti, 55, 131 n.304
Alvísmál, see *Elder Edda*
Ambrose, St., 43
amulets, 25 n.24, 40, 41, 46, 47
Anglian dialect (comprising Northumbrian and Mercian), 4, 5, 11, 13, 17, 18, 19, 20, 21, 112 n.79, 116 n.143b, 118 n.172b, 121 n.198, 137 n.386b. See also Mercian dialect, Northumbrian dialect
apo koinou construction, 117 n.158, 142 n.468
Arabic literature, analogues in, 23, 46, 59
Aristo of Pella, lost dialogue of, 54
Asatir, the Samaritan, 122 n.203, 124 n.205
Ashmedai (Asmodeus), 23, 27 n.8, 34, 59, 60, 119 n.180, 127 n.244, 128 n.255, 129 n.265, n.272
Asmodeus, see Ashmedai
Audelay, John, 28
Augustine of Hippo, St., 39, 43, 54, 135 n.357 (on twins)
Azza and Azzael, demons, 23, 59, 125 n.208, 127 n.247

Bede, the Venerable, 38, 44, 117 n.151b
Beelzeboul, 23, 34
Bel, 61, 123 n.203
Benaiah, servant of Solomon, 23, 60, 129 n.265
Benedictine reform, 14, 39
Berossus, priest of Marduk, 123 n.203
besom of devotion, an Irish prayer, 42 n.36, 111 n.66
Bilqis, see Queen of Sheba
blessing of food, 137 n.393
Bobbio Missal, 44 n.48
Boethius, 54, 62, 138 n.419, 139 n.434; Alfredian version cited, 12 n.3, 13, 69, 122 n.203, 135 n.346, 138 n.411
Boniface, St., 64
book, see riddles
Book of Cerne, 43 n.38
books, power of, 126 n.221, 127 n.228
Burton, Robert, 28
Byzantine Greek, Solomonic legends in, 24, 25

Cabbalistic writings, 21, 46
Calchas, legend of, 57
cattle, Devil's power over, 36, 117 n.153
Celtic influence on poems, see Irish literature
Chaldean(s), 5, 6, 45, 51, 53, 59, 61, 107 n. 20a, n.20b, 119–120 n.180, 121 n.198b, 121 n.199
Charlemagne, 38, 55, 56 n.16
charms, 41, 42, 125 n.211. See also amulets
Chaucer, 40
Christ, 42, 43, 44, 52 (at Doomsday), 111 n.66, 113 n.111, 136 n.373, 137 n.381; as exorcist, 23, 47; monogram of, 44, 112 n.99; reference in poem to, 66; Solomon in relation to, 22, 23, 47, 48
Cicero, dialogue of, 54
Clavicula Salomonis, 'Key of Solomon,' 21, 25, 46
Clovesho, Council of, 38
Cnut, Laws of, 39
Cōfor (see also glossary), 6, 45, 50, 59, *107 n.20a*
Contradictio Salomonis, 24, 29 n.7
Creed, the, 14, 38, 39, 41
Cyprian, St., 39

Dagon, 60 and n.7, 127 n.244, 128 n.255, 129 n.272
Danish invasions, possible influence on poems of, 12, 13, 14, 56
date of poems, 1, 2, *12–17*
Devil, the, 6, 8, 9, 22, 36, 39, 43, 44, 47, 69, 109 n.26, n.28, 109–110, n.45, 113 n.101, 111 n.66, 114 n.126, n.131, 116 n.149, n.151a, 117 n.151b, n.152, n.153, n.161, 129 n.272, 137 n.393, 154 n.489, 493. See also Satan
Devil's paternoster, 40 n.22
dialogue, *53–58;* classical d., 53, 58; didactic d., 53, 55, 56, 64; Jewish-Christian d., 53, 54, 56 and n.16. See also *Salomon et Marcolfus*, *Salomon und Markolf*, *Solomonic dialogues*
Didache (*Doctrine of the Apostles*), 37
dísir, 63, 132 n.325
Dius, 22, 45 n.2
Doomsday, 10, 11, 12, 14, 15 and n.16, 52, 62, 67–68, 128–129 n.263, 131 n.314

Edda, see *Elder Edda*
Egbert, Bishop, 38
Elder Edda, 57, 58, 110 n.46, 117 n.161, 132 n.325; poems of cited, *Alvísmál*, 65; *Hávamál*, 48, 65; *Sigrdrifumál*, 48; *Vafþrúðnismál*, 58, 65
Elli, "Old Age," 64
Enkidu, 61, 121–122 n.203
Ephraem Syrus, 15
exile, theme of, 63, 64
expanded lines, 7. See also metre

fallen angels, 62, 140 n.443, n.446, 141 n.454. See also Azza and Azzael
fate, see Wyrd
fire, 23, 59, 69, 115 n.136, 137 n.393, 138 n.396, n.400, n.411
five, as magic number, 115 n.136
Flood before Doomsday, 14, 15, 52, 131 n.314
food, see blessing of food
Freidank, 26, 30
French dialogues of Solomon, 27

Gelasian decree, 24, 123 n.203
German dialogues, see *Salomon und Markolf*
German romance, see *Salman und Morolf*
Germanic themes, see exile, runes, treasure, Wyrd
Gilgamesh, 61, 121 n.203
Glanos, the fish, 128 n.255
gnomic passages, 7, 65, 66, 69, 112 n.99, 126 n.216
Greek legends of Solomon, 23, 24, 25, 26
Greek magic, see alphabetic magic
Greek sources, possibility of, 23, 24, 25, 26, 112 n.99, 113 n.111
Gregory the Great, 55, 67
Grendel, 48
griffon, 127 n.244, 128 n.256
Guardian Angel, 67, *68–69*, 142 n.472, 143 n.477, 479
Guido of Bazoches, 29, 30

Halitgar, Bishop of Cambrai, 42
Hávamál, see *Elder Edda*
Heavenly Jerusalem, 67 and n.1, 68, 126 n.221
Hebrew literature, 8, 23, 41, 47, 61, 70,

121 n.198, 122–124 n.203, 125 n.208, 211. See also alphabetic magic
Heiðrek, King, riddles of, 57, 58, 64, 65
Hell, 110 n.46, 141 n.459, n.464
Hervararsaga, 57
Hiram, King of Tyre, 22, 28, 29, 34, 45 and n.2, 58, 59, 106 n.13
Hiruath of India, 127 n.244
Hisperic Latin, 43 and n.38
Holy Ghost, the, 69, 138 n.400
Homer, legend of, 57; cited, 131 n.304
Honorius of Autun, 135 n.350, 144 n.489
hypermetric lines, see expanded lines, metre

idisi, see *dísir*
ie, Early West Saxon spelling, 3, 16
Irish literature, analogues in and possible influence of, (15), 25, 41, 42 and n.36, 43, 57, 109 n.28, 111 n.66, 112 n.90, 127 n.244
Isidore of Seville, 44

Jerome, St., 31 and n.9, 49, 54
John the Scot, dialogue of, 55
Josephus, 22, 27 n.3, 28, 29 and n.3, 46
Jupiter, 33
Justin Martyr, dialogue of, 54

Kentish dialect, 18
kettle, 110 n.46
Kitovras, 25, 27 and n.8, 34, 35, 119 n.180

language, 4, *18–21*. See Anglian, Mercian, Northumbrian, West Saxon dialects
Last Judgment, see Doomsday
Latin dialogue, see *Salomon et Marcolfus*
Latin loan-words, 9 n.5, 13, 17, 25, 105 n.4, 106 n.12, 107 n.17, 110 n.53, 111 n.71, n.88, 119 n.184, 185, 120 n.186, 124 n.205
Latin source, 25, 26, 33, 45, 47
Leofric, 2
Letters of Pater Noster, *36–37*, 112 n.89, n.93, n.99, 113 n.101, n.107, n.108, n.111, 114 n.118, n.123, n.124, n.134, 115–116 n.136
light, see fire
lines 497–505, *8*, *10–12*
litotes, 121 n.198, 139 n.439
lorica, 42 and n.36, 111 n.66
lost leaves, see missing lines
Lucifer, see Satan
Luther, 28
Lydgate, 28

magic, see alphabetic magic, Solomon
Manuel Comnenus, 46
Manuscript A, *1–5*, 8–12, 16, 18–21, 37, 50, 109 n.30, 112 n.89, 130 n.299, 137 n.389, 144 n.497
Manuscript B, *1–5*, 16, 18–21, 105 n.6b, n.7a, 109 n.30, 112 n.89
Marcol, 27, 29
Marcolf (Marcolfus), *26–35*, 59, 118 n.180
Marcolus (Morcholus), 30, 31, 34, 119 n.180
Marculf, 28, 118–119 n.180, 123 n.203
Markolis, 31, 33 n.9, 119 n.180
Martin of Bracara, 41
Megara, tablet of, 41
Melot, 23, 129 n.265, n.268
Menander of Ephesus, 22
Mercia, 17
Mercian dialect, 19, 21, 133 n.330b
Mercurius, 31, 119 n.180
Merlin, 22
metre, 3, 7, 12 n.3, 13 n.7a, 14, 15, 16, 37, 120 n.192a, 126 n.227, 130 n.289, n.291, 132 n.323, n.325, 133 n.328, 135 n.358, 137 n.391, 143 n.479
Midrash, 31 and n.9, 122 n.203
Minucius Felix, dialogue of, 32 n.3, 54
missing lines, 1, 2 and n.3, 8, 9, 10, 11 and n.11, n.12, 37, 49 n.1, 50 and n.3, 53, 115–116 n.136, 130–131 n.299
Moloch, 23 n.14, 32, 108 n.20b
Mopsus, legend of, 57
Morcholus, see Marcolus
Morolf (Marolf), 27, 33, 34, 35, 132 n.321
mountain of darkness, 23, 60, 127 n.247

Nimrod, 33, 51, 61, 62, 107–108 n.20b, 121 n.198b, 121–123 n.203, 124–125 n.205
Ninus, 33, 107–108 n.20b, 123 n.203
Northumbrian dialect (and possible

Northumbrian original), 12, 17, 19, 20, 21, 105 n.6a, 107 n.18, 113 n.107a, 118 n.171, 127 n.227, 133 n.330a
Notker Labeo, 27 and n.3, 28, 29, 33

Octavius, 32 n.3, 54
Odin, 48, 58. See also Woden
Og, the giant, 122–123, 203
Old Age, see riddles
Oriental influence, 14, 15, 22, 27, 43, 45, 59. See also Arabic literature, Hebrew literature
Origen, 46, 54, 129 n.272
Ornias, a demon, 23, 34

palm-tree, 10, *43–45*, 116 n.143a, 117 n.167
papyri, 40, 46 n.7
Pater Noster, 6, 8, 9, 10, 13 n.10, 14, 22, 25, 35, *36–43*, 40 and n.21, 45, 48, 49 and n.29, 106 n.12, 109 n.39, 110 n.45, n.51, n.53, 110 n.63, 111 n.66, 112 n.89, n.90, 113 n.107, 114 n.123, 115–116 n.136, 117 n.161, n.167, 126 n.221. See *Devil's paternoster*, *paternoster verde*, *white paternoster*
paternoster verde, 40 n.22, 43 n.39
Paul, St., 52
Philistines, 23, 50, 51, 53, 59, 60 and n.8, 61, 62, 121–123 n.203, 124 n.205, 127 n.244, 128 n.255
pilgrims, influence in Solomon legend of, 24
Platonic dialogue, 52, 53, 58
Poem I (selected references): analogues of, 37–49; analysis of, 35–37; character of, 5–7, 56; date of, 12–17; language of, 18–21; MSS of, 1–5
Poem II (selected references): analogues and sources of, 26–35, 54–70; analysis of, 49–53; character of, 5–7, 10–11, 53–59; date of, 12–17; language of, 18–21; MSS of, 1–5
prose dialogue in MS A, 1, 8–12, 20 n.17, 26, 36, 56, 109 n.39, 118 n.169
prose dialogue in Cotton Vitellius A XV, 7 n.6, 20 n.17, 26, 55 and n.13, 56
Prudentius, 42
Psalms, magical use of, 46
Psychomachia, 42

Queen of Sheba (Bilqis in Arabic legend), 22 and n.7, 34, 58, 59

Rabelais, 28
Raimbaut d'Orange, 29, 30
Rätselwettkampf, see riddle-contest
rhyme, 7, 13, 17, 113 n.107a
riddle-contest, 22, 45, 57, 58, 64, 106 n.13
riddles, 58, 64, 65, 129 n.273; riddle of Book, 51, 58, 126 n.221; riddle of Old Age, 50, 51, 58, 62, 64, 129 n.273, 130 n.288; riddle of Shadow, 52, 133–134 n.330b
Robert of Sicily, 22
ropes of doomed man, 52, 132 n.325
runes and runic magic, 35, 42, 48 and n.23, 49, 64, 112 n.89, 114 n.118, n.134, 117 n.116
Russian legend of Solomon, 25, 27, 35. See also Slavic literature

Sachr, king of the djinns, 23, 34
Salman und Morolf (German romance), 27, (34)
Salme, wife of Solomon, 27
Salomon et Marcolfus (Latin dialogue), 26 and n.3, 27, (29), (30), (31), (33), (34), (35), 118–119 n.180
Salomon und Markolf (German dialogue), 26, 27, (33)
Satan (Lucifer), 11, 39, 40, 62, 67, 128 n.263, 139 n.434, 140 n.446, 141 n.454. See also Devil
sator-rebus, 41 n.26
Saturn (selected references): as Chaldean prince, 5, 7, 10, 33, 35, 51, 53, 59, 61, 105 n.1, 107–108 n.20b, 118–119 n.180, 121 n.199, 131–132, 320; character of (in dialogues), 6, 11, 45, 49, 63, 66–67, 132 n.321; in Old English literature, 108 n.20b; in prose dialogue, 8; Latin form of in Old English, 118 n.177; opponent of Solomon in dialogues, *26–35*, 57, 59; relation of to Asmodeus, 35; to Bel, 123 n.203; to Marcolf (Marculf), *26–35*, 119 n.180, 123 n.203; to Marcolfus, 30; to Mercury, 31, 119 n.180; sons of, 106 n.15
Scandinavian literature, see *Elder Edda*, *Hervararsaga*, Odin, Thor

Serlo of Wilton, 29
seven, as magic number, 126 n.221
Shachruch, 59
Shadow, see riddles
Shepherd of Hermas, 68, 143 n.477
Shinar, field of, 51, 121 n.198b, n.199
Sigrdrifumál, see *Elder Edda*
Sigurd, 48
Simurg, 59, 23 n.12
Slavic literature, 24, 25, 27, 34
Sleep and Death, 51, 131 n.304
Solomon, King (selected references): as champion of Christianity and forerunner of Christ, 5, 23, 47, 56, 62, 63, 67; as magician, 21, 22, 23, 35, 40, 47, 59, 126 n.221; in romance, 22, 27; legend of, 5, *21–35*, 45; ring of, 21, 23, 46, 59; seal of, 24, 46, 47 and n.18, 115 n.136; writings attributed to, 21, 23, 24, 25, 26, 47 and n.13, 126 n.221. See also *Contradictio Salomonis*, *Testament of Solomon*, Solomonic dialogues
Solomonic dialogues, 8, 9 and n.5, 22, 23, 24, 25, 26, 29, 31, 32, 34, 56, 57, 59. See also Poem I, Poem II, prose dialogue, *Salomon et Marcolfus*, *Salomon und Markolf*
Stoic philosophy, 54, 69
Strabo, 57, 110 n.46
sð for *st*, Early West Saxon spelling, 3, 16, 108 n.22a
Sulamith, 23 n.14
sword, superstitions concerning, 36, 48, 117 n.161, 126 n.214

Talmud, 8 n.2, 21, 60, 64, 122 n.203
Tertullian, 39 n.15
Testament of Solomon, 23, 24, 34, 46, 127 n.244, 128 n.254
Theodulf of Orleans, 38 and n.7
Thomas Aquinas, St., on amulets, 42 n.32
Thor, 64
Titans, 106 n.15, 122 n.203
Tower of Babel, 35, 59, 61, 62, 121 n.199, 123 n.203, 125 n.211, 131 n.320
Tractate Gittin, 23 n.10, 129 n.265
treasure, hoarding of, 131 n.310

Utrecht Psalter, 44 n.52

Vafþrúðnismál, see *Elder Edda*
valkyrs, 63
Vasa Mortis, 15, 22, 23, 35, 51, 59, 60, 61, 62, 67, 127 n.244, n.249, 129 n.263, *n.272*
Vercelli Homilies, 69, 143 n.449
Vespasian, the Emperor, 46
Virgin Mary, the, 42, 111 n.66
vocabulary of poems, 7, *20–21*

waste land, 121 n.198, n.203, 125 n.208, n.211
watchers, 128 n.253
water, 23, 59, 69, 137 n.389
weapons, superstitions concerning, 48–49. See also sword
Werferth, Bishop, 17
West Saxon dialect, 3, 4, 5, 12, 16, 17, 18, 19, 20, 21, 108 n.22b, 133 n.330
white paternoster, 40
William of Tyre, 2, 27 n.3, 28, 29, 30
Woden, 124 n.204, 125 n.211
Wolf, 51, 60, 61, 119 n.180, 121–123 n.203, 124 n.204
Wulfstan, 8 n.2, 38, 39
Wyrd (including fate), 11, 50, 51, 53, 54, *62–63*, 66, 67, 68, 132 n.325, 136 n.362, n.365, n.376, 138 n.419, n.427, 139 n.434ff., n.434b

year 1000, 15 and n.16

THE MONOGRAPH SERIES